I0119406

YOU ASKED FOR IT

SELECTED INTERVIEWS, VOLUME 1

by

GREG JOHNSON

Counter-Currents Publishing Ltd.
San Francisco
2017

Cover design by
Kevin I. Slaughter

Published in the United States by
COUNTER-CURRENTS PUBLISHING LTD.
P.O. Box 22638
San Francisco, CA 94122
USA
http://www.counter-currents.com/

ISBNs
Hardcover Edition: 978-1-940933-66-5
Paperback Edition: 978-1-940933-67-2
Electronic Edition: 978-1-940933-68-9

Library of Congress Cataloging-in-Publication Data

Names: Johnson, Greg, 1971- interviewer.
Title: You asked for it : selected interviews / by Greg Johnson.
Other titles: You asked for it (Counter-Currents Publishing)
Description: San Francisco : Counter-Currents Publishing Ltd., 2017- |
   Includes bibliographical references and index.
Identifiers: LCCN 2017016206 (print) | LCCN 2017040720 (ebook) |
ISBN
   9781940933689 (electronic) | ISBN 9781940933665 (hardcover : alk.
paper) |
   ISBN 9781940933672 (pbk. : alk. paper) | ISBN 9781940933689 (ebook)
Subjects: LCSH: Conservatism. | Conservatives--Interviews. | Right
and left
   (Political science)--United States.
Classification: LCC JC573 (ebook) | LCC JC573 .Y68 2017 (print) |
DDC
   320.973--dc23
LC record available at https://lccn.loc.gov/2017016206

CONTENTS

PREFACE

I have loved reading interviews with intellectuals ever since I discovered Bryan Magee's *Modern British Philosophy*, a collection of interviews with leading scholars and theorists of analytic philosophy which is still the best introduction to this tradition in existence. I went on to devour Magee's other interview collections, *Men of Ideas* and *The Great Philosophers*, and to seek out similar volumes devoted to writers like Flannery O'Connor, Walker Percy, and Ayn Rand, and to my favorite director, David Lynch.

Interviews, like letters, force people to communicate complex ideas more directly. The common denominator of both genres is that one is addressing a specific individual, not the world of letters at large. It is paradoxical that in many cases, when one envisions the broadest possible audience, one ends up actually communicating to very few people. Whereas when one focuses on a single individual, one often speaks in a highly accessible manner. Thus one of the best forms of communication is to allow the world to "eavesdrop" on one's spoken or epistolary conversations.

I have done a lot of interviews over the years, and they have developed a large following in an age in which people listen to podcasts on long commutes or while working out. But I have made a practice of having my interviews transcribed, since this is the age of the Internet search engine and there are still fans of the written word. I think many of these transcripts are worth publishing in book form. I already have enough material for a second volume, so this is just the first volume in an ongoing series. The interviews I will no doubt be giving to the likes of *The New York Times* and *Playboy* will begin to appear in volume three.

These interviews tend to be wordier than my written work, and often vaguer, but many of the ideas and images that appear in my writings were worked out spontaneously in these conversations. In editing these transcripts, I have introduced paragraph

You Asked for It

and sentence breaks, dropped false starts, supplied missing conclusions, gotten rid of hosts of "sort of," "kind of," and "and so forth" expressions, and quietly corrected some mistakes. But it would take a complete rewrite, not just a few nips and tucks, to transform these interviews into semblances of my written works, so the quality of the spoken word remains.

I eliminated chit-chat whenever doing so did not interrupt the flow of the conversation.

Since these are interviews, the words in quotes that I attribute to other people are not verbatim quotations but my summaries of the gist of their ideas.

I was pleased to see that my ideas have grown over the years. For instance, in the earlier interviews I echo the false notion that Americans and other European colonial peoples are simply deracinated, generic white people rather than new white ethnic groups. I correct that mistake in the later interviews. In my interview with Tom Sunić, I signal strongly against "petty" nationalism and extol a pan-European sensibility, but it would be a mistake to conclude from this that I endorsed, then or now, grandiose schemes for a pan-European superstate. I believe that sovereignty should reside at the level of the nation-state, which is the greatest political achievement of the modern world.

I want to thank the original interviewers: Francesco Boco, Mike Enoch, Georges Feltin-Tracol, Dennis Fetcho, Ruuben Kaalep, Matt Parrott, Laura Raim, Robert Stark, and Tom Sunić. I also want to thank V. S., who transcribed most of these interviews, John Morgan and Michael Polignano who helped bring them to the press, and Kevin Slaughter for this work on the cover.

This book is dedicated to an intrepid interviewer, Hugh MacDonald, who taught me something about bravery.

Budapest
June 11, 2017

The Alternative Right

Interview with Laura Raim[*]

Greg Johnson: Hello?

Laura Raim: Hello! Hi. Can you hear me well?

GJ: Hi! I can hear you well. Thank you.

LR: OK. I put on the video, but it may be not necessary.

GJ: I can see you. I can see you very clearly.

LR: OK.

GJ: I'm trying to see the titles of the books on the shelves behind you, but they're not that clear.

LR: You're not going to like them!

GJ: Yeah, the first thing I do—it's a very bad habit—but the first thing I do if there's a bookshelf I try to see what's on the shelf.

LR: I do the same. But I'd say it's mostly Leftist propaganda, mostly.

GJ: OK. I have a bit of that myself actually.

LR: Oh, OK. Really? What kind?

GJ: Well, practically anything written in the 20th century is Leftist propaganda. But I have about a half of a bookcase of Marx and the Frankfurt School. I was just re-shelving all my books, and so I found that recently.

---

[*] On August 22, 2016, French Marxist writer Laura Raim interviewed me for 2 hours on the Alternative Right for an article on "La « nouvelle droite » américaine," *Revue du Crieur*, no. 5 (2016). The audio is online at http://www.counter-currents.com/2016/09/greg-johnson-interviewed-by-laura-raim-about-the-alt-right/

LR: OK. So, as I was writing in my email, the first question is "What are the intellectual roots and references of the Alt Right?" I've read that some people think it's Samuel Francis or James Burnham before that, but what would you say would be the most important intellectual roots and references?

GJ: Well, the term Alternative Right was coined, I believe, around 2008 by Paul Gottfried. He gave a lecture where he basically declared the paleoconservative movement dead, and I think in the same lecture he also called for the creation of an "alternative Right." So, I see the Alternative Right as primarily emerging from the paleocon movement in American political thought, and the paleoconservatives would be people like Samuel Francis and Joseph Sobran and Patrick Buchanan.

Now, Richard Spencer was working for *The American Conservative* which was founded by Patrick Buchanan and Taki and a couple of other people to be a flagship for paleoconservatism. Paleoconservatism defined itself in contradistinction to neoconservatism, which they were trying to combat.

The paleocon movement got old. A lot of its leaders died. It never effectively institutionalized itself. It never effectively mobilized large donors. Of course, Patrick Buchanan has written many best-selling books and had a lot of media access. He was the main face of it, but he's getting old. *The American Conservative* lost steam. Taki left. I can't remember when, but he did create *Taki's Magazine*. Richard Spencer ended up editing *Taki's Magazine* for a while, and then he left *Taki's Magazine*, and then he created *Alternative Right* at the beginning of 2010. Sometime after that, the fellow who was running Washington Summit Publishing and National Policy Institute, Louis Andrews, died after a long battle with cancer, and so those organizations were handed over to Richard Spencer.

So, I see primarily a continuity between the paleoconservatives and the birth of the term Alternative Right. However, when the *Alternative Right* webzine was created there was a fairly self-conscious attempt to bring in a lot of different thought currents under that very vague umbrella, and so that included things that were not necessarily welcome in paleocon circles, and that would include things like neo-pagans and paleo-masculinity and White Nationalism. And so under that broad umbrella a lot of different thought currents came together.

I actually wrote something about this at *The Occidental Quarterly Online* just after the *Alternative Right* webzine launched, so if you want to cite that or quote that, that's there. It's up there somewhere.[1]

After a couple of years, Spencer, I believe, lost interest in editing *Alternative Right*, and other people took it over, really, on day-to-day functioning, and then he shut it down and launched his *Radix* publication. I thought in some ways that was a good idea because he felt like he had lost control of the brand, but on the other hand already at the time Alternative Right was becoming a generic term, and if you have a product that becomes synonymous with a whole genre—like Xerox or Walkman or something like that—the last thing you do is throw away such a valuable brand. But he did. He walked away from the brand, and Colin Liddell and Andy Nowicki have kept that alive.

In the last two years, of course, the brand has become much more mainstreamed. Because of its vagueness, a lot of figures that are, again, closer to the mainstream of conservatism than I am have embraced it. I would define myself as a White Nationalist and as a New Rightist and not as an Alternative Rightist, although I would use that term because it's a broad enough umbrella to encompass me.

LR: But more specifically a White Nationalist.

GJ: Yeah, exactly. And I don't feel the need to use vague, broad umbrella terms, but other people do just because they're not comfortable with being more specific. I'm all for people being as explicit and involved as they want to be and just respecting those decisions.

So, people like Milo Yiannopoulos, Mike Cernovich, Vox Day—all of them fairly prominent and connected with some of

---

[1] http://www.toqonline.com/blog/richard-spencer-launches-alternative-right/

the edgier reaches of the mainstream Right—have started using that term as well. Also, people like Andrew Anglin of *The Daily Stormer*. As soon as the term got popular, he started branding himself as Alternative Right, and it's a douchey move on his part, a trollish thing, to just try to take advantage of the popularity of the term, and I don't blame him in the least for that.

Anyway, it is a very broad umbrella term, but the main intellectual root of it comes out of the paleoconservative movement.

Now, as to what defines it today, I think the real core, the heart of it, the energy of it really is White Nationalists and New Rightists and people like that.

LR: Yeah, I got that from what Richard Spencer writes. For me, it's a White Nationalism sort of identitarianism thing.

GJ: Yes. European identitarianism: that's another term that we borrowed from Europe. It's a good term. It's analogous to libertarianism. It states what's most important in your ideology, which is the preservation of your distinct racial and cultural and historical identity. So, it's a good term.

And that really is, I think, where all the real energy is, and that is what's generating a lot of the intellectual excitement, if you will, on the Right from the creation of memes and trolling and arguments.

You know, in the past year-and-a-half or two years, things that have come out of our sphere have actually started to shape mainstream political discourse within the Republican Party, for instance. I think it was in 2012 that Gregory Hood at Counter-Currents referred to mainstream conservatives as "cuckold conservatives," and that was really the inception of the cuckservative meme, which, when it became more widespread through Twitter, became a really effective barb that drove a lot of mainstream conservatives wild because it was so true. So, we started shaping the discourse, and I think that's very valuable.

Now, another current of thought that is flowing into the Alternative Right that's very important is the breakdown of the libertarian movement. This is very important. I used to be a libertarian years ago, and I followed this intellectual journey a long time ago. But in 2008 when the Ron Paul movement was getting started, I started noticing how overwhelmingly white Ron Paul supporters were, and it was an implicitly white thing. They weren't aware of the fact that this was a very white form of politics. It made sense more to white people than to any other group.

I was betting at the time that a lot of these people would start breaking away from this and moving in the direction of white identity politics. When I was the editor of *The Occidental Quarterly*, near the end of that time, I actually set in motion an essay contest on libertarianism and white racial nationalism. The purpose of that was to get our best minds to think about this idea and create an analysis and work towards creating talking points that we could use to ease the way of a lot of people towards our position.

I don't think that bore any fruit at the time, really, at least I didn't see any, but a few years later after the 2012 election campaign and the end of the Ron Paul movement basically, within the libertarian sphere there was a real push by cultural Leftists to basically just take it all over and to eject anything that seemed conservative or patriotic or whatever. It became this Leftist, globalizing, and really sometimes quite explicitly Jewish takeover.

What happened is a lot of people were pushed out by just revulsion. There were these intense discussion groups online where people would be battling one another about this, and a lot of people just left in disgust. One of those online groups, a Facebook group, actually became the source of *The Right Stuff*, therightstuff.biz which now has *The Daily Shoah* as their flagship podcast.

Those people are all ex-libertarians, and they have moved out of libertarianism towards white identity politics in basically the same way I did and a lot of other people have. So, that really is a broad tributary that is flowing into white identity politics and into the overall Alt Right umbrella, and it's a very vital force too.

Most of the people involved in this are quite young. Most of

them are quite educated. It's very, very interesting. I had a dinner recently with some new young people who have come into
it in the past 6 months to 2 years and then some people who
have been around for decades. The contrast could not have
been more marked, because really the people who had been in
this for decades were all misfits. They were socially awkward
and weird people. And the younger crowd coming in were
mostly quite impressive: fratty, preppy, squared away people,
many of them with recent military careers, most of them in
their 20s or around 30 and just a very different look and feel to
this. People with a lot of agency and discipline and organization.

Now, there are a lot of people who we call autistes, who
are—if not outright autistic—at least on that spectrum. They're
socially awkward, and yet they do perform valuable functions.
They're great meme-creators and number-crunchers.

But there's also a large number of people coming to this
who are very normal in their presentation and their background. They're the kind of people who psychologically would
not be inclined to get involved in any kind of radical identity
politics. But there's a wind in our sails now, and they feel not
only conviction, but they also feel that this is something that
they can put their effort into, and it might actually bear fruit.
So, there's a great deal of excitement and intellectual vitality
here.

And this is very interesting also. One of the things that is an
internal, I guess, rift within the Alt Right umbrella is, of course,
the Jewish Question. I believe the term really was first coined
by a Jewish writer Paul Gottfried. The paleocons have always
been somewhat friendly with Jews, publishing them and associating with them at their conferences and things like that, and
within the White Nationalism sphere there's a strong group of
people who are quite critical of Jewish power and influence in
our societies. People like Milo Yiannopoulos and Mike Cernovich are Jewish to some extent in their identity. It's disputed in
Cernovich's case, because he once said he was Jewish, but he
put out his DNA profile, and none of it came up as Ashkenazic
or Jewish at all, but there were people who left Russia claiming

to be Jews who weren't, so he might be descended from that kind of line.[2] But anyway, that is a factor. There is a Jewish camp and a Jewish-friendly versus Jewish-critical camp split within the Alternative Right.

One of the interesting things that I've now been hearing about is young Jews, including young Orthodox Jews, which seems like a very unlikely category, are now being drawn into this. They're reading *Heartiste*. They're sharing Alt Right memes.

LR: *Heartiste*? I don't know *Heartiste*.

GJ: *Chateau Heartiste*. It's a blog run by this fellow who used to go by the name Roissy. Now he goes by the name Heartiste. Autiste is a play on Heartiste. But anyway, it's a "game" blog. It's on a higher level than "how to pick up girls," but it deals with realism in the relations between the sexes, and it's enormously popular, and he identifies himself as an Alt Right figure. It's part of the manosphere, which is a sphere that overlaps with the Alt Right.

But anyway, we're finding these young Orthodox Jews are now into Heartiste and into Alt Right memes. One of the things I think is going on here is they're just drawn to something that's intellectually vital and exciting. So, this is something that I've been seeing signs of in recent months.

LR: When you say there is a split on the Jewish Question, can you give me examples of those who are more friendly and those who are more critical?

GJ: Well, I'm quite critical. Kevin MacDonald is certainly quite critical. *The Occidental Observer* is his flagship publication. He also edits *The Occidental Quarterly* now. So, that would be one wing, and there is definitely a wing that calls itself Alt Right which is basically just rebranded National Socialism and, of course, they are quite judeo-critical.

The people who are more neutral or friendly on the Jewish

---

[2] Since I gave this interview, Cernovich has claimed to be of Croatian descent, not Jewish.

Question would be people like Jared Taylor, who runs *American Renaissance*. Some of the people who were involved in the original *Alternative Right* are neutral or friendly on the JQ, as we call it, and then of course there are just outright Jewish figures who contribute to this and that would include the grand old man, the dean of it I suppose, Paul Gottfried now, and beyond that there's Milo and Cernovich.

And within our camp there are people who say, "Well, look, we can be White Identitarians, but we also" — and they love to tweak this PC language — "should seek 'allies of color.'" And so their Jewish allies would fall under that umbrella.

One of the interesting things about this — and specifically the tributary coming out of libertarianism — is that although libertarianism and the Ron Paul movement were overwhelmingly white, there were certain outliers who were, say, black Ron Paul people or Asian Ron Paul people or South Asian Ron Paul people, and in the battle after the collapse of the Ron Paul movement after 2012, a number of these non-whites have been swept along by the logic of it and also by their personal relationships into being allies of White Nationalism.

Personally, I'm happy to have any allies I can get, and so I'm in an awkward position where some of the people who share the best memes with me and are showing up in my Facebook feed, well, you know, one's a black guy, and a couple of them are South Asian — Muslims, actually, which is even more awkward in some cases. But they put up with me and my "remove kebab" rhetoric, and we're all friends, and they have an intense moral and intellectual interest in this.

So, the broadness of the Alternative Right category really helps, I think. It allows a lot of people to participate in this, but also the broadness of it is threatening to some people because in the end these are not just ideas and fun on the internet. We really do have a vision of society.

Personally, I would like to see racially and ethnically homogeneous societies emerge, and so what we have is a strange moment in time where people in this multicultural context — some of whom are multicultural and multiracial — are coming together in a movement that is aiming at separation someday. I admire the people whc are involved in this. They're very, very principled.

Some of them say, "Look, you know, I don't feel at home in a multicultural society either. I feel less at home than you do." Speaking in the United States or Canada, "You guys created this society, and you feel more at home here than I do, but nobody feels at home anymore in multicultural and multiracial societies." And so we're finding that we do have allies of color, because one of the dominant traits that we're talking about, one of the main themes ultimately boils down to alienation.

LR: Mhm.

GJ: Everybody should have a homeland. Everybody should have a room of their own where they can go and be themselves. A home of their own. And then, logically, a homeland of their own. It's nice to have a place where everything is familiar, where everything is intelligible, and where you don't feel alienated, you don't feel a lot of stress and anxiety. Multicultural societies really are creating high stress situations, low trust situations, and the breakdown of community. So, we're communitarians, if you will.

LR: And your idea of the . . . What did you call it? The racially, ethnically . . . What was the word that you used?

GJ: Homogeneous.

LR: Homogeneous. This would be for the United States, right? So, what do you do technically with the black citizens, ideally?

GJ: Well, ideally, what I would like to do is . . . The landmass of the United States is quite large. And we do have to make some distinctions here.

First of all, there are indigenous people, and certainly they have rights here, and I would not in any way expel them or remove the remaining indigenous peoples, but I would give them maximum autonomy within their little ethnic reservations, and I think that's the only fair thing that can be done at this point.

As for blacks, most of them came here involuntarily, and they're descended from slaves. The fair thing to do would be to give them their own territories and their own autonomy and basically separate that way.

LR: Where, for example, could they go?

GJ: Well the South. There are large, heavily-black states in the South. There are a couple of those, and they certainly have ample resources, ports, and things like that. Everything that somebody would need to have a thriving country. Some states in the South might make a good black homeland.

Now, as for post-1965 immigration, that is really the main problem. Since 1965, America has gone from a country that was 90% European in descent to a country where we don't even know anymore, because the government has been maintaining that there are 11 million illegal aliens in this country for decades. We know that number has changed. It's more like 30 million or more than that. So, we honestly don't even know what percentage of our country is European-descended, but it's approaching 60%. It's going down to 60%, and where there are statistics about children being enrolled in school there are large numbers of states where among 6- and 7-year-olds we're the minority now. Just a distinct minority. Most of that is due to immigration into the United States in the last 51 years.

My view is the following: I wrote an essay called "The Slow Cleanse," which sounds like a dieting thing, but it's about ethnic cleansing, to use an ugly term.[3] But basically it says we shouldn't allow ourselves to be seduced by these apocalyptic scenarios about race war and cataclysm and things like that. We should recognize that the contemporary situation was created over a 50-year period, and it was created by instituting demographic trends that are not favorable to the European majority. We can fix it in the same way. We simply need to create positive trends for the European majority.

So, what would those trends be? Well, first of all, stopping immigration from non-white countries. Second, sending back

[3] http://www.counter-currents.com/2014/06/the-slow-cleanse/

all of the people who have come here illegally. That would be a good thing. Just make it impossible for them to draw welfare, hold down jobs, put their children in schools. Basically, take away all the incentives that led them to migrate here in the first place, and then they will deport themselves.

Beyond that, then there's a large population of people who are sometimes second and third generation now. They do have homelands. A lot of these people do have close contacts with people overseas, and we know that because they're constantly trying to bring more relatives over here. Lord knows I'm all for keeping families together, and what we need to do is reverse that kind of chain migration, family reunification tendency.

Many, many people move in America all the time. We are a very rootless society. People have to move because they live in a city where there's a real estate bubble, and their rents become too high for them to afford. And we just accept, "Oh well, rents are going up because of speculators. You have to move." No one sheds a tear about that. People's jobs change. The factory they work in closes and is rebuilt somewhere else, in Mexico or Indonesia. We don't shed many tears about that kind of forced uprooting of people.

My attitude is that we should not shed any tears about up-rooting people for something far more important than just the whims of the market and the private interests of capitalists. We should basically have an attitude that people move all the time, and if there are non-white families that work for large corporations that are global corporations, the next time they're relocated we want them relocated overseas.

At many, especially West Coast, American universities the majority of students are now Asian. I think we should encourage those Asian students, many of whom are bi- or trilingual and have fairly shallow roots in America if any at all, we should encourage them to pursue higher education in Singapore or Japan or China, and if they do it there they'll not come back.

Basically, if you just start nudging things in those directions we can wait 50 years, but one of the things that I constantly stress is that we would not have to wait 50 years before we

could reap some of the psychological benefits of knowing that
as a group white Americans now have a future, because a lot of
white Americans feel that as a group they don't have a future. I
think this is part of the reason why the mortality of whites, especially working-class whites, has gone way, way up, because
a lot of people are hopeless, they see nothing but diminished
prospects for themselves and their children, they turn to alcohol and drugs and risky behaviors. This has been rather epi-
demic, especially in the last 4 to 8 years since the current economic depression set in.

I think that if people thought they had a future again in
America—or the French, if they thought they had a future as a
people in France today—they would start feeling a lot more
optimistic. Probably they would start new businesses and have
babies. So, we reap a lot of psychological benefits today even
though it might take 50 years for us to get back to status quo
1965.

In terms of my ultimate goals, I love the idea of neat, homogeneous, partitioned homelands, but as a reasonable political
goal that I want to put forward within the present political context I'd say let's return to status quo 1965. That was when
American workers were doing the best, when America was
sending a man to the moon, when our cities were clean and vibrant in a good way. Vibrant with commerce and culture rather
than Rastafarians and druggies and things like that, jungle music, whatever. It would be perfectly reasonable to do that.

The 1924 Immigration Act set ethnic quotas based on a certain base year. We could have a status quo 1965 principle, and
if we got back there I think we would be at a point where white
Americans would probably feel so de-stressed and happy
about their future that they probably wouldn't even think that
we'd need to go all the way to separate homelands. I would
want to. You know, in 2065 when I'm dead, I'd want the next
generation of our movement to be moving the goalposts in that
direction, but the fact of the matter is that it doesn't need to be
some kind of cataclysm or apocalypse like a lot of Old Right—
and by Old Right I mean Fascist and National Socialist-
influenced people like William Pierce, for instance—envision.

LR: OK. Thanks. Back to my initial question about the references. Who would you say are the main thinkers of White Nationalism either contemporary or older political thought?

GJ: The main thinkers of contemporary White Nationalism first. The people who are the most read and commented on would be Kevin MacDonald and Jared Taylor. They're contemporary writers in their 60s and 70s, and they're very, very influential. William L. Pierce of the National Alliance is certainly a huge enduring influence on White Nationalism in the Anglophone world and outside of it for that matter. He's an ambiguous influence. There are many things I disagree about with him.

LR: William Pierce?

GJ: William Pierce, yeah. He's a very important figure.
Samuel Francis had a great deal of influence on it. He never really defined himself as a White Nationalist explicitly, but he participated in *American Renaissance* conferences and wrote many things that deal with race.
J. Philippe Rushton wrote on human biodiversity and racial differences in his book *Race, Evolution, and Behavior* and many other papers. He was certainly a major influence in White Nationalism today. Probably the most canonical statements about racial differences for most White Nationalists are Rushton's writings.

LR: That would be based on evolutionary biology? That kind of thing?

GJ: Yes.

LR: Could you sum up for me William Pierce? What does he bring?

GJ: Well, Pierce was basically a neo-Nazi. Early on, he was a follower of George Lincoln Rockwell's American Nazi Party. He joined that party, and after Rockwell was assassinated he carried on one strand of that National Socialist vision in America. He created the National Alliance and ran it until his death in 2002. It was a largeish organization. Certainly the largest organization in the United States of its type. They published books and magazines, held conferences, and encouraged people in various forms of activism.

His most influential book, unfortunately, is *The Turner Diaries*, which is a kind of revolutionary potboiler with a race war apocalypse in it. It fascinates a lot of people, but I think that it also serves as an impediment to thinking about serious policies that one could actually put in place that most people would not just shriek and run away from.

He was a somewhat contradictory figure because, on the one hand, he was an elitist. He had a Ph.D. in physics. He had a stratospherically high IQ, although he tended to have an engineer's mentality. He was basically a kind of Leninist in his views about politics. He thought of himself as an orthodox National Socialist, but he was pretty much a Leninist in his revolutionary attitudes.

On the other hand, he was constantly taking shortcuts and compromising with what he himself called the "buffoonery of populism," which led him to, for instance, buy a skinhead music label and recruit in the subculture of skinheads, which didn't work out well for him.

So, yeah, at his best he's very, very good, and he really did influence me on a number of points. I remember in 2000–2001 listening to his weekly radio broadcasts where he would analyze primarily current events, and he would stress over and over again the relevance of basically the power of the organized Jewish community in America in shaping events and just hearing that repeated over and over again over a couple of years and seeing the relevance of it to the things I was following was very, very convincing to me.

Before that, I had read Kevin MacDonald's work and intellectually it made a lot of sense. He's dealing with psychoanalysis, the Frankfurt School, deconstruction, and intellectual trends like that. But to have Pierce bring it home to contemporary unfolding political events was very powerful for me, and it showed the relevance of that analysis. And really that was his greatest influence, I think. His radio broadcasts. That and

The Turner Diaries. Of course, he's no longer commenting on current events, but *The Turner Diaries* are still being purchased and read.

LR: When you say he's a neo-Nazi, is there an effort in the Alt Right or at least in the White Nationalist branch to have a filter from neo-Nazis? I mean, to bound them?

GJ: Well, yes and no. There are really three attitudes towards neo-Nazis. One is there are people who *are* neo-Nazis, and they think everybody else should think their way. Two is there are people who aren't neo-Nazis and want to engage with them somewhat constructively because a lot of them are really young, they're naïve, and they're highly idealistic people, and they can grow intellectually.

And so I've tried to be somewhat constructive in my engagement and to say, "Yes, I see the relevance of this. However, it's more complicated. It's not quite so simple as you thought, and basically historical re-enactment of interwar fascism is not the answer."

Then there's a third group of people who basically want to create a *cordon sanitaire* around them and just keep them out completely. Those are the three tendencies within the Alternative Right.

LR: OK. And you're in the second category.

GJ: I'm in the second category. I think that unreconstructed National Socialism and interwar fascist movements — let's just call it that — are certainly not the way forward. These people were aware of a lot of truths, and I won't deny that, and I do think that something like fascism, in a very generic sense, is what every society ends up with if they try to do things like reconcile different class conflicts — interests of labor and capital, for instance — and if they take their own side in international conflicts. I do think that a kind of organic idea of society is somewhat fascistic, and societies move in that direction whether they want to call it social democracy or something else. They still move in that direction as they reconcile internal contradictions and as they educate people to be patriotic and so forth.

But, on the other hand, the thing that's worst about these ideologies is, to me, they're not realistic about how we're actually ruled. They emerged at a time when they were literally fighting Communists in the streets, and to beat Leninists they adopted their tactics. They had to. You take a knife to a knife fight and a gun to a gun fight, and when you're fighting Leninists you have paramilitary parties and militias and things like that. That's what they did. Unfortunately, they adopted quite a few traits of Communism, including some of its worst traits, and in the end they didn't beat it.

Today, we're not ruled in a hard, Leninist fashion. The Left controls us through soft power. As Jonathan Bowden put it quite strikingly, we have something that between the wars would have seemed utterly impossible and paradoxical: we have a Left-wing oligarchical society. We are ruled by an oligarchy, and yet all the reigning cultural values are Leftist. Leftist values, especially Leftist identity politics, are no threat to the reigning oligarchy. In fact, people like Chomsky have pointed out that they actually lead to the breakdown of identities that impede globalization and the globalization specifically of what we call capitalism. I just want to call it oligarchy.

And so, we have a Left-wing oligarchy. How did we get a Left-wing oligarchy? Well, after the Second World War, the Left basically realized that organizing the proletariat was something that the Right could do very effectively against them, and also that putting dictators in power can certainly turn against them. Stalin was a very scary figure. And so they launched, basically, a different path, a New Left if you will, of creating intellectual hegemony. This march through the institutions that the Old Left was already engaged in continued under a New Left, and we have now arrived at a point where basically all the dominant values put forward through the media and the popular culture and the educational system and mirrored in the political realm are all Leftist. There's a hegemony of Leftist ideas and values, and just as you take a knife to a knife fight and a gun to a gun fight you take ideas to a battle of ideas.

Really, the French New Right is my inspiration here. The French New Right realized that aside from riots in the streets and student protests in the '60s, the real battle was a battle for cultural hegemony, intellectual hegemony, and so to fight the Left in its current manifestation, which was cultural and intellectual hegemony, you have to deconstruct their hegemony with better ideas and create an alternative hegemony. That's really what the New Right is about, and that's why I call myself a New Rightist.

So, this is the speech I'm constantly giving whenever called upon to people who think that we just need to have some kind of Leninist party, and then we'll fight a race war. No, it doesn't work that way! And if you think that you're going to fight an armed struggle against the military and the police forces of any modern Western society, you're deluded. They can't even beat the mall cops and security guards of any modern Western society. It's just delusional.

LR: So, you're saying you have to fight the cultural war, the intellectual war.

GJ: Yes. It's a cultural, intellectual war. Yeah. And that's what the New Right is about. That's why I define myself as a New Rightist.

What I see the Alt Right as is a great front in that cultural and intellectual war, and there are a lot of culture-creators involved in this now. Very creative people. It's quite exciting. The people creating parody songs, memes, podcasts, videos. It's tremendous the amount of creativity that's being mobilized, and a lot of these people are very young, again.

The guy who's been running my YouTube channel just graduated from high school, right? He just turned 18 this summer. He does very good videos though, and he's been doing this since he was 13.

LR: It's interesting that you say Leftist values. I see what you mean by Left identity politics and things about diversity and things like that, but it's not the Left in the sense of working in the interests of workers, working against income inequality.

GJ: No. That's gone! But, you know, the Left makes gestures in that direction, right? Yet, in the United States, it's been democratic administrations, center-Left administrations, that are completely onboard with globalization. That's been massively destructive.

LR: Yeah, there isn't a Left anymore. It's liberals.

GJ: I wrote a piece called "The End of Globalization," and I'd recommend it to you.[4] I'm working on creating a video for it for YouTube. My values on most issues are Leftist. I talk about how globalization is undermining most of the things that progressives hold dear, most of the things that were actually won by the Left.

I used to be quite a patriotic American, but as I got to know more about American history I really came to the conclusion that the most glorious chapter in American history was the history of the labor movement. Not the frontier and not cobbling together an empire and not constant interventions in the Latin world, but the labor movement.

But what's happened with globalization is that the things that have been fought for like shorter work weeks, higher pay, making it possible for women not to work in factories (remember when that was a leading Leftist cause?), children not working, and things like that. All of these things are being undermined, plus environmental regulations as well.

The reason why these things worked, really, is there were limits to trade, right?

LR: Yes.

GJ: You were dealing with societies that were not global but somewhat autarkic. They did engage in trade, but they had mercantilist policies in place. When you globalize the marketplace, wages will fall to a global level.

LR: Yeah, you don't have to convince me of that. I'm a socialist and against free trade and a protectionist.

GJ: Good. Well, we're on the same page then on that issue.

---

[4] In Greg Johnson, *Truth, Justice, & a Nice White Country* (San Francisco: Counter-Currents, 2015).

LR: Isn't that somewhat contradictory with the libertarian trend?

GJ: Yes, it is. It's contradictory, and what's going on is its unraveling. Libertarians, of course, believe in globalization and open borders, and you're free to do whatever you want. Marry your boa constrictor or whatever. And now they're realizing that there are things more important than trade and individual choice, and that is identity, living in a functioning society, and so forth. And so they basically say, "This isn't important."

It's so interesting to hear people who three or four years ago were ferocious partisans of free markets now saying, "None of this is important. None of this matters."

LR: Really!? They say that? So, they're just not libertarians anymore?

GJ: They're just not libertarians anymore. They would like to live in a society where there's lots of freedom, where it's easy to create a business, but they realize that globalization is actually hollowing that out, and so they want to be "libertarians in one country," if you will. They want libertarianism with protectionism. They realize that that's really the only way you can have these things, because libertarianism is an ideological product primarily of homogeneous, high trust Northern European societies, and it would work in those sorts of societies as long as they maintained certain barriers to entry.

For me, I think they're a little too sanguine about that. I think social democracy works well in those societies, too! This is really the way that some of these former libertarians talk now. It's like, "Look, it doesn't matter what kind of economic system we have. What matters is that we have a society where it's just us, where we feel like we have a future, and where we can wrangle about women's rights and labor and all these other things amongst ourselves rather than having different parties basically bringing in alien groups to ally themselves with and use as leverage in their political battles against people who are of their own race and nation."

For me, Anglo-Saxon capitalism is a terribly evil system. For me, the Anglo-Saxon capitalist model is a plantation, and the globalizing impetus of Anglo-Saxon capitalists in America has been basically the recreation of plantation economies. Also, I oppose the social hollowing out of Western countries, and also I oppose the increasing destruction of economic and especially technological progress, because there are really two ways of raising productivity: one is you make better machines that allow you to do more. The other way of increasing "productivity" is simply cutting the costs of labor, right?

LR: Right.

GJ: As a mathematical construct, productivity treats those things as equivalent, and yet as a social phenomenon those are radically different routes. By restricting labor markets and keeping labor expensive, one of the things that the labor movement has done is constantly push for improvement of capital, which makes everybody more productive. Once labor markets are opened up and people can increase profitability simply by cutting costs, one of the main impetuses that we've had toward technological progress has been removed, and really one of the things that was most exciting to me about the recent Republican Convention was when Peter Thiel spoke. I read his book *Zero to One*, and one of the things he maintains is that globalization is incompatible with technological progress, which is really interesting coming from . . .

LR: Wow!

GJ: This is from a guy that works in Silicon Valley. He talked about this a bit in his brief speech. He said that all of America used to be hi-tech. When he was a kid, they were sending men to the moon, right? Today, we have 140 character tweets. Most of the technological progress that happens today is in the realm of computers, and most of that is simply improving ways that we can amuse ourselves during our decline.

I think that's very, very powerful. There's a lot of truth to that.

So, yeah, in the future, if we get what we want, we're not going to have free trade, we're not going to have globalization, we're not going to have destructive competition that's basically a race to the bottom, and instead we're going to create conditions where middle-class incomes and working-class incomes continually rise, and there is a constant spur to technological progress that's going to make us all, someday, out of work. The machines will put us all out of work someday, and then we'll have arrived at utopia.

LR: Talking about Libertarians, how does the neo-reaction movement fit in?

GJ: The neo-reaction group is a somewhat peculiar group of people. They're somewhat snobbish and secretive. Some of them are friendly with me. A lot of them come out of libertarianism. A lot of them are in two industries: technology and finance, which is why I think a lot of them are very, very secretive because they work for huge companies that would frown upon their shenanigans.

I think it's a highly interesting, highly intellectual group of people. I read their blogs, I read some of their books, and I value it. I think they try to remain aloof. It's an apolitical stance like you get from the late Ernst Jünger or post-war Evola. You know, "We'll just rise above all this stuff and not get involved in politics." I think politics is moving in our direction, and not getting involved is not an option at this point. It just makes you irrelevant. Still, they have lots of interesting ideas.

One of the things that I most like about the neo-reactionaries is that they've learned a lesson that I learned years ago. For years, the most influential book on me was Ayn Rand's *The Fountainhead*, the most influential piece of fiction, but that changed, and eventually I realized that the piece of fiction that's had the most influence on my thinking is Frank Herbert's *Dune*.

The thing that fascinates me with *Dune* is its combination of futurism with archaic values and social forms which is basically what Guillaume Faye talks about in his book *Archeofuturism* as the way forward. We need to reinfuse modernity with certain things that are treated as archaic, and that means identity politics, an aristocratic ethos, a warrior ethos, and things that have been bred out of us by consumerism and bourgeois modernity.

So, Herbert basically applied himself to this question: what social form is consistent with mankind ascending to the stars and colonizing the galaxy? And it was very obvious to him that that was not consistent with democratic politics which has a very low time horizon. It requires grand politics, grand visions, a grand strategy stretching forward over generations, and we had that briefly under the pressure of the Cold War and because Kennedy was a visionary, but politics as usual took over. Space exploration has faltered, "because democracy."

What you would need to reignite that is some kind of society like we had pre-modernity where we had aristocracies that thought in dynastic terms, where you had orders like the Catholic Church that thought in very long terms over time and perpetuated themselves over time.

What the neo-reactionaries take from Hans-Hermann Hoppe in his writings on the failure of democracy is basically this point. Hoppe said, "Look, democracy is a failure and undermines civilization because it shrinks time horizons down, and that means you can't pursue grand strategies and civilizational goals. You're just thinking about the next quarter if you're in business. You're just thinking about the next election if you're a politician." So, the neo-reactionaries take this critique of democracy and modernity very seriously, and so the question then becomes, "What kind of social form do we need basically to get ourselves toward a technological utopia?"

On the other hand, however, I have also defended a certain form of populism and a certain form of democracy. I have an essay called "Notes on Populism, Elitism, and Democracy." It's in my book *New Right vs. Old Right*.[5]

You do need some kind of popular counter-balance to elites. There's no question about it. I'm a populist in this sense. I believe in classical republicanism as opposed to liberalism. I believe in an organic model of society. I believe, like the classical

---

[5] Greg Johnson, *New Right vs. Old Right* (San Francisco: Counter-Currents, 2013).

republicans believed, that the main force in a society that guards liberty is a strong middle class. However, liberalism and globalization undermine the middle class. Therefore, if you value liberty you have to value protectionism, and you have to impose certain restrictions on the operation of capitalism to make sure that the rich get richer and the poor get richer and the middle class get richer. So, I don't believe in strict equality, but I do like the Aristotelian idea that inequality has to be somewhat proportionate. There can be distributive justice, in other words, which is a concept that libertarians just completely reject. They write that out of their system of ideas.

LR: So, you would still be for keeping democracy?

GJ: Democracy to some extent, but . . . we've become too democratic, I think. Average people have lower time horizons. The more power that average people have and the people that ride to power on the votes of average people, the shorter the time horizons are. However, if you just get rid of any popular representation you're just leaving yourself open to abuse by elites.

So, the classical republican view — and this really did influence the founding of America far more than, say, Lockean liberalism, which is a myth that libertarians put forward — and modern republicanism *à la* Montesquieu was an organic view of society. You had to have limitations on commerce, you had to protect the middle class, and you had to have checks and balances. So, you had, in effect, the mixed regime.

The model of the mixed regime comes from Aristotle's *Politics*, it's in Montesquieu, and it's in the United States Constitution. And really every good, functional Western European society, ancient and modern, has had some form of a mixed regime. You've had a monarchical principle, whether it's a hereditary king or a president or whatever, you've had an aristocratic principle, and you've had a popular principle. Those things have to be kept in balance, and so I believe in the mixed constitution, the mixed order. I just think that we've strayed excessively towards a combination of democracy and oligarchy, and we don't have leaders who think long term about the common good anymore.

Again, libertarianism doesn't have a notion of the common good. They've got procedures, and whatever comes out of the sausage machine at the end is blessed, right? No matter what it looks like, because it's going through their procedural notions of what is right.

I now have ex-libertarians who routinely talk about the common good or the good of society. There's a resurgence of these classical republican notions like the common good percolating around within this context of the Alt Right, and I'm happy that I'm one of the people who has been promoting that.

LR: OK. But you would still keep elections? Something that does represent the will of the people? Because it's one thing to have checks and balances and another having some way of representing the will of the people.

GJ: Yeah, well, the will of the people is a really complicated notion. This is something I do like to point out against the most anti-democratic people in our circles. The fact of the matter is that if we had direct democracy where people voted with their television set or their smartphone or their computer, we would actually have better policies than we do today on things like immigration and trade. There's no question about that.

So, in situations like that the people actually know what's right. Better than the elites, which need to be brought to heel, brought into line. They need to be replaced, basically.

But what is the will of the people? The people wants what is best for it, but what's best for us is not necessarily what we want at every given moment, right? So, we really want that cigarette right now, but that's not what's best for us in the greater scheme of things. So, you do have to give power to the populace to check elites, but you also have to have people who are wiser and more public spirited than average in positions of authority so they can basically say, "No, we're not just going to have bread and circuses and free cigarettes." There are bad popular policies that can come about to through direct democracies. So, you do have to have a moderating influence.

This is a standard thing that Rousseau talks about when he

talks about the general will. The general will is not necessarily what the populace wants at any particular moment. It's what they want when they're thinking most rationally about things in the long run.

The origin of this idea, fascinatingly enough, is Plato's *Gorgias*. Socrates in the *Gorgias* says there's a distinction between what you want and what you *think* you want right now. What all men want is the good life, they want well-being, but what they think they want at any particular moment might not necessarily be conducive to well-being. And if freedom is getting what you *really* want rather than what you just think you want right now, then that leads directly to Rousseau's conclusion that you can be forced to be free. You can be freer if you are paternalistically prevented from throwing away your freedom and your future by, say, getting addicted to heroin or gambling away your week's wages before taking it home to feed your family.

LR: So, at the end of the day, you'd still be for some elections?

GJ: Yeah, definitely!

LR: OK.

GJ: Definitely. And there are different ways you can do that. There are forms of popular representation that don't require people standing for election. You can have sortocracy. You can have systems like they had in the past where people are randomly pulled out . . .

LR: Right. Like in Greece. Like in Athens.

GJ: Yeah, like in Athens or like people who do jury service in America today. You're just pulled out randomly to do jury duty. But there are all sorts of ways that you can do that. But yeah, representative democracy is one way to do it.

Another way of doing it is plebiscites. Plebiscites tend to be quite favored, actually, among authoritarians of the Right, and honestly if Marine Le Pen ever ends up running France she's probably going to have to be using plebiscites more than getting things passed through the legislature.

LR: To what extent is neo-reaction something that influenced the Alt Right? A lot of the articles that I read in the US media about the Alt Right made it seem that neo-reaction was at the core of it.

GJ: It's not. It's very peripheral. You see, this is part of the problem with the news coverage in America. It's extremely lazy. They do a quick Google search, and they find a few articles about neo-reaction, and they think, "OK. I can run with this. It sounds kinda edgy and sinister even." Yet the fact of the matter is that it's always been marginal, and it holds itself aloof from most of what's going on in the Alternative Right sphere. It has not influenced it all that much.

It parallels what I think in some ways. I can't say it hasn't influenced me at all, honestly. I see where they're coming from. I can complete some of their thoughts. It's *simpatico*, but it hasn't been influential on the Alternative Right, and it's just lazy reporting that leads people to say this kind of stuff, basically.

LR: I would say that one of the points in common seems to be the rejection of equality.

GJ: The rejection of egalitarianism. A kind of elitism. But a lot of us are really populist, right? I mean, the core of this thing is a populist attitude. You might believe that the best way to serve the good of the whole is to have a certain elitist element in government, but you can't even just say that elitism *tout court* is completely the way to go. Like I've been arguing, you need a mixed regime. You need a popular element.

We are populists, and they are elitists, and that's really the big gap between us. They tend to be really interested in technology and things like that. Well, we're very interested in that too. There's no question about it. We tend to be engaged in actual things that we hope will produce political change, and they're trying to posture as being above all that.

Basically, they're signaling, "We're no threat to you, system that might destroy us or fire us from our job at Google or whatever! We're no threat. We're just harmless little fuzzballs.

We're just harmless eccentrics circling around on the internet." And I can understand that as a protective coloration, but a lot of them really do seem to take it seriously, and until they stop that sort of posturing and start actually recognizing that the world today needs changing, and they can actually effect it, they're somewhat irrelevant. Interesting, but irrelevant.

LR: Right. Another difference I would say—tell me if I'm correct—is that if they are strictly anti-modernist and the Alt Right is too modernist in the sense that identitarianism and nationalism are still a product of modern times.

GJ: Yeah. One of their memes—I call it the 1789 canard—is that they claim that the modern nation-state is a very modern invention. Yes and no. When you read Machiavelli, Machiavelli was calling for what? The unification of the Italians to chase out the barbarians who were invading their country. There was an Italian nation in the Middle Ages, and the Italians recognized each other from the Piedmont down to Sicily as a common people, divided politically, but a common people. The ancient Greeks regarded themselves as a common people. They were politically divided, but they were the Hellenes as opposed to other people. So, there were national identities even in antiquity. There weren't necessarily nation-states.

LR: Yeah, the nation-state is a product of modernity.

GJ: Yeah, and I think it's one of the great products of modernity. This is one of the ways I differ from these people who are all traditionalists. Oh, if you're a traditionalist you believe in empire. No, I'm not a traditionalist in that sense. I don't believe in empire. Empires are always created by murdering people and oppressing them, and I don't believe in that.

To the people in our circles who defend empire and colonialism, I always say that if you defend these things you're basically signaling to your neighbors that you're not above a little murder and theft when it suits you.

LR: Yeah.

GJ: And I think that's just a morally retarded attitude. It's morally retarded, and it's quite anachronistic, because we don't live in a world where white people are ever going to be running everything again. It's just not going to happen!

LR: Richard Spencer seems to have a fantasy of recreating a white sort of Roman Empire with Europe and America reunited like a big white empire.

GJ: Yeah, well, I have an essay called "Grandiose Nationalism"[6] where I'm somewhat critical of that.

His views on this have shifted a lot over the last couple of years. A few years ago at *American Renaissance* he was calling for the idea of the ethnostate, the ethnically homogeneous homeland. By the beginning of 2014, he then gave a talk at the Traditional Britain group—I forget when that was; I think it was 2013—about why we need Europe against the Brexit attitudes or the attitudes that led to the Brexit. After the Ukrainian revolution, suddenly he was basically turning *Radix* into an outlet for *Russia Today* propaganda and was extolling empire.

Basically, I think a lot of this has to do with the influence of his wife, who is a very, very strident Russian nationalist and basically spends a lot of her time pushing Kremlin propaganda about Ukraine. Suddenly ethnonationalism became a bad thing when ethnonationalism meant Ukraine demanding that it chart its own course rather than let Russia do it. So, I think that his thinking on this is overly influenced by political events and by the people he talks to. It's not as ideological of a position as it is something that is news- and personal relationship-driven.

LR: And as for neo-reaction, it seems to me that even though it says it's against anything that's happened since the French Revolution, what it seems to aim for is something that doesn't have anything to do with what existed in the past but more this idea of the small company units dismantling countries and competing companies, basically. I don't know if you read about that.

GJ: Yeah.

---

[6] In *Truth, Justice, & a Nice White Country*.

LR: It's something else entirely. It's neither traditionalist nor modernist. It's more just like geek or corporate.

GJ: Corporate geeks. Yes, this is a fascinating trait of theirs. Some of them are traditionalists. Others are techno-utopians. Others are quasi-libertarians. They're all interacting with one another.

The corporation can be a model. It can be reconfigured in a quasi-feudal way. I think the Japanese have done this. Corporations can, in principle, think very, very long-term. More long-term than politicians.

They're toying with ideas about different social forms that are compatible with long-range thinking. That's really the core thing that a lot of neo-reactionaries are concerned with. Questions about time horizons and how these things impact civilization and technology and progress.

LR: It's good that I'm speaking to you, because I was feeling that I was a bit misled by these articles that seemed to put neo-reaction with the Alt Right. But, for example, there are points in common like neo-reaction talks about "The Cathedral" and the Alt Right talks about "The Synagogue." Sounds like it's the same thing.

GJ: Well, it is the same thing, but one thing you have to understand is that there is a certain amount of our discourse that is not sincere, and this is the thing that's most troubling to me, because I don't say things just to get rises out of people. I don't say things for effect. I say things because I think they're true, and I don't believe in lying propaganda or dissimulation, because I just don't think that's where our strength is.

There's this whole troll culture where trolls will say things that are patently false or insincere just to get a rise out of people. When people talk about "The Cathedral" and others talk about "The Synagogue" it's a trolling thing. It's like, "No, it's a synagogue! There! I got ya!"

But they are opposed to the existing elites. There's no question. They do have that in common. The reasons for their opposition and their rationales, their visions of society that they have, they differ somewhat, and in the end they still are fairly marginal to what we call the Alt Right, and they want to be.

In recent months, I would say in the last nine months or so, I've noticed that some people who are friends of mine who are coming out of the NRx sphere are much closer to me, and others have receded behind a wall of opsec (operational security). They've become much more secretive in their interactions. Some of their little gatherings are open. Some of them are blogging less for the public and writing for one another in their little groups. Things like that.

LR: Oh, OK.

GJ: So, they're becoming a little more occulted, if you will, whereas others are being more open.

One thing that has, I think, excited the whole Alternative Right and some people in the NRx sphere as well is the Trump campaign, because he's, well, a populist for one thing. But there are certain dimensions of his thinking and behavior that resonate with some of the NRx concerns with technology and also some of the NRx attitudes about long-range thinking. Because Trump isn't the kind of person who made billions of dollars by currency trades and arbitraging like George Soros. He builds things, and he builds things that last a long, long time.

He also thinks dynastically. He's got these kids he's trained to be part of his organization, and he also runs his company like a feudal baron. He can be very crass and sounds like Archie Bunker sometimes. He can be very crass, but by all accounts in his handling of his employees and the way he relates to them he's extremely lordly but magnanimous and gentle with people, very forgiving, and he gives them a lot of latitude. He has some aristocratic virtues about him that are one of the reasons why he's a very effective builder of big companies.

So, those are some of the things I think unite us when we look at the Trump phenomenon. There's something here. There's something really exciting here even though he doesn't really agree with us on a lot of the most important issues.

LR: Just so I understand, back to the question before of the differences, of course you're more populist and they're more elitist, but you would both share anti-egalitarianism?

GJ: Yes, to some extent. Equality is a nice thing, but it's not the most important. That's the way I put it. Liberty is a nice thing, but it's not the most important thing. There are higher values that might cause us to want to trim the liberty of the individual and trim social equality, and to the extent those higher values exist I will compromise on those issues.

I do think a certain republican attitude about having a society where there's a broad middle class, where there are lots of property owners, where people are more self-employed than employed by large corporations, and where people don't work on plantations for big bosses. That is a kind of egalitarian attitude that I have.

On the other hand, I would love to see an ethos like you have in Japan where corporate CEOs would be embarrassed to pay themselves as much as Americans do in comparable positions. I'd like to see that because they're quite rich anyway, right? There are certain upper limits. There should be a certain sense of classical virtues like temperance that I would love to see come back.

But yeah, if people produce more value they should have more rewards. Income inequality is a fine thing, but you don't want it to translate into social and political inequality, if you put it that way, the breakdown of the functioning of a republic where you've got a lot of free people, self-employed people, and so forth. So, I would like to see limits on loan capital. Things like that.

And you see this throughout history, and it's been a theme of republican thinkers throughout history, if people can borrow against their property, if they can mortgage their property and then lose it, this is one of the ways that independent farmers and homeowners become renters and employees. So, you want to find ways of limiting that kind of stuff.

In ancient Athens, Solon instituted debt repudiation, because he realized it was threatening the republican liberties of Athens. More and more people were losing their land and becoming laborers on somebody else's land. The plantation economy was asserting itself, and so he introduced a shaking off of debts and broke up estates and gave small farms to farmers again and tried to recreate the middle class.

The same dynamic happened with the destruction of the Roman Republic, and in the 19th-century American context, the populist movement there was very, very concerned with preventing the impoverishment of farmers. They were opposed to the gold standard, because it was deflationary and harmed farmers especially.

All of these kinds of issues are things that I'd bring back, and those have an egalitarian bite to them, but it's not the idea of complete strict equality is the highest value in society.

LR: Right. For you, it's identity and order, you could say?

GJ: Identity and order. Identity and a kind of organic society. That's how I would like to think of it, and organic societies have differentiation in them. They've got hierarchies, but at the same time there has to be a moral obligation to make all those internal distinctions work for the good of everyone as opposed to this factionalist attitude that the people on the top are ruling for their benefit alone.

LR: What does it mean, "organic society"?

GJ: It means organic like an organism. Today we have an inorganic society where you've got different classes and different groups of people, and they're all pursuing factional interests. It's not a single organism with a common life and common interests. It's an economic zone where warring tribes are fighting over spoils. That's what most societies are like today, whereas in an organic society there is a sense that it is a whole and it has a common good. If there is not a whole then there is no common good.

That's all I really mean by organic. It's a whole, it has a common good, and the internal differentiations that exist in that work towards the common good, and when you start getting a part that's working for its own interests, well, that's analogous to a tumor growing in a body. It's an organ or it's a clump of tissue that's inimical to the common interests.

LR: And so you think there is a common good?

GJ: Yeah.

LR: How would you define it?

GJ: The common good for the French is to keep on being French.

LR: That's your point of view of the common good. So, what if someone disagrees that that's the common good?

GJ: Well, we can talk it over. But, you know, eventually someone's going to decide, and we hope that we can create the broadest possible consensus, and there will be about 10 to 15% who will probably never get on board. But we can deal with that.

But yeah, in the simplest identitarian sense of a common good, the common good of Hungary is that Hungarian people will have a home and there will be Hungarian people in the future, that the things that they value and love will continue to be valued and loved by their descendants, you know, until the sun burns out and we have to go and have Hungary on another planet somewhere. I'm being somewhat facetious, but not 100% facetious. But that's really the attitude I have.

For a European-descended American like myself, the common good really is that the things that we have created and valued will, first of all, be restored, and they will be propagated.

How to put this? I hate using these old 19th-century imperialist terms like "manifest destiny," but I do also think that we should strive for some kind of destiny to actualize our highest potentialities, and that includes things like perfecting us culturally and perfecting science. One of the things that I think is the most important is protecting the biosphere that is massively over-stressed. I would like to see human beings continue to explore the depths of the oceans and outer space, things like that. These things are glorious, and I think that they elevate us. We have that potentiality, and I think that when we see these things actualized we respond with awe. And that's a good thing. That brings us all together.

LR: Right. To what extent is the Alt Right in part a revival of the Old Right before the Reagan and Buckley conservative revolution, before *National Review* Republicanism? It used to be more isolationist. It used to be more protectionist.

GJ: Yeah. And let me just make a little point here. People have criticized the way I use "Old Right." I wrote this essay "New Right vs. Old Right"[7] where I stipulate that the Old Right for me just refers to National Socialists and fascists and inter-war totalitarian movements, but I did grant that there is an Old Right in the American tradition that is pre-WWII, and yes they are protectionist, they are anti-interventionist. To a great extent, the paleoconservatives were looking back to that Old Right.

LR: Yeah. Exactly.

GJ: Most definitely. After the Second World War, the Right was relaunched by William F. Buckley, and it was really defined in such a way that a lot of what constituted the Right before WWII was just thrown out.

LR: Yeah.

GJ: You know, nativism, skepticism toward freedom of trade, and things like that. There was a strong Right, populist critique of liberal economics and libertarian economics in the Old Right in America. All of that's totally valid.

That's one of the things that astonished me in my intellectual journey. Before I became a philosophy major, I was briefly an economics major, and I was very interested in economics and somewhat enchanted by the whole free market economics model. And then to discover that there's this whole raft of critiques from the Right of liberal, libertarian, free market, Manchesterist, and whatever economics. It was a great discovery, because all of that has been completely marginalized within the

---

[7] In *New Right vs. Old Right*.

economics profession, which is very, very interesting, because nominally a lot of libertarians and free market types are Right-wing. But the stuff that they really emphasize is completely consistent with the functioning of our globalized Left-wing oligarchy. The elements of Rightist critiques of neoliberalism and liberalism that they've completely hidden—things like distributism, things like the populist movement, the critics of gold standards, or the social credit movement, guild socialism—all of these things are incredibly rich traditions of thought, and they have these free marketeers absolutely nailed, which I guess is one reason they hide this stuff, because what they stand for doesn't stand up to that kind of critique.

It's very, very interesting if you go back into the 19th century when a lot of these movements are coming into existence, there's the "horseshoe effect" that people talk about where the political spectrum curves around and meets in certain ways. The things that are still valuable about socialism today were acknowledged and understood for the most part by Right-wing critics of capitalism before the First World War and Second World War, which I think is really interesting.

LR: Yeah. It's strange for me to hear you say "Left-wing oligarchs" when there's not much that I can see that's Left-wing except for the cultural aspects of it.

GJ: Yeah, but that's really what it's all been reduced to. It's "Cultural Marxism," as people like to say.

LR: Economy-wise, it's ultra-capitalist, ultra-financialized and globalized, free trade, and all these things are what I would call Right-wing in the sense of pro-market, pro-capitalist.

GJ: Right. But you do understand my point though.

LR: Yeah.

GJ: I would agree that it's bad for the public, it's bad for working people, the middle class, and it's bad for society as a whole, and yet there are lots and lots of Leftists who are perfectly comfortable with this system, and Left-wing identity politics, especially identity politics, is organically part of this oligarchy today.

LR: Yeah, exactly, but I don't consider them legitimate Leftists.

GJ: OK.

LR: But yeah, I see what you mean.

GJ: Self-described Leftists then, who are organically part of the oligarchy.

LR: Yeah. I get it. I think that's practically all of my questions. So, just out of curiosity, you majored in philosophy? That's what you told me?

GJ: Yes.

LR: And that means a Master's in philosophy?

GJ: I got a Ph.D., yeah.

LR: Oh, you have a Ph.D.?

GJ: A Bachelor's, a Master's, *and* a Ph.D. in philosophy!

LR: Oh, OK! What university?

GJ: I don't want to go into all these particulars.

LR: Oh, you don't want to say anything at all about that.

GJ: Yeah. There are 53,000 Greg Johnsons on Facebook alone, so that provides me with a certain cloud of unknowing that I can hide details in.

LR: Right. But you don't hide your political opinions in your everyday life?

GJ: No, but I don't want people throwing bricks through my windows and things like that.

LR: Oh, yeah, of course.

GJ: Or Theresa May — or I guess she's now the Prime Minister—but I don't want the Home Office sending me letters banning me from the United Kingdom, which I know they would do if they could just figure out which of those 50-some thousand Greg Johnsons on Facebook I am and send something to my address.

LR: Right. Do you still work in academia? Are you a researcher or teacher?

GJ: No.

LR: No.

GJ: No. My academic career was brief and inglorious, and I went directly from there to be involved in all of this stuff.

LR: You mean professionally? Is this . . .

GJ: This is my job. I make a living as a publisher and a blogger on the New Right.

LR: Really? Oh, OK.

GJ: Yeah, I employ myself and a couple other people, actually, with my efforts.

LR: OK. I should have asked this question at the very beginning but sorry for being all over the place. The Alt Right, you could say it starts around 2010? Would that be the date? The thing is that there's so many older trends and older movements that seem to come together that it's hard to put a beginning date.

GJ: I think in 2008 and 2009 was probably when it was coming together as an idea, and then in 2010 at the beginning of the year the webzine *Alternative Right* was launched. So, I guess it was coming together in 2008 and 2009 then it rolled out to the world at the beginning of 2010.

LR: Right. OK. Well, thanks a lot for taking all that time to develop all these points. It was very helpful.

GJ: Well, thank you very much. I enjoyed this actually. This was fun.

LR: You're not interviewed a lot, no?

GJ: No, actually I've been dodging interviews with the American press for a couple of reasons. The main reason is I want Donald Trump to win, and American reporters have been contacting me basically because they're trying to get juicy quotes to smear him with by associating him with all sorts of crazy, unappetizing radicals like me, and I don't want to play their little game.

I figured, you being in France, you're far enough away from that particular low agenda, and so I figured why not.

LR: It's not even web-based. It's an actual paper publication, so you can't even go online.

GJ: Yeah, I tried to do a little research about you, and I was like, "Wait. This is ink and paper. How archaic!" But that's great. I actually like that fact. And when the lights all go out it'll still be around. So, it's a good form.

But yeah, I made a reference recording of this. Would you mind after your article comes out or whatever if I were to make that public?

LR: Our interview?

GJ: Yeah! I thought it was very interesting.

LR: Um. I definitely do not want to be filmed.

GJ: No. I just have the audio.

LR: Well, I have to think about it. I didn't really contradict you at all, because it wasn't really a debate but I suppose . . . I suppose. I'm not sure I would want my name associated . . . Well, I'm not going to hide that. I'm using the interview. I suppose there's nothing wrong with it, I guess.

GJ: Right. Well, I can send you the recording if you want to listen to it over again.

LR: OK. Sure. I would have paid more attention to being

more articulate with my questions.

GJ: Oh, no! You were excellent. You were quite good. I was really happy. I was feeling like I was searching and mumbling and woolgathering a lot.

LR: Fair enough. But I guess there's nothing wrong with it. I just wouldn't want my face to appear.

GJ: No. No, not at all. It's just audio.

LR: Maybe because some of your crowd looks kind of aggressive.

GJ: Oh, of course. Yeah.

LR: So, I don't know if I'd want to be attacked.

GJ: No, nobody's going to do that. Well, think about it.

LR: That should be OK. And OK. Thanks a lot for taking all that time.

GJ: No, it was a pleasure and just send me a link to whatever you write up. I'd like to see it.

LR: OK. It probably won't be online.

GJ: Oh, could you send me a copy of it then?

LR: Maybe I could make a PDF.

GJ: PDF. Yeah.

LR: It will be a very, very long article.

GJ: Well, good. I read French pretty well, so I will enjoy it.

LR: It probably, as you can guess from my honest presentation of myself, it will not be favorable, but it will be . . . Well, as you can guess, a Left-wing interpretation.

GJ: I can't ask everyone to agree with me, but I do enjoy having civil intellectual conversations and debates.

LR: Yeah, it should be possible to talk with even your adversaries. But what's also troubling and interesting is that . . . Of course, I'm not sensitive at all to . . . Race and identity doesn't talk to me at all, but on the other hand the critique of globalization and that part of it is totally compatible with my politics, so that's always sort of troubling to see. Points in common.

GJ: Yeah, well, it is interesting to me. I used to be a libertarian, and all of this stuff fell on deaf ears, and now I think of myself as Left-wing as one can reasonably be. In my essay "The End of Globalization," the main point that I make is that if you're going to draw a line and halt globalization, what's the natural line to draw it at? What is the natural end point? And I say that it's natural to draw the line at the nation-state.

It just makes sense, because you've got governments in place, you've got common history, you've got policies. A lot of things that were very good that happened over the last century happened within the context of nations that had protectionist measures in place. And so, in some ways, to end globalization you need to reset to an earlier form of what France was up to or what the United States was up to.

LR: Yeah, I completely agree with that. The thing is that then the discussion is how do you make a nation? Is it based on an idea of citizenship or is it based on an idea of ethnicity? And that's where we probably sort of diverge.

GJ: Yeah. The mainstream today is, at best, civic nationalism. Even the Front National is a civic nationalist organization. Donald Trump is a civic nationalist. There's no question about it.

LR: Yeah.

GJ: I would like to go to a civic nationalism. I think that would be an improvement. However, I think it's an inherently unstable form of government, and that there are ethnic fault lines within any civic nationalist thing that would have to be addressed next.

Civic nationalism is always trying to foist artificial forms of unity upon people, and why should we foist artificial forms of unity upon people when there are actual organic forms of unity that are already there? Even, probably, in you. You know, because you're French. You have a lot in common with other French people, and there's an organic connectedness that you have that is probably more rooted and more stable and more, therefore, conducive to a functioning, just society than artificial civic forms of nationalism that we're constantly trying to impose.

Here's another thing. Carl Schmitt is wonderful about this. He talks about how to function democracy is illiberal. Democracy and liberalism don't go together, because when a democracy is trying to function it tries to impose *unity* on the populace, and if it's a multicultural, multi-ethnic populace it will impose forms of unity that are often fake.

And one of the most interesting things is to look at the history of 20th-century fake nationalisms like Turkish nationalism, for instance. They invented a whole fake history for themselves. It's really quite remarkable.

LR: Oh, all nation-states do that.

GJ: Yeah! But it has to be imposed with a certain violence.

LR: For sure.

GJ: And, of course, what happened in the Ottoman Empire when they tried to create Turkishness as a unifying factor is they basically tried to exterminate the Christian minorities of the empire. There is a terrible logic to this, which is why I favor, if necessary, breaking up these nation-states, if they're mini-empires, so that you don't have to have fake forms of unity imposed really by doing violence to people's identity.

LR: Yeah. I think I'm more skeptical about being able to achieve that unity. Even maybe just because I believe, as a Marxist, I probably believe too much in class antagonism, and I don't feel close at all to the French boss exploiting people, you know? Maybe I feel that. That's just my Marxist approach probably.

GJ: Right. Well, you know, I'm not a Marxist . . . Obviously.

LR: I'm glad we got that.

GJ: We got that out there, yeah. In case you were wondering about that . . . Really there are all sorts of things that Marxists are zeroing in on that are bad about capitalism and modernity. But I just don't think that the Marxist framework is true or adequate. I don't believe in historical materialism. I'm really a kind of historical idealist.

I think, honestly, as a political philosophy and as an account of history, Hegel is disturbingly close to the truth for me. The great thing about Hegel, I think, is he rediscovers something that's central to classical political philosophy, which is the concept of *thumos*, the middle part of the soul, the spirited part of the soul. Which is what? It's attachment to one's own, including one's own identity ultimately. Not just one's personal identity, one's sense of honor, but also one's place, one's roots, one's homeland, one's people. That was, for all the classical Greek thinkers, the essentially political emotion.

Desire. Well, that leads to the global marketplace. Reason. That leads to the cosmopolis, the republic of letters. But the distinctly political part of the soul that leads to diversity of political orders is *thumos*.

Hegel believes that really *thumos* is the driving force of history. The master-slave dialectic is all about a struggle to the death over honor, which is the thumotic part of the soul.

One of the things that I've been working on just recently is a review of Peter Sloterdijk's book *Rage and Time*, because I found out that actually one of the strategists for Alternative für Deutschland is a student of his, and in *Rage and Time* Sloterdijk is arguing for the inadequacy of modern liberalism, and I would also say Marxism too, and psychoanalysis to understand the distinctly political emotions and passions which are connected with *thumos*. This fellow, whose name escapes me now [Marc Jongen], the Sloterdijk student, basically has come up with an argument for German nationalism that's very, very simple and bypasses all of the events from 1933 to 1945.

He simply says, "Look, it's natural, normal, and right for

people to love their own, to have a love of one's own, a prefer-ence for people who are closer to them over strangers." And that's really the basis for ethnic nationalism. I think it's a very powerful argument, actually.

If you look at Carl Schmitt's *The Concept of the Political*, really the hidden assumption there is the power of *thumos*, because he says there will never be a global polity. Politics is always plural for him. What does that mean? It means that inherent in the political is a particularizing force that always will posit an "us vs. them."

LR: Yeah.

GJ: And that, I think, is a dimension that for me really opened up the book of history. I don't think that people really understand history by looking back at it from materialist lenses. I think that most of the cultural realm is based on an economy of, if you will, *thumos* rather than desire. Human be-ings are articulating their distinctness as a species by creating artificial worlds that are not governed by the economy of de-sire.

And so, I look at someone like Bataille in his Nietzsche-influenced writings about culture as having something essen-tial that he's saying that fits in with the Hegelian and Platonic notion of *thumos*, because we create culture precisely by negat-ing materialism. We raise ourselves above the realm of necessi-ty by creating luxury. And so I think that history has to be un-derstood not through materialism but primarily as a negation of materialism, which creates this realm of culture.

That's why I'm not a historical materialist.

FORCED TO BE FREE

INTERVIEW WITH MIKE ENOCH[*]

MIKE ENOCH: Alright. So, I'm here with Greg Johnson—you know him, you love him, hopefully—of Counter-Currents.com.

We're just going to have a chat about . . . We'll just start and see where it goes. We talked a little bit beforehand, and the first question Greg wanted me to ask was, "What do you think of our site? What do you think of TRS and what we've been doing?"

GREG JOHNSON: Well, Mike, thanks for having me on the show. I've been a big fan of you guys for a long time. I think TRS is great. I love *The Daily Shoah*, and I like the *Lampshades* interviews as well. What I like about you guys is that you are really witty and enjoyable, and I am not the kind of person who likes to tune into talk radio and listen to people like Opie and Anthony shooting the breeze. A friend of mine tried to introduce me to Opie and Anthony when we were driving in a convertible down the Pacific Coast Highway, and after a few minutes I wanted to leap to my death on Big Sur, because I couldn't stand it.

ME: That's funny because sometimes my partner, Seventh Son, and I talk about how Opie and Anthony is sort of like our spirit animal, if you will.

GJ: Right.

ME: Because we were both . . . I confess we're both sort of middle-class guys from the tri-state New York/New Jersey area. We had very similar upbringings growing up. We didn't meet until recently, but we grew up similarly. We were both fans of Opie and Anthony when we were younger, and I get why it's not everyone's cup of tea. I think that we actually do get into more intellectual topics. Like they're mostly just dick jokes.

---

[*] On May 21, 2015, Mike Enoch's interview with me appeared on Between Two Lampshades on The Right Stuff. The audio is no longer available online.

GJ: Yeah.

ME: It's funny because we just sort of by default adopted that format, but I completely get why it might not be everybody's thing.

GJ: Well, it's the ideas that are attractive of course, but it's your personalities too. I think you guys are really witty, really funny, and it's just enjoyable to hear you get together and talk.

It's also important from a metapolitical point of view, because you guys are educating yourselves in public and drawing a lot of really smart people along in your wake. When Bulbasaur was talking about Kevin MacDonald, and you guys were talking about him more generally on the show, I think that was really important. I think that a lot of people started reading *The Culture of Critique* because of that.

ME: They did. I've sent out many copies of it just through email to people who requested it. I thought about putting it on our site as a permanent link, but that's of dubious legality so I won't do that. But people can still email me and I will send you an e-book copy of it.

GJ: Well, that's great. I don't think Kevin MacDonald would mind.

ME: I don't think he would mind, but there might be somebody that minds.

GJ: I think that he actually owns the copyright to it now. I think the whole thing is on his website now.

ME: Oh, that's great then. One way or another get your hands on it. Read it.

And you're right about us sort of educating ourselves in public, because as you know we came out of a libertarian background. And when libertarianism became too retarded, if you will, we all had to kind of shift to something else, and we started playing around in neo-reaction. That didn't feel quite right. And we started looking at all these questions that were floating around on the Alt Right, and we are sort of gelling around a narrative, and I think we are getting very close to a coherent narrative now.

Kevin MacDonald was a big influence on me. I know there are other things I need to read, but yeah it continues to develop.

GJ: Yeah, and I think NRx is a really exciting field, frankly. Personally, I came out of libertarianism myself, and I started out when I was in high school really becoming a libertarian. I was always individualist minded, and I was always something of an elitist. My staunch Democrat, union father and I would go around and around about things, and I saw the Milton Friedman *Free to Choose* program. Part of it, I think, was that it rustled my father a little bit. That was just a bonus, right? I thought that the arguments were really compelling. I read Ayn Rand when I was a senior in high school, and I read *Atlas Shrugged* when I was a freshman in college, a bunch of her essay collections when I was a freshman. I was a bit of a boy Objectivist, a bit of an asshole, for a couple of years because of that.

But you know, I was really genuinely interested in philosophy before I read Ayn Rand, and because I was still interested in philosophy, I sort of read my way out the other side of Ayn Rand into other things, and I became more of a conservative, more of a kind of paleoconservative. Oddly enough, one of the books that really influenced me in that direction was a black conservative, Thomas Sowell's book called *A Conflict of Visions*.

Sowell lays out this distinction between constrained and unconstrained visions of society, and the constrained vision is for him exemplified by Edmund Burke. It's an anti-rationalist, tradition-minded conservatism, and the unconstrained mentality is William Godwin the anarchist writer. I read that, and I could tell that the Godwin view was false, and the Burke view was closer to the truth.

But damn it, all of my assumptions were very Godwinesque! I was a classical liberal. Very rationalistic. I had been reading Rand. Also in my second year of college I read through all of *Human Action*, and I thought it was a fantastic book. I read *Socialism* the same semester. So, I was into the Austrian school. I was into Ayn Rand. When I read Sowell I started getting more interested in Hayek because he had the same kind of evolutionary, skeptical, anti-rationalist sociology and anthropology, but still basically classical liberal political conclusions.

When I got into graduate school I was crashing for a few days with some graduate students while I looked for my own place, and I picked up a copy of *The New Criterion*, and I thought, "This is a really impressive magazine," because I was a culture vulture. I was really into classical music. I was really interested in art history. When I was a kid I wanted to be an archaeologist or an art historian. I was just really, really interested in ancient civilizations. I realized it was primarily an interest not so much in digging in kitchen refuse dumps like archaeologists actually do, but the history of civilization, the history of art, the history of the mind, and so forth. That attracted me.

Anyway, I was very interested in culture, and so I got this kind of Right-wing, neoconish culture magazine. Picked it up and really got into it. Started subscribing to it. Started reading *Commentary*. I had been a really big fan of Hannah Arendt my last year or two of college. I read her in political philosophy class and got into phenomenology and Heidegger and all these other areas.

I rapidly figured out that there was a strong Jewish slant to neoconservatism. *Commentary* is published by the American Jewish Committee.

ME: About what year was this? If you don't mind revealing that. You don't have to if you're not comfortable revealing it.

GJ: I guess I can't even remember the year, but I was 22 or 23 when I started reading *The New Criterion* and *Commentary*.

I liked the quality of the writing. I was somewhat pro-Zionist at the time, but then I started realizing there was a definite Jewish bias to this, and it wasn't necessarily my bias.

In graduate school, I started reading Leo Strauss and being around Straussian professors. I thought they were really impressive people. I think Strauss is a tremendously impressive writer. And yet again I could see there was a particularly parochially Jewish angle to this.

ME: The only reason I asked the question about the years is because when I started getting into . . . When I started getting out of my Left liberal upbringing, and I started getting interested in other ideas and I was into libertarianism and paleoconservatism, one of my early influences was *Antiwar.com*. So, it was made clear early in my politicization, if you will, that neocon was a Jewish conservative outlook. I hesitate to even call it conservatism. What the neocons would always say is, "Oh, 'neocon' is just a code word for Jew," and *Antiwar.com* was upfront about that. It is, and it doesn't matter.

GJ: Yeah, *Antiwar.com* wasn't around. The internet wasn't really around when I started.

ME: Yeah. So, I was aware of the . . . I used to couch it in terms like "Zionist." Now, I just say Jewish because that's what it really is. So, I was aware that neocon was a distinctly Jewish movement early on. But this is like the year 2000.

I feel like I'm old when I'm around TRS people, but I think I'm younger than you.

GJ: This was back in the '90s. I started getting more and more keyed into the Jewish slant on things. Living around Jews, rubbing elbows with them, I had some Jewish graduate student colleagues, one Jewish professor actually. The real thing that crystallized it, though, was I really started getting into Heidegger, and I really like Heidegger still. He's one of my favorite philosophers. I was getting a Ph.D. in philosophy, and I actually thought I might write a dissertation on Heidegger.

Anyway, the controversy around Heidegger's National Socialism really called forth a lot of rhetorical thuggery, let's put it that way, on the part of Jewish commentators, and it just didn't sit well with me.

ME: I know the feeling.

GJ: I remember, actually, having disputes with Jewish graduate students that I would bump into about this stuff. A few years later I read *Mein Kampf*, and Hitler goes on about his encounters with Jews in Vienna and the formation of his worldview, and he talks about how he would patiently spend hours debating and destroying the arguments of these Jewish socialists, and then the next day he'd hear them trotting out the same arguments.

ME: I know the exact passage you're talking about. Yes.

GJ: That's when I knew this guy was telling the truth. That was so powerful. I'd seen that with my own eyes. There was just no gainsaying it. That was something else. It just didn't sit well with me. I was becoming increasingly sort of paleoconservativeish.

One of my favorite Heidegger scholars, a guy named Thomas Sheehan, wrote a couple articles that I dug up because I was just going through his bibliography and reading everything he wrote. One was an article about Alain de Benoist and Julius Evola. The other was just about Evola entirely. And I thought, "Wow! This is really interesting stuff!" So, that was my first encounter with the European New Right of Alain de Benoist and then the ideas of Evola. I bumped into an Evola book not long after that. I got *Revolt Against the Modern World*. I also started getting stuff by Alain de Benoist, and I really found these people quite impressive.

But you know, there was this weird thing going on where, logically, if you asked me, "Are there other people out there who believe these things?" — because clearly there have to be other people out there if these books are being written and published — I would have granted that. But I had this deep inhibition about actually seeking out such people, because I guess I thought they'd all be a bunch of weirdos. I had some conservative friends in grad school with whom I could talk about *some* of this stuff, but we kept it between us for years, until I bumped into this guy. I was living in Atlanta, and this was 1999, I believe. I was in the Borders Books in Buckhead, and there was this guy in a black t-shirt standing in the philosophy section. He had short hair and a black t-shirt and tattoos on his biceps. And I thought, "Hmm . . . Looks like a bad boy." I think he picked up Kojève's *Introduction to the Reading of Hegel*, and I said, "That's a really great book." And we got started talking.

This turned out to be Joshua Buckley who is the editor of the journal *TYR* now. He was an ex-skinhead and really, really intelligent. Pretty much self-educated. High school drop-out, highly intelligent, self-educated guy, ex-skinhead. And he was the first actual concrete person that I met who was on the Right, aside from myself and some friends of mine. I found it really eye-opening. Not just eye-opening, world-opening. This whole world opened up around me.

ME: Yes, I can also relate to that feeling.

GJ: Yeah. He introduced me to the neofolk music scene and a lot of other stuff that I thought was really fascinating. At that point, I kind of made the plunge into not just privately thinking these ideas but not doing anything more . . . Because, essentially, deep down inside I just felt it was all hopeless anyway, right? It's like the world's going to hell, and there's nothing anybody can do. I actually started thinking, "Well, maybe something can be done." So, I started educating myself and getting more into this.

I think it was Labor Day of 2000 when I took the next step. I went out to a diner in Buckhead where David Irving was going to talk. There were people there, and some of them seemed a little like seedy haters from Hollywood central casting. But you know, I'm one of these essentially liberal-minded white people. I'm open to "the other." I carried around *National Geographic* magazines when I was a kid, to the ridicule of my peers, because I was so fascinated with ethnography, and I was one of those white people Christian Lander talks about who's always trying to become an expert on somebody else's culture. That was me. And along with that comes a willingness to take certain social risks.

So, I said, "Fuck it. These people look a little weird, but I'm going to take the risk."

ME: You know, it's funny. I'm sorry to interrupt, but it's funny you say that because I think that for many of the kind of liberal white people, they're not so liberal on that. I mean, this might be a little bit of a derailment of your story, but . . .

GJ: Oh no, exactly. Because white people have this weird dual consciousness. One the one hand, the liberal-minded white person is extremely . . . I'm in Seattle right now. It's just *über*-Nordic culturally, and still the population is very Nordic. In Seattle, they have the biggest Norwegian Independence Day parade outside of Norway, for instance.

ME: I've been to the *Syttende Mai* parade in New York City, and it actually exists, and it's not that small although it's been probably 20 years since then. Maybe a little less than that since I went. But I have Norwegian ancestry. My mother's house is completely decked out in Norwegian stuff. But yeah, there's actually one in New York City, and it's fairly large. It's probably not as big as the one in Seattle though.

GJ: Yeah, but it's a very Nordic place. One of the things about Seattlites, and one of these things about Pacific Northwest people—and I'm one of them—is if a stranger comes up to you, somebody from out of town, they're speaking English a little oddly, they ask directions, and you're just like, "Oh, yes! It's over here." And everybody's super welcoming to strangers. But on the other hand if they sense that one of their own people is not on board with being super welcoming to strangers, they come down on them like a ton of bricks.

ME: Well, this is the sort of paradox of the high trust society. Kevin MacDonald talks about this when he talks about . . . I don't want to call it the weakness of white people, but it's the trait, it's the character that is able to be exploited by other elements and Jewish philosophers and media critics and things like that in particular, I would say, because they are very skilled verbally. This high trust notion that we have high trust amongst each other, and one of the ways we maintain it is through monitoring. It sounds kind of creepy when you put it that way, but it's not really. It's like we all sort of look at the behavior of others in the community and make sure they're on board with the norms, but when those norms become perverted then problems happen, if you get what I'm saying.

GJ: Oh yeah, I totally agree with this analysis. One of the reasons why European societies and especially Northern European societies were so capable of creating highly functional scalable institutions that allowed people to cooperate to do great things is because we are essentially very individualistic and we are prone to trust, and we also have enough conscience as individuals to not betray that trust. So, we are constantly taking social risks with strangers, and we are constantly goaded by our own conscientiousness to keep our promises with those strangers, and that makes it possible for us to create great civilizations. Whereas people who are not as willing or capable of trusting strangers and not as willing or capable of keeping promises to strangers or people who are outside your closely defined ethnic in-group, those societies are brittle, and they cannot create and sustain large-scale institutions. The ones that they do create tend to be, if you peel the veneer off, simply ethnic mafias, family mafias or tribal mafias. But those are weak institutions because if you are constrained by nepotism you cannot put the best person in the job. So, they are corrupt, they're nepotistic, and they are consequently brittle under pressure, and they have very, very marked strong—how to put it—limits on their ability to scale up. Because you can't just bring in anybody to your ethnic mafia. They've got to be your 4th cousin or something, and if you run out of 4th cousins, well, you run out of people you can trust, and that means that your government or your business or your tribe, whatever it is, is going to be limited in its capacity.

ME: Yeah. I don't know if you've ever heard of Curt Doolittle. Do you know about Curt Doolittle?

GJ: I listened to his interview. I thought he was really interesting.

ME: Yeah, because the things you guys are saying using slightly different language and terms are basically the same narrative here. He has developed highly specific terms for things like this. White people, Northern European white people particularly, are high trust. Absolute nuclear family centered. Create commons. Because of this high trust, etc.

And that's basically what you were talking about. He calls

the strong institutions commons because it's not simply the property owners of the institutions but the whole society that benefits. One of his lines is like, "White people, particularly Northern Europeans, consider telling the truth as paying a tax into the commons, and we willingly do it because we understand that everyone's better off when we do it." And that's a trait that's specific to our people, our ethnic group.

I'm mostly Northern European, some Southern European and some Slavic, but mostly Northern European, and this touches something deeply inside of me if you can relate to what I'm saying.

GJ: Totally. One of the philosophers that I've studied the most is Immanuel Kant. He has this formulation of the categorical imperative where he says that the only moral maxims you should follow are those you could will to be universal laws. Now, that is a very peculiar idea.

ME: Yes.

GJ: He also talks about acting as if you were a citizen of a Kingdom of Ends, a particular kind of order where people are rational agents who are ends in themselves, and you have non-exploitative relationships with them. It's basically talking about free individuals. There's an idealism there because the fact of the matter is you don't live in a Kingdom of Ends, but what you're doing is *not* acting according to the real world you're living in; you're acting according to the world you'd *like* to live in. In so doing, you are incurring risks in this world. But we feel very high-mindedly committed to the idea that we should still take these actions because we are creating a better world.

ME: That's true across Left and Right for white people.

GJ: Oh yeah. Totally. And this is why it's very, very difficult to convince them to change their course because in a certain way the fact that it might not be working out right now, the fact that they might be being exploited or subverted in some ways because of their idealistic course of action . . . If you bring that up they're going to say, essentially the reaction is going to be,

"Well, look, you're just being small-minded, petty, and selfish. If we persevere in this course we will overcome this, and we will create utopia." It's only mean, petty people who give up at this stage of the way.

The trouble is that this is not a functional attitude anymore. That particular kind of high-mindedness. We actual measure the sublimity of our actions by the difficulties that it creates for us personally.

ME: Yep.

GJ: And we can't do that forever because we are locked in a struggle now with people who are evolutionarily and culturally calibrated to exploit those characteristics as weaknesses.

ME: Yes, completely. And the thing I like to say, or other people have said to me and I have now adopted, "If it's not re-ciprocated, you're not really living by the principle."

GJ: Exactly.

ME: It's not being reciprocated.

GJ: Yeah, exactly. It's not being reciprocated. But the idea is, "Well, yes, it's not being reciprocated *now*, but eventually if we can just show them our good will and show them how wonder-ful we are . . ." Because white people really do believe that we are wonderful, that the way that we live is the best possible way, and that literally everybody would want to live this way.

Go to some *über*-white place like Stockholm or something like that, and you see how beautiful everything is, how everything works really well, how kind people are. Why wouldn't you be-lieve that the whole world wants that?

ME: I want it.

GJ: I want it. Everybody else must want it too! We have the assumption that everybody's just like us, and they're not. We've finally encountered people that we cannot assimilate to our in-group. One of the things that's most beneficial about this open-ness to strangers, and Kevin MacDonald talks about this as evolving with hunter-gatherers in the Ice Age of the north, is that if you're a small group of people and you encounter another group of people that you can actually trust and cooperate with then your chances of surviving that long winter have gone up.

ME: Yes.

GJ: Because we have been open to strangers, and the strangers we've been open to have basically been the same kind of people as us who will reciprocate in kind, we have been able to build a great civilization. But that civilization has gone out all over the world, and we've encountered people who are not like us and who look upon us as basically marks.

Jews basically come to our societies like hackers—this is something Matt Parrott used, and I think it's really good—they come to our societies like hackers come to a website. They probe it for its weaknesses.

ME: They find the exploit. That's hacker terminology for you.

GJ: Yeah, and that's what they're doing. The *goy* is always friendly with strangers; he's willing to give strangers the benefit of the doubt, and they will exploit that over and over again. Even when it doesn't work out in their favor they will still keep doing it because their high-mindedness is so pegged to the idea that if they can just show they're big . . . They're big, you know? We're big. We can take it, and if we just persist in this liberal, open course we will convert these people into being part of us, and we'll have utopia.

It's destroying us, and we need to make ourselves conscious of this dynamic so we can inhibit it when it is no longer functional for us. It helped us create a great civilization when we encountered people like us. Now that we're not encountering people like us it's a weakness that's leading to our downfall.

ME: Yeah and I think part of it is also—the thing that makes it difficult—in some sense when the people who aren't like us are Africans, that's one thing. The differences there are so obvious there actually was racism and exclusion and in South Africa they formed territories, "Here's for whites, here's for blacks," and even in the American South because the differences were so obvious and apparent that they couldn't work out.

But when you have a very small group like the Jews, and they're very high in their verbal IQ, and they are able to present as us, and then they can kind of hack this narrative as we've said. They can hack the high trust mechanisms that we use to have created our civilizations. It's very damaging. And then what Kevin MacDonald calls the culture of the holocaust where this idea that we have to constantly be atoning and we can out signal each other.

Signaling is a term that we've hit on. It's one of our TRS terms that we've hit on. Increasingly, we've been calling people out for their signaling. Moral signaling is a fundamental communication strategy that we have, but it also has been hacked. I agree with you, it's been hacked. So, the moral signaling is that we have to atone. We have to never let this happen again. It's because of our fundamental barbarity that we can never let it happen again, that this horrible thing in the past happened and any kind of prejudice that's shown will lead directly to this. So, now white people compete with each other. It's really a very competitive thing to be the one who out morally signals the next. And it's unhealthy. We have to stop.

GJ: We have to stop that. And the idea that another holocaust is going to happen is the most ludicrous idea in the world. Jews have their own country now which has a mountain of nuclear, chemical, and biological weapons. There will never be another holocaust. Get it through your heads. Stop this emotional blackmail. I'm so fucking sick of this whining and emotional blackmail from the most powerful people on the planet.

ME: Yes.

GJ: But still, even though they're the most powerful people on the planet—and would have no hesitation in destroying the planet if they felt their own existence were threatened—these people still have the psychology of cornered rats who think that every issue is existentially threatening to them.

ME: Yes. Even what we're saying now would be considered some sort of existential threat. And I'm like, "Look, there's a country. You could go there. I don't see what the issue is."

GJ: Yep. Exactly. Even in the privacy of our own skulls if we have thoughts against them they consider that to be an existential threat.

Let's just call them what they are. They're a race of paranoid lunatics. One of the things we talked about before we started recording is this strange oscillation in people who suffer from mania between grandiosity, where they feel that they are God, or God is in them, or that everybody's God, and they have this ebullient grandiosity where they literally feel like they're the whole universe; they are God. Then what happens is when people don't respond to you appropriately when you say that you're God, you start feeling that they are evil in some way. You start getting the touchy, paranoid, hateful side. The side that feels victimized and persecuted.

Well, that basically just sounds like Jews to me, because they have the grandiose notion that they are God's chosen people, that they're a light unto the nations, they've given the world all these wonderful things. And when people don't treat them in ways that coincide with their grandiose self-image they assume always that these people have some problem, that these people are evil, malicious, they're plotting against them, they're trying to destroy them. It sounds like a nation where insanity is basically the norm. We need to send them to their nuthouse in the Middle East. Preferably disarming them of all their nuclear weapons at the same time, because you don't give a gun to a child or a person who's in a psychotic episode.

We've given control of our societies, submarines, nuclear weapons, biological and chemical weapons to people who are basically insane, and it's really got to stop.

Anyway, you guys are doing a great job in getting people aware of this and giving people permission to think about this, to laugh about it, and I just think it's a tremendous service that you're doing. Because nothing is more important, I think, than getting the organized Jewish community off our back and disempowering these people and sending them away so we can finally live and breathe and have our own countries again. Anyway, TRS is doing great work in that area.

ME: Yeah, and I think that laughter really is—it's a cliché, but—the best medicine. It's a way to disarm the issue and it's funny because we've all been psychologized into this mentality where "bigotry is bad," "thinking bad things about out-groups is bad," and particularly any bad thoughts you might have about Jewish people. "Bad, bad, bad." This has been drummed into our heads by the media and the school system. The two biggest influences other than your family in your life, schools and media, are consistently hitting you with this narrative, and if your family is hitting you with it too it becomes particularly hard. I even sometimes start to think . . . I don't really any more, but I did for a long time. Now it's like: just make it a joke.

ME: A friend of mine said something to me pretty funny the other day. We were just chatting online in a sort of IM message, and he said, "It's funny because you're one of the least edgy people I know on the Alt Right." And I said, "What are you talking about? Look at what we say. Look at what's on my website." You know what I mean?

GJ: Yeah.

ME: And he's like, "Yeah, but you're a normal guy; you've just got politically incorrect opinions." And that framed it for me in an entirely different way. Because I'm like, "Man, what we're doing is like . . ." I couldn't stop doing it if I wanted to. I have to do it. But I'm thinking, "Man, if people see this my career could be ruined, my family, etc." But he put it in this frame, and I thought, "You know what? You're right. I'm just a guy with politically incorrect opinions. Fuck you!" You know what I mean? And that's kind of the attitude I want our fans and listeners and our friends . . . I hope all our fans become our friends. I've consistently been bringing people in. When people comment on the site a lot and they email me and we talk. Then we become friends, and that I think is how we're broadening our community. And everybody feels this feeling that we're just guys, and we think politically incorrect thoughts, and we say them, and we have fun doing it. That's our thing.

GJ: I think it's great, because people can and do identify with you people just as people. That's very important. When I was editing *TOQ Online* I started this series called Why We Write, or Why I Write is what it should have been called. I was thinking of the old Frank Capra *Why We Fight* series.

ME: We *know* why we fought!

GJ: Yeah. The purpose was just to have our writers talk about why they write. What makes them tick. The purpose of that was to allow people to identify more personally with these people so we're not just names putting out information, but we're real people with real stories. I think telling stories about people's lives, situating things, being a real 3D person, speaking on the radio rather than writing—all of these things are very, very important for building community, building identification on the sort of sub-rational interpersonal level, not just ideas but people. We relate first and foremost to people not just disembodied ideas.

So, you guys are giving a really appealing embodiment to a certain trajectory of self-education and political incorrectness that I think is bringing a lot of people along in your wake. That's why I follow your site. I'm really happy to be finally interviewed on it.

ME: Oh yeah, for sure. The only reason we didn't do this before was scheduling issues. We played email tag before for weeks.

GJ: Oh, I know. I know. I'm not saying, "It's about time!" I have a terrible time scheduling interviews, and I do interviews myself. I've been moving around a lot. I've been traveling a lot, etc. But yeah, it's great to be here.

One thing I wanted to address is you said you couldn't stop doing this. That's how I feel about this. One of the things I would like to stress—because there's so much negativeness and back-biting and "in-fighting" in the movement—a lot of people get the impression that it's a really negative thing. It's like being tied up in a bag full of weasels clawing at you. And I get why people have that impression, and there are a number of people

I'd like to tie together, put in a bag, and drop off a bridge. But, that said, the fact of the matter is that on balance this has been far more fun and far more rewarding personally to me than anything else I could do with my life.

I have met the best people I know. I have met the most interesting people I know. Sometimes not the best, but you meet really interesting people. I've met some of the worst, craziest, most crooked and corrupt people I've ever met too. But once you get outside their baleful influence or if you avoid it, it's still very, very interesting. So, I have a really interesting life, and I'm going to keep doing this. Not just because I think it's really important, but because I think it's personally rewarding. I think that if you're just doing stuff because you think it's right, it's your duty, that's sublime. That's admirable. That's Aryan. But it can't sustain you. It can sustain you to pull yourself together and charge the machine gun nest or something like that. But it can't sustain you for years and decades or a lifetime. You also have to have some personal rewards built into the process, and it is very personally rewarding on a psychological level.

The only thing that really bothers me about this life is the financial insecurity. But it finally occurred to me one day that financial insecurity is something that everybody has to deal with. I know people who are literally worth hundreds of millions of dollars, and they are consumed with financial insecurities. Once that dawned on me it was like, "Well, the last regret that I have has basically flown out the window."

I really love this life. I think it's very, very important, and I think that not only does it potentially make a difference in the most important issue that we face—this is the great battle of our time. I don't just think of it as for the interests of white people. Although that's my primary interest. I do think that this is something that aligns with the interests of the whole world, the welfare of the world, and I think that if we don't save our race this planet is going to be nothing but a burnt out cinder someday.

ME: I agree, and it's funny because the conceit of the Jews is that they're the light of the world. Really? When you look it's Europeans that are. We created the greatest civilizations across two continents (North America and Europe), and if we're gone that's it. There are East Asians, and I respect East Asians, and I'm friends with a lot of them. I think that we can always be friends with them and have bonds of mutual respect across borders.

But European civilization is really nothing like it, and if that goes then it's gone. The world will be reduced into a ball of barbarism like you said, and there will be nothing beautiful and enlightening. It's sad, and I don't want to see that. As you said, I've gotten to the point where now I'm primarily concerned with saving the white phenotype, the white genotype, the white race essentially and keeping us going, keeping us from destroying our native homelands in Europe and our adopted homeland in North America. I'm still holding on to hope. I know there's a lot of people in our sphere who are like, "Give up America." But why should we give up America? We civilized it. Why should we give it up?

GJ: The people who say, "Oh, it's hopeless. We can never get rid of all these people." Look, it's never been more feasible to move large populations.

ME: In North America, there are 230 million white people, people of European descent living in North America. That's almost as many as there are in Europe. I don't see why we have reason to think we need to give up this piece of territory.

GJ: No. The fact is that these people all came here in the last 50 years. The vast bulk of these people have come here in the last 50 years. They can go over the next 50 years. It's not going to take some great cataclysm, some apocalyptic race war, some "Day of the Rope" scenario and all that kind of fantasy literature. If we just had a ruling elite that decided from this point forward that we are going to put our race back on the path towards life, health, flourishing — and what that requires is that we are going to change the dynamics of immigration so that there's a net emigration of non-whites each year — we could wait 50 years.

But, you know, even if it took 50 years for our continent, our country, to be entirely white, we would be reaping all the psychological benefits of that today. I think a lot of white people deep down inside are demoralized by the fact that they the feel that the race is on the path to suicide.

You look at the baby boom or you look at the Third Reich. Objectively, a lot of things had not changed between the end of the Weimar period and the beginning of Hitler's Germany. What had changed was there was a sense that finally things were on the right path. That confidence did a lot of the rest of the work. After World War Two in America, there were all kinds of shortages and problems left over from the war, and yet there was great confidence that we were on the right path, and so we had this great baby boom that lasted really almost 20 years and a prosperity bubble that lasted even longer. That kind of self-confidence is something that we could win back and enjoy today if we just made the decision that white people will henceforth have a future in North America. We don't have a future now, but if we decide to have a future we will reap all the benefits of having a future in the present.

ME: Yeah and I know there are various groups that have different narratives on the post-war boom in the United States, but it's interesting to me that the post-war boom, regardless of whether you're an Austrian or a Keynesian or a Monetarist or whatever the hell you are, was a boom of the confidence of our people, and it was optimistic. What killed it was the counter-culture of the '60s, the Civil Rights movement, the immigration law of 1965. That's when the hope and optimism in the country started being crushed by this counter-culture, which was mostly led by Jewish revolutionaries and intellectuals, and that's what put us on the path that we're on now.

Those that were born in the baby boom had been highly influenced by this. That's my parents, and I know it's the parents or even grandparents at this point of many of our listeners. They become sort of infatuated when the mission of America became social justice and justice for everybody.

But it's demoralizing to white people, fundamentally, and even though there is a lot of us here people don't feel any connection.

It's interesting that we're having this conversation today because just this morning on my way to work I was walking down 17th street (I don't know how well you know New York City) and Irving Place . . . Irving Place is one of the wealthiest parts of New York City. It's actually one of the few parts of Manhattan where there's a private park. The people that live in this area have a private park where you actually have a key if you own or rent a home in the area. It's one of the few places in New York City where that exists. Really, really wealthy area. But it's also right next to some of the scuzziest areas. This phenomenon happens, interestingly, all over the United States. Wealthiest areas near the scuzziest areas. There was a high school I walked by. I believe it was right there on 17th and right before Park Avenue.

There was a fire drill at the high school, and the students started pouring out, and I'm thinking, "Holy crap! 1 out of 15, maybe 1 out of 10 of these I'm seeing are white faces." And I became incredibly demoralized. My heart sunk. It literally sunk, and I felt bad, I felt empathetic for those white kids that were coming out. I can't really project my own feeling on to them, but I imagined myself . . . Because I went to a high school that was about 40-45% black, and now the high school I went to is 55% black. But I was thinking they really can't be loving this, and if it was 90% white those kids would be having so much of a better time.

GJ: Oh yeah. There's no question. We know this, because we know that's the way the human brain is wired.

ME: Yes, there's ample psychological evidence of this. Then I went up to my office and I thought, "Wow, so I've gone from the life that a high school student has to live in New York City to now the life of a middle-aged (and I hate to say it, but I'm approaching that), middle-class professional in New York City, and everyone in my office is white. Some Jews, but mostly white or Asian. Asian, but like white-presenting Asian or Asian-Asian but silent. In an office of 200 people, maybe one or two very white-presenting blacks. This is a different world from what the high school student is encountering. So, I could see the dynamic in one glimpse.

You have parents of people in New York City that are probably middle-class professionals, and this is their experience, and their children's experience is completely different, and there is no way to communicate across that gap. I know some of them have so imbibed this liberal ideology that if their children even tried to talk to them about it or even had the language with which to express this they would be . . . I don't even know what would happen.

GJ: They'd send them to a psychiatrist.

ME: Yeah. They'd probably try to break them of it. It just made me sad. I went through sort of a . . . I hate to sound like I was overwrought and emotional, but for like a half hour at work I was just sitting there thinking, "Oh man, that sucks."

GJ: It's hard to feel like you don't have a future. My grandmother on my mother's side had three children, seven grandchildren, and she had three great-grandchildren. Of her seven grandchildren, only two of them had children. What did they all do with their lives? What have I done with my life? We've all had our careers, we've all had our hobbies, we've all had our trips, we've all had our lavishly doted upon Golden Retrievers, but no kids. She must have looked at that and felt sad near the end of her life. She died last year. What are the chances it's going to continue, with that pattern?

It is sad. Every SWPL, every white person I know who dithers about having kids, I say two things to them. This is advice from someone for whom that ship has probably sailed. First, all of the things you're running around doing with your life instead of having kids or are putting off kids to do, none of these things are going to matter if there's no next generation.

ME: Yeah, you're totally right.

GJ: And second, if you are worried about having kids, or you're not sure if it's a good idea, or you're not sure if you're up to it, or you're afraid that you're bringing them into a terrible world, just think about all of the ancestors that you had going back to the very beginning of our race. Every one of these people probably had it harder than you.

ME: Way harder.

GJ: Way harder, right? And somehow they overcame all of their qualms and life continued on. Are you going to be the whiny little maggot who brings all of their striving and struggles to oblivion because you just can't get your act together and decide to go off the goddamn pill or stop using condoms or whatever and just take the plunge and carry the race forward one more generation?

ME: You know, I don't even think with those that aren't having children that it's necessarily a fear or anxiety. I think it's selfishness, frankly. And I think part of it is because the value of it was not inculcated to them, and there's other factors that go into it that we discussed. But it's selfishness, and it's not even fear and anxiety. I think maybe for some people it is, but . . .

GJ: You're right. The best people are afraid. White people are the only race that abort their children because they're afraid their children won't have an upper middle-class lifestyle. That's insane.

ME: But, you know, when you actually look at stats on abortion the overwhelming majority of abortion . . . Upper middle-class white women very rarely have abortions. I don't know how familiar you are with Charles Murray and his recent book *Coming Apart*. He actually outlines a sort of split between . . . You may or may not agree with this. I'll just sort of lay out what his thesis is, which is that there's two white Americas, and he's saying there's been a split where the upper or "oven," as we say, middle-class and wealthy white America has gone one direction, and lower class white America has gone another. The problem in terms of behavior isn't really with the top half. The top half continues to get married at higher rates than the bottom half, have high investment children at higher rates, are religious at higher rates. Essentially, all the positive traits for carrying on civilization happen at the top 50% of the white income bracket, but that top 50% is also overwhelmingly liberal and doesn't care about any of the things we're talking about.

GJ: Right.

ME: And the lower half is having abortions, they're doing drugs, they're not getting married, they're having children out of wedlock, they're mixed race children. It's a mess. That's really who's being screwed over right now. In the long run, we're all going to get screwed over, but right now it's the bottom rung. It's the bottom 50% that is getting really fucked. In the long run, it's going to be all of us. So, us upper middle class need to get our shit together.

GJ: Well, one of the things that we have to do is overcome this wound in our body politic, which is the attitude I see amongst my liberal relatives, which is that they always define themselves in terms of not being like *those* white people.

ME: Yeah, that's got to end.

GJ: Those lower 50% white people. "Oh, we're not like those people. We're liberal and coastal and eat goat cheese and arugula. We're not like those gun-toting hicks in Montana or something like that." I get that all the time. It is the lowest, most vile form of prejudice.

ME: It really makes me mad.

GJ: Until we realize that, "Look, you're talking about your first cousin here. You're talking about your sister!" These are our people, right? These are our people out there in flyover country that are being mocked, and we need to bristle and stand up for them. Yeah, if there are parts of our race that are being ground down and degraded, we have to come to their defense not feel superior to them.

ME: I completely agree. I remember when I first came to this realization. It happened somewhat when I was in a libertarian milieu, and it fully happened once I moved over towards the Alt Right, for lack of a better term, but now—fuck it—I'm friends with rednecks. You have a problem with that? Yes, I'm friends with rednecks, hicks, hillbillies, whatever you want to call them.

Guys that have ten AR-15s in their basement. They're my friends. Fuck you!

GJ: Yeah. I'm a big snob about a lot of things. There's certain kinds of food I won't eat. There's certain neighborhoods I won't go to. There's certain kinds of television I won't watch. I'm a big snob.

ME: I would recommend not watching any of it.

GJ: "*Breaking Bad* is really good!" But anyway, the kind of snobbery that I hate is the class snobbery, the liberal upper mid-dle-class snobbery against other white people. I'm friends with rednecks, I'm friends with ex-skinheads, and I will defend these people's honor and integrity and their intelligence. I would love to see them matched in debate with some of the executives and board members of charities and snooty Ph.D.-level people that I know, because I know these people would wipe the floor with them, even though they don't have the self-confidence that they otherwise should because they're largely self-educated.

I'm a big populist in this sense. I'm an elitist and a populist. I'm a populist in the sense that the only just system is the system that serves the common good of the society, and that means that you cannot have a just system if it's premised on the ruthless exploitation or exclusion or shitting on a large percentage of your people. On the other hand, I recognize that the best way to have that kind of society is to have an elite that is organically connected with the rest of society.

And I do think there's a role for certain elements of democra-cy. I believe in Aristotle's idea of the mixed constitution. You need to have aristocratic and democratic elements to the consti-tution. The American Constitution was based on the Aristotelian idea of the mixed constitution with a monarchical, aristocratic, and democratic element to it. It's not a bad system. It's a system that is not shallow. It's not rooted in modern liberalism.

ME: I agree.

GJ: All these sort of NRx, anti-modernist people can be dis-missed. It's rooted in the Western political tradition.

ME: I completely agree. Would the US Constitution be so terrible . . . For those who think the United States was just a completely failed project, and I'm not even necessarily whiteknighting for it, but let's imagine the United States was still 90–95–100% white people. Really? Do you think the US Constitution would be such a bane on society then? No, of course not.

GJ: No. And one of the things that I have come to believe as I become more of a racialist is that, in a way, I am somewhat dismissive of people who are too concerned with things like constitutions.

ME: Yeah. I'm right there with you.

GJ: My attitude is white people create order and civilization wherever we go, and it might be a Scandinavian-style welfare state with a constitutional monarch or a republic or something else. But no matter how we slice it or dice it or organize it, if it's white people doing it, it always tends to work out to be orderly, prosperous, and civilized. That's all I care about.

ME: I can't even tell you the level to which I agree with that. For so much of my political life I was focused . . . Like libertarianism, and you can relate to this of course because you were libertarian as well. Where I was like, "No. Free markets! Absolutely free markets! Unregulated . . . blah blah blah" and all this stuff for so many years. I still bristle a little bit when people start talking in, my opinion, overly socialistic terms, but it doesn't even matter because if we had a white state these would be issues that would be hashed out, and it wouldn't go so far. Obviously, I think we can both agree absolute Communism is completely out, but other than that whatever and I'm not going to get so hung up on needing this sort of laissez-faire free market economy, although I do favor that, but that's secondary.

You know what I mean? You and me might not even come down on the same page there, but it doesn't matter because if we had a white state then it wouldn't matter. We could have that political disagreement, the state would still be prosperous, the people would be prosperous, we could deal with X level of social democracy, whatever.

GJ: Yeah, you see, the way I put it in one of my essays somewhere. I've written hundreds of things now, and I lose track of them. I said, "Look, I'm all for pluralism. There's just one thing that's going to be non-debatable under the system that I want to create, and that's that our race is going to be degraded and destroyed." That's going to be off the table. That's not going to be an option. That's going to be non-negotiable. Everybody's going to be on the same page about white people having the right to exist and prosper. Everything else will be up for grabs, and we will be arguing about abortion and feminism and socialism and taxes, but it will be an argument amongst white people, and none of the partisans in those arguments will have the capacity to bring in non-whites as allies to gain an advantage over their own flesh and blood.

That is my vision of utopia. It's very broad-brush and sketched out, but that's fine. That's all we need. We do not need everything worked out. We do not need people who are writing constitutions and designing logos for the ethnostate. It's just silliness.

ME: It's fun though. Somewhat.

GJ: For me, in terms of economic things, the essential thing is the fundamental principle of society. In terms of fundamental principles, I am a collectivist. I think there is such a thing as a common good that can be defined for a people. I think that individualism is part of our nature. It's part of what makes us highly functional as a race. We need to find a way to give maximum scope to individual creativity, maximum scope to individual preferences, private life. All of these things are good things, except when these things conflict with the common good, and when they conflict with the common good we say, "Wait. There are limits here." I think that would leave as much liberty as one could reasonably want, as much individualism as one could reasonably want, without it turning into some kind of false absolute idol which undermines civilization. That's what I think libertarianism does.

ME: Yes.

GJ: Libertarians start out coming up with this wonderful model of voluntary interaction, and they have this science of economics which shows how this works with the marketplace and the price of milk and stuff like that.

ME: And it works on that level.

GJ: And so they just imagine, "Oh, let's extend this model out to its absolute limits. Let's have marriages run on the same model as businesses. Everything's voluntary. Everything's selfish. Everybody is serving their given preferences by interacting and trading with one another."

The trouble is that when you absolutize that, it's bad, because it destroys social capital that made possible that limited realm where it actually works well.

ME: Yeah. I completely agree. I know that we have libertarian listeners. I know there are those Right-wing libertarians for whom our site is a guilty pleasure. That's actually the market I am trying to reach, in their parlance. I am trying to hit that niche because that's where I come from. That's where my friend Seventh Son comes from. Basically, TRS came out of that. We were libertarians that rethought it and came to a different perspective. That's the market I am trying to hit, and I know we're going to strike a chord with them, and it's not because I don't understand your talking points. So often libertarians think, "Oh, you're strawmaning us. You're not understanding what we're talking about when we talk about free markets, when we talk about individualism." No, I get it. I know it, and I know you know it. I know Greg knows it.

We're trying to hit you on another level. You can't have those things outside of a white society.

GJ: Exactly. It presupposes a social capital that cannot be created by the market, and when you absolutize the market it actually undermines that social capital and will destroy the market and will destroy civilization. Therefore, we need to rein this in and keep it within the boundaries in which it is actually functional and beneficial.

ME: In libertarian terms, the market needs to be protected by a bubble of violence, a bubble of force, and I know that's maybe a harsh term. A bubble of force like the state. It's the state. The state is the bubble of force around the market for those people that are protected within it, and that's how it has to work. The state, in my opinion, the boundaries of it should be ethnic. Because why should it not?

GJ: Because why not?

ME: There's no reason why not. If you're into libertarian morality, I challenge you to come up with a reason why not.

GJ: Yeah. The way I look at it is that individualism presupposes that you have a certain high trust culture.

ME: Yeah, because there's a reason—sorry to cut you off—why every freaking guy I've ever met at a libertarian meeting was a white guy. You know what I mean?

GJ: Yeah and it presupposes a certain high trust culture, and it doesn't work if what you have is what John Robb calls . . . I like this euphemism. He has to use euphemisms, but I don't . . .

ME: No euphemisms here. Say whatever you want.

GJ: Yes, I know. "Parasite tribes." Jews, Gypsies, there are a million of them in the Indian subcontinent, whence the Gypsies come. Tightly endogamous groups that have dual moralities. If you're strangers, you're food basically. You'll be exploited. These people enter an individualist, libertarian society, and they will destroy it. Why? Because in any interaction the individualist will try to treat them as individuals, and if they have the best price, the best product, they get the money, they get the job, whatever. But when they are in decision-making positions, they don't act as individualists. They are thinking about the interests of their tribe.

So, yeah, you might be more qualified than cousin Abdul from Peshawar or wherever, but he's going to get the job. So, these societies get infected with these growing ethnic mafias that will destroy liberal individualism once they become big and powerful enough. The only way therefore to maintain and preserve an individualist market society is to have a state that draws boundaries and keeps parasite tribes out.

ME: I agree with you like 8000%. 1488% I agree with you.

GJ: What that means though—and this is where the game is up, libertarians—is your individualism and anti-statism depend upon the state and collectivism to work.

ME: You need a group of people to use violence to protect your individualist market society.

GJ: Exactly.

ME: And I'm a laissez-faire guy. I love laissez-faire. I am for that. I am not a socialist in those terms. Socialist in terms of the mechanism of violence to keep outsiders out. You and I might disagree on that.

GJ: I mean, look, I'm a little bit more of a social democrat. My dad was in a union.

ME: This is a fight you and I can have in the future ethno-state.

GJ: Exactly. There's another argument that I want to make about laissez-faire capitalism: just as it presupposes the social capital high trust society, which it cannot preserve without flipping over into statism and collectivism, it also presupposes the social capital of a pre-individualistic, non-voluntary society and tradition.

What I mean is simply this: The Randian sort of individualist reads *Atlas Shrugged*. He's 14 years old or 16 years old, or he's 18 years old like I was, and he says, "Damn it! This is right! From henceforth I am only going to enter into relationships that serve my interests." Well, if you really stick with that, you'll be 39, and you will have never entered into any relationships that challenge the values and outlook and maturity of a 19-year-old. That means you're going to be a 19-year-old when you're 39 and when you're 49 and when you're 59.

The point is that human spiritual growth and maturity often require that we take harder roads, and instead of satisfying our "given preferences," we learn that they're inadequate, and we learn to give them up. That requires that we approach social institutions and other human beings not just as ways of satisfying our given preferences, because that just makes us 14 forever or 19 forever, but rather as something that has the authority . . .

ME: 14.88 years forever. I'm just kidding. That was actually a bad joke. Sorry.

GJ: Well, when you put it that way . . . But yeah, it means that we have to have this attitude where we can approach other people, other institutions, as things that can challenge who we are. We're not good enough.

When I was teaching in college I would say things that would shock my students. I would say to them, "You know, the reason why you're here is that you're not good enough." And they'd go, "Wah! What are you saying!?" They'd been told that they're wonderful in every way. And I'd say, "You're not good enough, because you're ignorant, and you need to learn things! You're not good enough, and you're going to get better through this educational process. If you believe you're good enough just the way you are, then close the book."

ME: Why not just leave?

GJ: Why not just leave? Yeah. There's something about a strong individualist, egoist ethic that I think undermines what Hegel calls ethical institutions. He has this distinction in his *Philosophy of Right*, which I think after Aristotle's *Politics* and Plato's *Republic* is the greatest work of political philosophy. He has this notion of abstract right. Abstract right is like libertarianism. He says it doesn't work. It requires other things to function. One of the things it requires is what he calls ethical life. These are actual concrete institutions that do not service the given preferences of each individual but challenge and reject and replace the preferences of the individual with more mature preferences and therefore help us to grow as human beings.

I do think that individualism tends to freeze people. If they really are strongly individualistic, it will freeze them at whatever level of immaturity and ignorance they started out at.

ME: If you'll allow me to run with this for a second . . .

GJ: Sure, yeah.

ME: I'll even challenge the individualist notion by bringing in the concept of time preference where, say, you become a Randian or Rothbardian or whatever at age 19 or 20 as we've been discussing, and your preferences at that age are you want to make money and have sex or whatever you want to do, and you engage in the mutually beneficial, voluntary relationships which have allowed you to make the most money and have the most sex. If you continue those relationships, your individual interests, by the time you're 40 you'll be empty and hollow.

GJ: Exactly.

ME: I was a Rothbardian or a Randian, more Rothbardian. To some people there's no difference. I see the difference, but it doesn't matter. When I was in my early 20s that's what I was. Rothbardian, mutually beneficial, voluntary relationships, etc. I could have continued to just smoke weed and go to parties, you know what I mean? But my long-term actual self-interest, if I was still doing that at age 40—which I'm not yet but close—instead of finding a wife . . . You know what I mean?

GJ: Yeah. Exactly.

ME: At some point I innately recognize this, "Oh, I want a wife. I don't want to smoke weed and party." Right now, the idea of smoking weed and going to a party . . . I don't know. I would reject it. I would rather stay home with my wife. Because you change.

Inject the libertarian concept of time preference into the libertarian concept of individualism and freedom of action, and you'll understand that your individual goals will be better met by taking a longer-term view, and that longer-term view will lead you ultimately to, I hope, the view that both Greg and I, I think, are sharing, which is that you want to have your market activities protected by a bubble of force that protects the ethnic group.

GJ: Yeah and the longer-term view that you're talking about, I would put it in terms of a model of self-actualization. If you're just allowed to satisfy your given preferences that means that you'll always find a way of being comfortable at whatever level of maturity you're currently at.

I remember these ads I saw on TV: "Bad credit? No credit? No problem!" The point is there will always be people who will find a niche in the market to accommodate whatever level of vice or immaturity you might be frozen at. The market is not going to push you outside that comfort zone. The market is all about servicing that comfort zone, and so you've got to have other kinds of relationships.

ME: If in the moment you have the goods or the resources to trade for satisfaction, the market will do it. For most, it's neutral morality. Libertarians consider it to actually be a positive morality. I just think it's neutral. If you service your whims in the now, then OK. I'm not going to condemn it, but it's not a higher good. Libertarianism has perverted, I think, the idea of good to the idea of *that* is the good. People voluntarily transacting to serve their desires right now is the good.

GJ: Especially if it involves marijuana.

ME: Yeah! Particularly with marijuana.

GJ: It's one of my pet peeves. I have to say from the point of view . . .

ME: I dislike marijuana culturally, viscerally. That's just a personal preference. I'm sure many of our listeners smoke marijuana. Do your thing, but . . .

GJ: Guys, put down your bongs and listen to me for a few minutes. From the point of view of long-term self-actualization, I think marijuana is one of the worst, most insidious substances.

ME: I've got to agree.

GJ: I'm going to write an article about this before I go to bed tonight.[1] You'll read about it on Counter-Currents.

ME: I'll link to it from our site, because I completely agree. Marijuana culture is ovens.

GJ: When I went off to college my first year, I fell in with some stoners, and they gave me a little bit of their pot, and it didn't have much of an effect. So, I said, "Fine. I don't like smoking at all." I went off, got my Ph.D., ended up teaching, and a friend of mine during my first year of teaching visited me and said, "Do you know where I can get some pot?" I said, "Well, there's this place down by the record store that says 'Drug-Free Zone.' I bet you could get some there."

So, anyway, we went there and I went into the record store and bought a Marianne Faithfull CD, and I came back out and he had scored some marijuana. We went back to my place, and I tried it again. We were watching television, and we were watching that shitty show *Alias*, I remember. Then there was this commercial for this laundry detergent that came on, and suddenly I felt this commercial was this epic. It was this vast space where there was this woman who had the most compelling struggle of all. Namely, to get her laundry as white as possible. I was experiencing this commercial with all the intensity that I would experience an epic drama, and I thought, "Wow! This is really something."

So, my friend and I went out to the symphony. We went to the symphony the next day. We got high. We got high and had food. We ate at my favorite restaurant before we went, and the food tasted better than ever. Food tasted better than ever. We went to the symphony. It was Richard Strauss's *Ein Heldenleben*. It was the second part of the concert. Suddenly, I was *in* the music, and I totally understood what was going on. It's a tone poem. It tells the story of Strauss and his wife and his romance. I was totally inside it. I knew what he was getting at. It was the most profound musical experience I had ever had, and I said,

---

[1] "Against Pot," in Greg Johnson, *Confessions of a Reluctant Hater*, 2nd, expanded edition (San Francisco: Counter-Currents, 2016).

"This stuff is fantastic."

On the way home, we're listening to the radio and it's some shit-tier pop song, and I was thinking, "This is the most profound musical experience!"

ME: Yeah, I know exactly what you're saying.

GJ: Then on the way back to the house, I said, "I'm really, really hungry." So, we stopped in and we got some donuts, and they were really old crusty donuts. I started eating them, and this was the most profound culinary experience I had ever had. By the time I got home, I realized this was why pot is so insidious.

Because if Britney Spears is just as profound and pleasurable as Richard Strauss, and this day-old donut is as pleasurable as this great meal I'd had earlier in the evening, then why not just stay at home in your pajamas and eat cereal out of a box all day, and life will be fantastic with this stuff? I thought, "This is the most insidious stuff that's ever entered my life, because I can see how this would totally destroy me in terms of my ability to create and grow as a human being." Look around at the potheads I know. Bingo! That pretty much describes them.

ME: No, you're right. And that effect does wear off. I mean, I know exactly what you're talking about where I would think that I had discovered . . . And I even had experimented with other drugs and even other hallucinogenics. It's been years since I've done any of this stuff. With LSD or something, we'd be outside and on LSD, and you'd feel like you've discovered some profound truth, and a couple days later you'd think about it, "Oh, we were just thinking about this trivial bullshit." You know? And you thought you had broken some code to the universe or something.

It makes the mundane seem profound, and I suppose the effect wears off, but . . . I stopped smoking marijuana simply because I got anxiety from it, and every time I smoked it I would get anxiety, and I think that that happens. But yeah, I agree with you.

If people like it, I don't think people should be thrown in jail for it, but I just really recommend that you don't center your life around it. If you're going to do it, do it only on special occasions and make sure what you're doing is actually special because it gives you the idea that playing Call of Duty all night and then jacking off is a special event, and it's not.

GJ: It makes sex great, and it makes masturbation great. Who needs another person? It makes Britney Spears great. Who needs Richard Strauss? It makes donuts great. It makes Captain Crunch great. Who needs healthy food?

ME: Who needs filet mignon when Captain Crunch is awesome?

GJ: Yeah, exactly. That really is very destructive.

ME: That's the reason why they call it the herbal Jew.

GJ: The herbal Jew. I like that. That's brilliant. Consider that stolen. I'm going to work that in some place.

ME: Yeah, you can work that in. Don't get me wrong. I've been known, and people have accused me before, I'm a little bit on the side of the alcoholic, or the liquid Jew as they call it. It's definitely a vice of mine, but we all get one.

GJ: One of my friends from San Francisco, she said, "You know, I've tried every drug, and nothing compares to alcohol!"

ME: Alcohol is the best drug. Because it makes you better in social situations *to a point*.

GJ: Yeah, I don't get anything out of it. It doesn't do anything for me. I'll order it sometimes because I notice that people who drink feel uncomfortable if I don't share what they're doing, so I'll have a glass of wine, and I'll sip at it. I just don't get that much out of it, but I do understand that a lot of people do.

ME: It's a social lubricant.

GJ: It is a social lubricant, and for me—this is weird—I'm super psychologically attuned to the people around me, and I notice if I'm with people who are getting a little tipsy, I'll get sort of sympathy drunk anyway.

ME: Oh yeah. We've met in person several times and I was drinking in those situations. I don't know if you noticed that or not, but I remember we had great conversation that time at— well call it "the mansion"—I had a lot of fun that night.

GJ: Yeah. That was a great time. I don't think I had anything to drink, but I was just in a room full of people who were very convivial, and I felt great. I get that way. One time I had dinner with Mark Dyal and a few friends in Atlanta. This was back in March. I realized that I was getting sympathy drunk just hanging out with them over dinner. So, when the dinner was over I ordered a dessert wine just to keep the buzz going for a couple more hours.

But yeah, it just doesn't do that much for me, but I totally get why people drink.

ME: The thing is also the atmosphere of those parties was also like, "Hey! We're here. We're in person together. We can talk about whatever the hell we want." At some level, alcohol reduces inhibitions, but just being in that atmosphere reduces inhibitions. We're in a room with 20 or so people, and I can so whatever I want. How often do I experience that?

GJ: Yeah.

ME: That's the feeling I always sort of played on at those gatherings, and it's really only those gatherings where I felt that. In a way, it's a level of freedom that you're not used to, that we're not used to.

I really just wonder about potheads. Had I smoked pot in that situation I would have just withdrawn into myself and maybe been paranoid. But whatever. Enough about pot.

GJ: Well, one of things about the NRx gathering that I went to that struck me immediately is what a high trust group of people, because these people gave their address to a bunch of people they knew from Twitter, or people who knew people that they knew from Twitter.

ME: Oh yeah. Mhm.

GJ: Boy, oh boy! In the White Nationalist world, I would never do that! I would never do that because I've just gotten stung. I went there and thought, "Wow, this is a very high trust group of people and a high caliber, highly intelligent, highly articulate group of people." My feeling is that the NRx crowd that I've hung out with is on average about a standard deviation smarter in terms of IQ than say the people who go to the AmRen conferences. Bless their hearts! They're a bunch of bright people, but the NRx thing is even more IQ-loaded.

ME: It self-selects for that, if you will. In a way, I get what they're doing and I fit in with them and I enjoy their company, but I also get why . . . I mean, I've read Moldbug. They've all read Moldbug. I think that they, to some extent, are maybe too into it or it's like you're into Rothbard, and now you're into Moldbug. I get it, but let's also take another perspective on things. There's some wisdom there, but . . . I don't know. I can't really articulate what I'm trying to get across.

GJ: I look at it as an opportunity. Obviously these people are pulling in some super bright people, and they're giving them permission to think some really heretical thoughts, and I want to insinuate myself into that process. I want these people to know me. I want these people to read me. And I want to help finish the thought. For me—I don't want to sound like a monomaniac or a bore—but the thought they need to finish is, basically, they need to get their heads wrapped around the Jewish problem.

They need to do that desperately, because when I read *The Culture of Critique* . . . Going back to my education. I wish I could get back all the hours I spent reading people like Jacques Derrida and Lyotard and Foucault and Deleuze and all this Left-wing postmodern stuff.

ME: Oh jeez.

GJ: And I always felt that these bastards weren't putting their cards on the table, that there was something that I just wasn't getting, there was some little agenda here that was off, because it wasn't really Leftist. It's not Leftist, but something else. I read *The Culture of Critique*, and suddenly the scales fell from my eyes, and all of those paradoxes and puzzles just fell together. It was like, "Oh my God, words are weapons for these people, and they are weapons in ethnic struggles against whites."

ME: I even sometimes have wondered — and you comment on what I'm about to say — to what extent is there even a Left and is it not just a Jewish attack on white civilization.

GJ: I think there's a Left. I mean, there's a Gentile Left, and they want walkable communities and zoning laws and kindness to animals and things like that.

ME: I almost don't even think of that as Left anymore. Maybe it's my own sort of twisted view on things now. Because after reading *Culture of Critique* I had a moment where I was like, "Holy shit. Every idea that I've — not even on an intellectual level, but on a visceral level, on a gut level — that I've felt like has been an attack on me and on my people, it's come from this."

GJ: Yeah. I think it is. I think there's a Gentile Left, and I think that it's not a bad thing for the most part. I wrote this piece called "West Coast White Nationalism"[2] because I've noticed these people out on the West Coast who were objectively in every possible way, they were Leftists. It's just that also they were reading *Mein Kampf* along with their *Lord of the Rings*, and they really were aware of race and the JQ, and yet they were kind of West Coast hippy types and, you know, organic and crunchy and Birkenstocks and all that stuff.

I'm as Left-wing as I can reasonably go in some ways. The people I hang out with, the stuff I like to do, most people just assume I'm a liberal, and I'm going to art museums and sitting in independent coffee shops and going to independent used book stores and walking dogs. All that kind of stuff. It just fits.

ME: See, I see that as just a white culture thing. I don't see that as a Left thing.

---

[2] In *Confessions of a Reluctant Hater*.

GJ: That's right. You're right. One of the ways that I sort of look at it . . . Josh Buckley told me about some bumper sticker I think he saw at a farmer's market in San Francisco. It said, "Organic food: What our ancestors called food." And I think of all this stuff that's organic and SWPLy and hipsterish. Let's say, "Gentile Left: That's just what our ancestors referred to as white civilization."

ME: Yeah. And I'll be honest with you, I identify more with the redneck kind of thing. You know, "my property and I've got a bunch of guns. Screw you!" Not "screw you!" You know what I mean. Not all white people are the same, and in fact one of the funny things is, one of the keywords we were taught is "diversity," right? But there's actually, I think, more diversity amongst white people than there is outside of that. My cultural sympathies don't necessarily lie with SWPLdom. They're more towards the guy with the AR-15, and we go shooting, I drive a huge SUV, whatever. But ultimately these are all just different expressions of white identities.

GJ: It's peculiar. There are certain places in America where the Right-wing survivalist, "redneck" culture and the Leftie hippy culture fuse totally together, where you get these guys who are cleaning their AR-15s and talking about the meaning of the rose quartz crystal. How did this strange confluence happen?

ME: Yeah, but that's our people though.

GJ: That's our people, and God bless them. I love them. We have these Hobbit-like traditions that people are getting honestly, either because they grew up with it, or because they're sort of feeling their way back towards it as flannel-clad urbanites who want to keep bees and make their own beer.

You know, I think that's all well and good. I think we're all tunneling into the same mountain from opposite sides, and we're coming back to who we are. Again, if we can really get over this wound—I call it the wound in our body politic, and that's where the maggots are feasting—between us "good" white people and those "bad" white people.

ME: Yeah, that has to stop and, as you said, that has been created by a group of outside agitators.

GJ: I don't think it's necessarily created. I think it's been exploited.

ME: Yeah, it's been exacerbated.

GJ: America being a colony, a settler society, a society where basically everybody's a bourgeois individual, it doesn't have a past or class like Europe does.

ME: In some ways, I don't know if I'd really be able to fit in another kind of place, but I get why that's exploitable.

GJ: Because people need status, and because we do not have inborn status, even humble inborn status, we're all fluid and mobile, we constantly have to renegotiate our status every moment of our lives.

Tocqueville got to the heart of this, I think, in *Democracy in America* nearly 200 years ago. He was traveling around America and he said: "It's odd. Americans are the most individualistic people in the world and the most conformist people in the world." But the connection between the two is very simple. If we are all individuals and we all make our own way in the world, that means that the only way we can have any peace, if you will, any respite from constant insecurity is to reliably attain the approval of our peers.

ME: Yes. Exactly.

GJ: That means we have to be super-conformist. Super-conformist so we can maintain whatever little bit we've gotten for ourselves. I think another implication of that is in the struggle for status we look for other white groups to look down on because white people on some level, no matter how liberal, only think other white people really matter.

ME: Yeah, I know. You're definitely right.

GJ: Feeling superior to blacks, well . . .

ME: It's . . . a given.

GJ: Yeah, so you have to have other white people you feel superior to, and so we have this very poisonous snobbery amongst the middle and upper classes in America. It's mostly the middle classes, because upper class just means rich middle-class people.

ME: It's true. I don't think their attitudes are that different. They just have a lot more money.

GJ: Yeah, exactly. I think that snobbery is a bad thing, and it's got to go.

ME: To sort of bring it all back around and we can kind of round out the discussion: We were talking in the beginning about the prospects for nationalism or the different views of nationalism, and you were talking about how you didn't think it necessarily, you know, we can get past nationalisms of the past, the stereotypical view of nationalism of a sort of National Socialist thing, and I don't think that fits in the American context, but I think that ultimately we have to get back around to getting away from this class derision where the oven middle class . . . Even the term "oven middle class" in and of itself buys into it, but that's sort of our way of reversing the paradigm where it's always the upper middle class looking down on the rednecks. This is a way for the rednecks to reverse it, you know what I mean?
The funny thing is I'm oven middle class, and I think you are too, and I'll embrace the term.

GJ: Oh yeah, and I will go so far to say I am a self-hating WASP because I'm 100% WASP, and I see especially in my family the horribly dysfunctional snobbery and also grandiosity and unearned guilt.

ME: I know exactly what you're talking about.

GJ: It's breathtaking to me to be in the presence of this stuff. There's no group of people who is more capable of exalting themselves through ritualistic self-abasement. We're responsible for all the evil in the world, which means we're the only people who matter.

ME: And there's a Christian element to that too.

GJ: Oh, definitely.

ME: We're about an hour and 45 minutes into this to even start on this question, but yeah there's a Christian element to that and we've talked about that, and I've had guests on. You're friends with him as well, Graaagh. We've discussed this and the Mosaic distinction and all this. This might be more than we can even go into in this conversation, but certainly my mic is always open. We can always talk about these things further.

TRS has had kind of a not necessarily solid narrative the whole way, but one of the things I think we were onto very early was this idea of signaling moral superiority through self-abasement. Nietzsche called it slave morality, I believe.

GJ: Yeah, I'd love to talk about that. Maybe we can do this in another conversation.

ME: We'll do this again. This has been a great conversation. This was one of my favorites.

GJ: Well, good. This is one of my favorite interviews I've done so far. So, I've really enjoyed this, and it's not really an interview, it's just a conversation.

ME: Yeah, we're really just having a conversation. We're at now an hour and 50 minutes. Do you want to have any closing thoughts? I don't know. Maybe I'm closing this off too early. We could probably do this for 5 hours, time allowing.

GJ: No, seriously, I have a Golden Retriever who's climbing in my lap wanting a trip out, so we should probably wrap it up fairly soon. I'm sure people with sensitive ears are going to be hearing all this dog stuff going on.

ME: Amazingly, I'm not hearing it.

GJ: Good. Anyway, just to wrap up . . . Let's wrap up on a hopeful note.
(dog shaking)
Well, you probably heard that!

ME: I did hear that!

GJ: Let me just let her out. One sec.

ME: OK sure.

GJ: You don't need to edit this out. It makes it real.

ME: So, this is now Greg letting his dog out.

GJ: OK, let's wrap it up on a hopeful note. I have never been so hopeful for what we call the movement in general and more broadly for the future of white people. Yeah, objectively, the trends are all bad. Objectively, right now, we don't have a future as a race. But I've never been more hopeful that we can turn this around fundamentally.

Why? Because I've been involved in this for a little more than 15 years, and I am seeing so much positive change. I am seeing younger, smarter people getting involved in this. Younger people every year and smarter people on average every year. I am seeing social networks and vistas opening up that I did not think of as possible. I am now in contact with people who are solid white racialists who are one degree of separation, if not zero degrees of separation, from some of the wealthiest, most powerful and influential people in our society.

We're making progress, and I have never felt closer to getting a handle on the white mind and the liberal mind, because we have to understand the liberal mind and we have to hack it.

ME: We also have to understand how it's part of our mind.

GJ: Yeah. It's our mind, too. It's some of our bad traits exaggerated.

ME: Yeah.

GJ: In terms of nationalism, I do think that there is a controversy within our ranks. There are people who basically believe that the only authentic, real, honest, and courageous form of White Nationalism is something like National Socialism, and I've gone through that sort of phase. But the way I put it with a friend who is very much somebody who just wants to stand there like an honor guard by the eternal flame at the crypt of National Socialism is that I'd be right there with you, except I actually think we can win. Therefore, I don't think this whole thing is based upon the historical contingencies of Germany between the two World Wars.

What we believe is based on nature, on history, on reality that's accessible to every human being, every nation, all the races of the world. It's better for everybody to have this basic outlook and this basic system of racial nationalism, making biology part of politics, recognizing that biological differences matter, that there is a common good which is the nation that can overcome in some ways class divisions and heal some of these rifts in our society. Patriotism is a thing that overcomes class division.

ME: I really think that class warfare is an insidious agent in the polity, if you will. Upper, middle, and working classes work together to create the nation and all benefit from the actions of each. Class warfare is an insidious, destructive concept and I hate it.

GJ: Yeah, and I think if you really follow the logic of eliminating that I think you can put together the case for a moderate social democracy. For me, I just look at it as not redistribution of wealth. I think the idea of simply redistributing wealth to make people more equal is *prima facie* unjust.

I do, however, think that basically a kind of paternalism that in a sense requires people to put money into the commons, if you will, to provide, say, a social safety net . . . It's like forcing people to buy insurance.

ME: Let me just run with this for a second. As a libertarian and a staunch believer in individual rights and free markets, I can compromise with what you're saying and that is if you talk about this kind of thing right now, social democracy, we all give in for the benefit of the commons, I'm going to feel like I'm going to get ripped off. I'm going to get screwed over. I'm putting in all this effort, I'm contributing, I'm paying taxes, and someone who fucks up is going to get the benefit of that for making shitty decisions. That's a powerful argument, but now put that in the context of an ethnostate, of a white state. All of a sudden, I'm not balking at that anymore. You see what I mean?

GJ: Yeah. One of the main reasons why Americans are so resistant to these sorts of things is because we all know . . .

ME: It's because of racial diversity. This has been studied.

GJ: It would be racial redistribution, right?

ME: And this has even been studied by sociologists who are like, "Hey, people in Scandinavia don't have a problem paying 40% taxes to the common good. People in America balk at that. Why? Well, America is racially diverse and Scandinavia isn't." Or wasn't. That's what it comes down to. When I think about it myself, I'm thinking, "Hey, if I'm living in a high trust white community . . ." 40% might be a little much, but you get the point. I'm happy to contribute to the commons because I know everybody benefits. Right now in America? I don't know that I benefit. I don't know that everybody benefits from my contribution to the commons. I feel like I'm getting screwed.

GJ: And most white people are.

ME: We are getting screwed. It's unequivocal. We're getting fucking screwed.

GJ: No doubt about it. I wrote this essay called "How About Fascist Medicine?" addressing the socialized medicine thing.[3] I basically said the reason why healthy white Americans who have their acts together don't like the idea of socialized medicine is because they feel like they're going to be subsidizing the bad lifestyle choices . . .

ME: They're going to be subsidizing obese blacks. Let's be honest about it.

GJ: Exactly. So, why not fascist medicine? My idea of fascist medicine is if we're going to be paying for people's medical care we're going to send them all to fat farms.

---

[3] In *Truth, Justice, & a Nice White Country*.

ME: Yes. You go to fat farm, you complete the regimen. You'll be better off.

GJ: Yeah, exactly. Instead of just subsidizing pathological lifestyles. Maybe the state could actually — instead of subsidizing that and making it easy — they could raise the bar and make people healthier here. Anyway, that's what I threw out there.

ME: Instead of funding someone's carbohydrate diet that's obese, fund their fat camp.

GJ: Exactly.

ME: No, I'm completely with that. That's what I'm saying. You know I'm a laissez-faire type guy, but when it comes to this it's like, "Look, we're going to pay a tax into the commons. Let's make that commons in the interest of the individual rather than detrimental." If they don't have the time preference, we'll give them the time preference.

GJ: I believe in a kind of limited paternalism in this sense: When you're a parent and you've got a kid, you'd damn well better be paternalistic because it's in the interests of the kid. The thing is that every adult at some time in his life acts immature, makes stupid decisions, discounts the future radically in terms of the present, and so forth, and therefore it's reasonable for "society" to say, "Hold it there. That's not the right decision. You'd be better off not doing this." And to provide some nudges down the road to self-actualization.

ME: The worst conceit of libertarians is that nobody knows better for you than you. Actually, no, because . . . Let's just take an extreme example. Somebody who is a cokehead and snorting $500 worth of coke every day. I know better than that person what's good for them, you know? So, obviously that falsifies the premise that nobody knows better than you what's good for you. So, we can collectivize that.

GJ: Yeah, we could be a little paternalistic and say, "Look, there are certain points in everybody's lives where you are not qualified to make decisions for yourself because it's harming you. It's not in your interests."

ME: And it's not any one person. It's a collective wisdom of people that's doing it.

GJ: Yeah, exactly. Plato in his dialogue *Gorgias* . . .

ME: Oh, I love that dialogue. I really do.

GJ: Yeah, that has got the most powerful argument for a kind of objective notion of ethics and a kind of paternalism. Basically, Socrates says there's a difference between what you *really* want to do and what you *think* you want to do. What we all really want to do is be self-actualized in some sense. What we *think* we want to do is smoke our seventh cigarette of the day. We *think* that's what we want, but that's not what we *really* want. What we really want is to be healthy and self-actualized, but we're often mistaken about how particular things that we're doing contribute to what we really want.

Therefore, it follows — and Rousseau in *The Social Contract* is presupposing the whole Socratic analysis here — that if we really want to be self-actualized, then that's what freedom is. Freedom is getting what you *really* want, and that means self-actualization. If there are certain things you *think* you want that are getting in the way of that, it's possible for people to paternalistically step in and stop you from doing it by force, and therefore Rousseau's conclusion is, "Mankind can be forced to be free."

ME: Yeah and once you overcome that hurdle you won't be a libertarian anymore, and you'll come to the view that we have.

GJ: Exactly.

ME: I think that's a good place to end. We're at two hours now. So, that's great. This is great. I think our listeners are going to love it. I thought this is an awesome conversation. This is a lot of fun. I really enjoy talking to you. I would love to talk to you for three more hours.

Gotta get back to my wife. Gotta eat my dinner. But, you know, this was a great conversation, and we will do this again.

We have to do this again.

GJ: Yeah. I'd love to. Yeah, let's just call this one "Forced to be Free."

ME: So, down I went to the Piraeus today to talk to Greg Johnson, and this was a lot of fun and really great, and we will do this again.

GJ: Thanks very much. It was great being on the show.

INTRODUCING COUNTER-CURRENTS

INTERVIEW WITH TOMISLAV SUNIĆ*

TOM SUNIĆ: Good evening, ladies and gentlemen! Good evening, dear friends! This is your host Tom Sunić from VoR. Welcome back!

Well, folks, you already know me; I like discussing culture and politics, and I keep insisting, and I keep emphasizing, I keep pointing out the importance of culture as a main artillery that we need to have in our political promotion, our political activities, and our political goals. So, I'm very pleased indeed to welcome our guest, a friend of mine, Dr. Greg Johnson.

Greg, welcome to my show!

GREG JOHNSON: Thanks, Tom, for having me on!

TS: Well, thank you! It's a great pleasure. Indeed, long time no see. I understand you're on the other side in California. Am I correct?

GJ: Yeah, I'm on the West Coast now.

TS: First, let me extend my congratulations and my best greetings. I'm really pleased with what you're doing. . . . Could you please tell our listeners what is Counter-Currents, what is this edition all about, what is basically the goal of Counter-Currents? Could you please develop on this theme a little bit?

GJ: Sure, thanks. Counter-Currents Publishing Ltd. is a company that my friend and business partner, Michael Polignano, and I created, and the purpose of it is to publish books and spread ideas that are based in the European New Right, and the goal of that is to perhaps spark a North American New Right by which we understand a cultural, intellectual, metapolitical

---

* On August 9, 2011, Tom Sunić's interview with me appeared on The Sunić Journal at The Voice of Reason network, which is now defunct. The audio is no longer available online.

movement that may eventually lead to real political change in North America.

We've published six books now. We've been doing this a little more than a year. Our one-year anniversary was the 11th of June this past month. The books we've published are Michael O'Meara's *Toward the White Republic*, Michael Polignano's *Taking Our Own Side*, I put out a collection of essays called *Confessions of a Reluctant Hater*, then we published a couple of fiction works. You mentioned Andy Nowicki's book. It's called *The Columbine Pilgrim* and Ward Kendall's science fiction novel which is a re-edition of a book that came out about 10 years ago called *Hold Back This Day*. Our latest book, which is fresh off the press, is called *Summoning the Gods*. It's a collection of essays by Collin Cleary, who is one of the founding editors of the journal *TYR* and I'll be sending off a copy of that for you soon, Tom.

TS: I'm very pleased. In fact, you seem to have lined up some real heavyweights, and I'd like to tell you: I think I'm pretty much qualified to talk about this. I'm surprised how good the authors are you've lined up, especially Michael O'Meara. I've always admired this gentleman. In fact, he's not just a great author. He's also a great translator. And you yourself, Greg. Don't be too modest. You need to tell the folks that you handle the French language very well, and you're doing a great deal of translation. You also did help me on several occasions.

Could you just tell us a little bit, just in a few minutes about your background, your Ph.D. in the humanities? Could you tell me specifically where did you study, where did you get your Ph.D.?

GJ: Actually, I don't want to do that and for one simple reason. There are people in the United States and around the world who are trying to suppress the kind of intellectual activity that you and I are engaged in, and so far they have not managed to put together a coherent dossier about me. They're still wondering who I am. There are a lot of Greg Johnsons in the world.

TS: Oh, good point! That's a very good point!

GJ: So, I'm really loath to make their work any easier for them. I don't doubt that eventually they're going to figure it all out, but they are of course afraid of lawsuits, and if they were to identify the wrong Greg Johnson as the horrible hater who puts out these books and the Counter-Currents blog, well, they might be hit with a lawsuit themselves for a change. So, anyway, let's just leave that aside.

TS: No, no, that's a very good point that you've made, and I'm very pleased that you've said it. Unfortunately, my name is pretty much unique. Sunić even sounds like French unique. It's unique. The French language is full of those antonyms and synonyms. So, unfortunately, I don't have this chance of going under a different name.

But, anyway, could you just tell me what specifically your interests are? Definitely humanities and languages.

GJ: My main interests are philosophy, political theory, religion, the history of art and music, and contemporary political events.

So, what Counter-Currents is about is basically this: we realize that political change requires foundations. There are things that come before politics. We call those metapolitical things, and they shape the political and make political change possible. What we want is not considered morally right or even feasible, not even conceivable by people today in today's cultural climate. If we're going to halt the dispossession of European white Americans and create some kind of ethnically defined state in North America, the first thing we're going to have to do is get enough of our fellow white people to think that is not only a moral goal, but also a practical, feasible goal.

And so a lot of political movements start with the foundations. They start with metapolitical foundations and sometimes it takes decades before they can actually break through into the political realm.

The best example I can give of what we're going to do is actually not so much the European New Right, although a lot of the ideas that we look to are based in the European New Right, the best example from the United States is the libertarian movement.

The libertarian movement really started a little more than 50 years ago. It started in Ayn Rand's living room in New York City and other places on the East Coast. It was a small group of philosophers and economists and historians who got together and decided that they wanted to promote a certain vision of society, which turns out to be a radically individualist, capitalist vision of society. I don't agree with that vision. I think it's wrong. However, the way in which they went about promoting it was very effective. They started out with little meetings and little publications. They won more and more people over to their way of thinking. In 1971, a political party, the Libertarian Party, was founded, and it is the third largest political party in the United States today. Of course, it's a distant, distant third compared to the major two parties. They created institutes, think tanks: the Institute for Humane Studies, the Cato Institute, the Independent Institute, the Ayn Rand Institute. They have sponsored summer schools, essay competitions, a whole range of projects, and they have influenced the culture in mostly a subterranean way for decades now.

And then in the last quarter of 2007, suddenly this figure, Ron Paul, who is a very marginal Republican legislator from Texas, who would poll in the single digits even among insider Republicans when it came to potential presidential candidates for instance, suddenly he came out of nowhere and managed to raise $20 million in the last three months of 2007 to run for the Republican presidential nomination. As if from nowhere, all these Ron Paul supporters emerged, raised a huge amount of money, and sparked a very, very active, idealistic political movement. Of course, when he didn't get the nomination he took nearly $5 million in unspent campaign contributions and endowed an organization he called Campaign for Liberty that fights for his ideas.

That organization and the Ron Paul movement in general, after the election of Barack Obama, really sparked the Tea Party, which is an ongoing Right-wing, libertarian, somewhat populist phenomenon and that is still a very active force in American politics today. Ron Paul's son is in the US Senate now, and this is going to continue for a long time.

Now, some people were totally taken by surprise at the

emergence of Paul and his followers, but actually if you know how ideas percolate through society and how they influence politics, it really didn't surprise me at all, because I had been following this movement for decades, and they were laying very carefully the metapolitical foundations of political change.

I should say that I follow the New Democratic Party, the NDP, in Germany, and they talk about three elements to their political struggle. One is spreading ideas, the other is building community or community organizing, if you will, and the third is actually trying to get political power. Those first two things, namely getting ideas out and community organizing, those are what I call metapolitics.

TS: Greg, I was wondering, what does the American New Right . . . I understand that you're not an official, but you're sort of a leader or spokesman of it. How does it fit into this scheme, this vision that you have just mentioned a while ago?

GJ: If we're going to have the kind of really radical political change that we need in North America, we're going to have to lay the metapolitical foundations. That means we're going to need a movement and, for better or worse, I am going to call it the North American New Right. I am waiting for somebody better to come along to be the leader of this and raise the banner, but no one's done it yet, so I decided I might as well just try and get this thing rolling and see if we can attract a lot of interesting new people, including better minds than my own.

The purpose of the North American New Right is again to lay metapolitical foundations for creating a white, ethnically defined society somewhere in North America. That's how I describe it.

The main ideas really come out of Europe. However, there are a couple of places we differ from the European New Right. In Europe, you still have real, living ethnically defined nations and sub-nations. You've got the French, you've got the Germans, Croatians . . . All of you still have real national identities which can be foci around which you can organize for your collective interests, whereas in the United States and in other what you can call European diaspora societies, European colonial societies like Canada, Australia, New Zealand . . . What you have here is really a core population that was from the British Isles, but generation after generation of immigration from other parts of Europe have really created a blended European identity. We really don't have a distinct core ethnic identity in this part of the world. We have tried to make do with a set of universal propositions from the Enlightenment, but that is really destructive of peoplehood. It's very destructive of peoplehood in the United States. It's very destructive of the French people in France. This republicanism, this ideology of liberty . . .

TS: . . . This is a fascinating point you've just made, and I hope that our listeners, especially our younger students are listening to what you're saying. However, this is an irony of history. Keep in mind, and I'm sure you're aware of that. After all, you have the same degree, you have the same background that I do. But precisely this "tribal nationalism," Germans, English, French, Croats, what have you, very often functions by default and this is the problem. I hate to say it, but I'll give a speech on that in DC, but you can develop on that shortly. The problem is that we often hear in Europe to assert our nationalism by excluding the other European ones. Do you see what I mean?

This is the great advantage of White Americans. From Arkansas to Alaska there is one language, one culture, one people. Of course, of European roots that at least logistically gives them greater strength.

Would you agree with that? I'm sorry to interrupt you.

GJ: Yeah, that's a very good point, and I do agree with that. This is how I look at it. Because we don't have these compact, historical European national identities over here, we do need to emphasize another commonality. For me, it cannot be some kind of propositional nation based on Enlightenment ideals, because those are applied universally, and they are destructive of peoplehood.

For the North American New Right, biological race is an important thing, because that is a distinct commonality that sets us apart whereas in the European New Right, biological race discourse is not as necessary, because you can fall back on your European national identities.

However, you are completely right to point out that . . .

TS: It's a good point. It's a fascinating point that you're making. I'm very pleased that you mentioned that in American White Nationalism race is a biological determinant. It's much more important than in Europe. This causes a great deal of misunderstandings and tensions, especially with my French friends here. But go ahead, please.

GJ: There are two issues here. I do agree, however, that European nationalism can be turned against the interests of Europe. I remember a few years ago people were very excited about this Hungarian nationalist party called Jobbik, and so I started reading about them. It turns out that Jobbik is all about being mad at the Slovakians and the Romanians.

TS: Absolutely! You're reading my mind! This is exactly what I'm talking about!

GJ: There are all kinds of people who are genuine aliens to Europe living within the borders of Hungary. Jobbik is not worried about Gypsies or Jews or people from the Middle East or whoever is there. They want to recreate Greater Hungary at the expense of the Slovakians, and I think that is a madness that in the United States we don't have, and so that's a strength.

One thing that I think you can say is a benefit of these European diaspora societies with their mixed European identities is that, in a way, it's at least possible, that what we're doing here is reconstituting a pan-European identity that existed in Europe too before the emergence of these modern nation-states and nationalities. In Europe in the High Middle Ages, you had a pan-European culture. You had a common language. You had the capacity to unify Europe for geopolitical struggles against Islam, for instance. But then that disintegrated into the smaller, petty nationalisms of Europe today, and that has been something that has weakened us as a race.

So, I do think that some of the deracination, if you will, of these European colonial societies actually can strengthen us as a race, and I think that is a positive thing, and you're absolutely right to point out the problems with these petty nationalist parties in Europe today.

TS: Greg, I am so glad you've mentioned it. Believe it or not, I am not trying to flatter you. You've given such a nice speech that many, many academics in Europe would not be able to deliver. I'm not joking. I'm very pleased that you have mentioned that. Look, we're not fooling each other here. Nationalism has its good side, particularly in the United States where it could have great opportunities. But I know it first hand after this terrible, stupid war between Serbs and Croats quarreling about different mythologies, different lies, different religions. So, folks, rest assured that nationalism always has to be evaluated with the appropriate intellectual and historical context.

Anyway, this is a fascinating topic, but let's just move a little bit ahead. Let's talk a little bit about Counter-Currents. Are you actually talking about this on your forum? You were also in charge of *The Occidental Quarterly* some time ago, or the main editor, so you do have baggage, so to speak, intellectual, academic baggage to be quite versed in different spheres and different fields. Could you tell me exactly how you deal with those topics? My second question is how do you define your relationship with the French New Right, with my friends Alain de Benoist (I'll be seeing him shortly) and how exactly do you think this cohesion can work together, how you can blend them together? Why do we always have to say, "He's French" and "He's an American"? I'm getting tired of those little, petty quarrels and tribalistic wars.

Go ahead.

GJ: Let me answer the second question first about how we relate to the European New Right. Basically, I think that what Alain de Benoist and Guillaume Faye and Robert Steuckers and other European New Right thinkers are up to is largely correct. I think there are two places where our approach differs from theirs. I mentioned one, which is a greater emphasis on biological race as a commonality. However, I do want to say that a lot of us are not reductionists or determinists when it comes to biology, but we do think it's an important factor nonetheless. But that's a genuine debate within our ranks. There are hardcore ma-

terialist, Darwinist types, and then there are people who are followers of things like Traditionalism, which obviously consorts
uneasily with Darwinism in a lot of ways. So, we are genuinely
divided in that, and I'm hoping that maybe someday we can
work out some kind of synthesis.

The other area where I think that we differ is that in the United States we certainly are, I think, much more explicit about the
whole so-called "Jewish Question" than the European New
Right. There are real debates on that. Guillaume Faye's book, *The
New Jewish Question*, for instance. I think that with the European
New Right it's possible for you to deal with a lot of these issues
that we deal with under the rubric of the Jewish Question indi-
rectly, in effect by proxy, by just being anti-American, to put it
crudely. But really the United States is the citadel of Jewish
power in the world, and I think that we have to name the problem and deal with it explicitly. So, that's one thing that we try to
do.

However, I do want to specify that I don't want to compete
with Kevin McDonald's work on this topic, and *The Occidental
Observer* is a very, very good publication. So, it's an issue for us,
but it's not our main focus, if that makes sense.

TS: Of course, we have to point it out to all of our listeners
that what I personally like about Counter-Currents and your
publications is that you don't seem to be obsessed just with one
single issue. Of course, you talk about race, you talk about the
Jewish Question in a very critical manner which we cannot even
imagine or think about here in Europe for obvious reasons
which we don't need to be that explicit. But I am pleased that
you actually extend the horizons, that you cover poetry and you
cover art and other fields. And this is something I'd like to focus
on now in the second segment of our show.

So, go ahead. Could you just give me a short summary of
how you actually grapple, how you cope with that?

GJ: OK. I am obviously an intellectual, not a businessman,
because if I was really a businessman the first thing I would
have done is given the web address for Counter-Currents right
up front. So, let me give that now. It's counter-currents.com and

that is the website of our publishing imprint, but the first thing you'll see is a kind of blog, and five days a week we put up articles and reviews. That is really the thing that I spend 60–70% of my time working on, just the webzine. Then we also publish books.

The focus of the webzine eventually will expand. I hope to have full coverage of all the important works coming out of Europe. I hope to have a lot more coverage of High Culture, if you will: art criticism, music criticism, things like that and also pop culture and musical sub-cultures on the Right. That's a very important area. We just don't have the coverage yet.

What we are trying to do though is we want to cover everything. Why? Well, because the European heritage encompasses everything. You don't have to go too far back in history, either, before you find that every great philosopher would be considered a Right-wing extremist by contemporary standards. We want to recover that tradition for us and show that the Western philosophical tradition, the Western theological tradition, Western literary and artistic tradition really point in the direction that we want to go rather than in the direction of this kind of homogenized, global, multicultural, commercial melting pot.

So, we have a lot of stuff on literature, a lot of stuff on art and music and also film. Film is probably the thing we've got best under control.

TS: That's very important, the film.

GJ: I actually think that what Wagner was describing as the complete work of art that integrates all the other artworks was realized better by film than by opera. I think that film is the most powerful intellectual tool for creating a world-view. Unfortunately, for the most part, it creates a bad worldview and reinforces it.

TS: . . . Please do tell just in one little sentence or one little paragraph, if I can put it that way, what exactly is the difference between the European New Right and the North American New Right? I don't see any, but just try to make those distinctions quite clear for our younger audience, for our younger students here.

GJ: Well, I don't think there's that big a difference, but I do think that within the North American context, and also the context of countries like Australia and New Zealand where you have more of a blended European identity and the old European national identities are disappearing, that the commonality that we need to stress is going to be based on a common European history, but also a racial identity, racial distinctions.

TS: Talking about commonalities, I'm glad you mentioned that. Are you in touch with your colleagues, with our friends from Australia, from Down Under? Mr. Herfurth? Welf Herfurth? I've just written a preface to his book that should be out shortly. Do you know the gentleman?

GJ: Oh yeah, I met him. He was in San Francisco last year, and I met him. He's a nice fellow. He's a National Anarchist. I've never quite understood what National Anarchism means, but I think he's a very fine person. I enjoyed listening to him speak and talking to him, so I wish him the best.

I know a lot of people Down Under. There are a lot of really good people in Australia and New Zealand.

TS: I just want to make sure that our folks don't get sidetracked. Alain de Benoist has probably told me two dozen times, and I'm sure you're aware of it, but we're using this term that's a little bit clumsy: the New Right. It's not a self-chosen word. It was actually labelled on us. It was pasted on us by our opponents. So, I just use it by default, so to speak.

GJ: Well, yeah, we are using categories that have been imposed upon us by our opponents. That said, however, we do have to recognize that whatever we are, our roots are now primarily on the Right. And not the Right in the sense of the American Right, which is basically classical liberalism, but the European Old Right which is rooted in more traditional, hierarchical model of society. We do embrace that. A lot of things that are conventionally Left-wing by contemporary standards are not so different from things that were defended by Traditionalists in Europe in the past. So, we tend to have a critical attitude about capitalism, we tend to be opposed to the despoiling of the environment or the destruction of history, of walkable communities, of processed, crappy food, and things like that tend to be in many ways, in terms of lifestyle and aesthetic tastes and things like that, aligned with people who are contemporary Leftists. But I would ever say that the contemporary Left has roots if you go back far enough where things blend together with things that are more Right-wing, if you will, or let's just say European traditional forms of society.

So, one of the things that I talk about is what I like to call West Coast White Nationalism, because a lot of the people that I know on the West Coast who think in terms of wanting a racially defined new order of society you could take one look at them and you'd think they're hippies or you'd think they are liberals. Their lifestyles and their attitudes embrace a lot of things like being into Eastern spirituality, drinking fruit juice and wearing sandals and granola and vegetarianism and organic food and organic farming All these sorts of things that you think are kind of hippy things. Well, if you look at the roots of a lot of West Coast hippy culture and also the hippy culture in Europe for that matter a lot of it comes from Tolkien. What doesn't come from say the Frankfurt School and things like that, a lot of it comes from Tolkien, which is pretty directly connected with European traditionalism.

So, we are sort of beyond Left and Right. Especially beyond Left or Right in terms of the superficial Left-Right distinction that you have in American politics. But we still have roots that are, I think, objectively on the Right, especially when you talk about what was the Right at the time of the French Revolution or something like that.

Evola when he was put on trial said, "Look, you can say that I'm promoting Fascism, but the ideas that I promote were the ideas of every serious thinker before the French Revolution."

TS: Absolutely, that's a good point.

GJ: So, these are very deep roots, and when you pursue those roots back far enough we don't represent Left or Right. We just represent the center, the core values of European civilization.

TS: Greg, let me ask you this. This Counter-Currents project,

actually it's a press, is this a one-man show? Is this just you pick-
ing up the tab, if I can put it that way? Or do you have some as-
sistance? Because, as I said a while ago, you've lined up some
real big shots, some real big guys like Michael O'Meara, who
does some good translation. Indeed, I was struck by the good
translation of Guillaume Faye, because I know Guillaume Faye.
He actually caught his style, or rather meta-style, he caught his
sentiments. I know Guillaume Faye very well. Are you doing
that all by yourself or is somebody assisting you other than Michael Polignano?

GJ: Well, Mike Polignano is the guy who deals with the sort
of technical and business side of things, and I deal pretty much
with all the editorial work of this project, and so I work very
long hours, because I also do outside work to pay my bills. It's
challenging, but it's also very enjoyable, because it's what I really want to do, and so when you're doing what you really want
to do it's always possible to find energy to do a little bit more. I
am hoping to get more collaborators involved. So far, we have
virtually no money, so it's almost impossible for us to pay authors for their work. But yet we have managed to get a lot of really good authors to write really good pieces without paying
them just because we have managed to appeal to their idealism
and stoke their idealism, and you can go a long way with idealism. The only trouble with idealism is that if there aren't other
objective frameworks like institutions and money and incentives
like that, a feeling of community, a feeling that you're moving
forward and positive feedback, it tends to run out.

So, one of the things that we're trying to do now is raise
funds so we can pay authors. We're also trying to create a community of contributing editors who have a sense of ownership in
the project, and we're hoping that will draw more work out of
people and sustain their interest of the long run. Because the
way I look at this project, this is what should have started 50
years ago.

TS: Exactly.

GJ: And I'm not going to point fingers and blame people for
not doing this. There's nothing productive to be gained in that,

and every bit of energy that one could use doing that should be used to move things forward, so that's how I tend to focus. But I do think this will be a multi-decade process, if not a multi-generational process.

I do, however, take solace in one fact and that is that whatever we have to do we are certainly not going to have to overthrow the United States government or anything grandiose like that. My feeling is that the system that holds Europe and the United States in its grasp is self-destructive.

TS: It's a good point.

GJ: Although, the only question is will it destroy us before it destroys itself?

TS: That's an even better point! Excellent, Greg! Greg, if you don't mind, you're a very prolific author, so I must again thank you for all the books you have sent me. What's your last book about and could you just give me the crux of the message and why is the book important?

GJ: Well, I hope it is important. It's important to me. It's a collection of essays called *Confessions of a Reluctant Hater*, and the basis of it was an email from one of our readers who said, "Look, why don't you put together a collection of your simplest essays and reviews that I might be able to give my brother or cousin who's not quite on board with us yet and would be somewhat seductive to them. It would be sort of an introductory collection of short works. Some of them rather topical, commentaries of news events and things like that." So, I thought that's a good idea, and I opened a file where I keep a list of all my writings, and I started shifting things around, and within a few minutes the whole thing sort of fell together.

It's in three parts. One is called *Finding a White Voice*, which just basically talks about how I and others can start thinking explicitly in terms of racial identity in all these political struggles that are going on about multiculturalism and so forth. The second part is called *Polarizing Moments* and that deals with political events that I thought were interestingly polarizing in the United States, like the Henry Louis Gates controversy, the 9/11 mosque controversy, the election of Barack Obama, and things like that. The last section is called *White Lifestyle Politics* and that's where I develop some of my ideas on West Coast White Nationalism, and I try to show that you can be a racially conscious person without necessarily being a reactionary or a Republican. It's an attempt really to show that you can get outside of that American Left-Right dichotomy and so there are essays in there about drug legalization, race mixing, I have a review of Jim Goad's book *Shit Magnet*, which is kind of a funny review, and things about Christmas. It's all over the board. And I have two essays at the end about Alan Watts, who is one of my favorite thinkers.

Watts is really a fascinating guy, because he was one of the great popularizers of Zen Buddhism and Taoism and Vedanta in the English language. He was a profound thinker, I believe, in his own right, and he was also a man of the Right. It was not apparent to most of his followers, who were sort of New Left hippy types, but he was deeply rooted in what we would call Traditionalism, and he was a fascinating figure. I think he was in some ways a hero of mine, although there are certain things about him that I don't admire. But still he's an example of how a lot of our best minds really fall outside that Left-Right dichotomy, and they're radical thinkers.

Kerry Bolton has written lots of really good essays that I am now going to publish as a book called *Artists of the Right* about artists in the 20th century, some of the greatest 20th century artists, who were men of the Right. The Right in the traditionalist sense that we talk about. A lot of them were modernists like Ezra Pound or Wyndham Lewis. So, we have to expand our minds to grapple with that kind of paradox of the radical artistic modernists like the Italian Futurists who were also men of the Right. So, that's one of the projects we're trying to do.

The long-term goal of this, again, is metapolitical. It's cultural. What I would love to do is in some way work as a midwife or as an encourager of a new artistic movement. There's a lot of artistic activity going on in the European and American racially conscious community, and yet a lot of that goes on cut off from the earlier tradition of the great 20th century writers like Pound and

Knut Hamsun and D. H. Lawrence and others like that that these people could look to and take inspiration from. So, one of the things I would dearly love to do is enrich and encourage this artistic subculture that's going on, and that's absolutely necessary because art reaches more people than intellectual work ever can and it reaches them on a deeper, more emotional level.

TS: Just like the movies, right?

GJ: Exactly. The Tolkien *Lord of the Rings* trilogy that Peter Jackson did: that is one of the great works of cinema, and it's a very powerful thing for our cause, if you will. I think it's one of the great subversive achievements of the Western film industry. So, I would like to see more work done in that vein. I'm very delighted that Peter Jackson is now directing *The Hobbit*.

TS: Greg, let me ask you. Your website and publishing efforts are really fascinating. I enjoy talking to you.

I also know other people from other publishing companies who also have their "institutions" and publishing things. I don't know if you're familiar with a gentleman, he's a good friend of mine, Richard Spencer, who runs *Alternative Right*? A website with very good publications, very good pieces. I was wondering if there was a chance of fusing our efforts together or regrouping or scooping up those people that I know personally like Australia Down Under, I know folks in England as well like Arktos? You mentioned Arktos. It's a fascinating publishing company. They published a book of mine. Aside of our little rivalry, and of course I understand we all have a little bit of egos, is there a chance of just pulling all our efforts together and bringing them in one single place?

GJ: Well, that's a good question. When I created Counter-Currents the initial idea that I took to Mike Polignano when we discussed this was I really wanted Counter-Currents to be the publisher that would bring out English translations of all the major works of the European New Right. Well, we just didn't have the capital or the staff to do that, and Arktos came in and got Alain de Benoist and Guillaume Faye to sign contracts with them.

Well, there are two ways you could look at that. One is you could feel all hurt and jealous and everything like that. The other way is to say, "Well, there's no shortage of work that needs to be done, and everything that they're doing means that there's something else that I'm free to do." And that's how I look at it. I look at this as an opportunity. It's certainly not a zero sum game. I'm on very friendly terms with John Morgan at Arktos and on cordial terms with other people at Arktos. I wish them all the best, and what their *coup* has done is force me to reconfigure, reconceive what I am going to do. That's good.

Now, *Alternative Right* is a very attractive looking webzine. We have a slightly different editorial focus than them. I do look around and think, "You know, there are very few websites that are putting out good material in English that really excite me." In some ways, we are slightly duplicating one another's efforts.

What I think is necessary is this: we need to get together, Richard Spencer and John Morgan and I and a few other people, Kevin MacDonald who runs *The Occidental Observer*, and we need to do some colluding. Alex Kurtagić is another person I would definitely like to get in on this conversation. We need to sit down, and we need to collude so that we do not duplicate one another's efforts but rather we compliment one another's efforts. I think that is very important, because there are very few of us, and we have a lot of work to do if we're going to change the world. So yeah, this is an important thing, and I've been taking steps in the direction of trying to get people together so we can engage in some of that collusion.

I think that in the years down the road we are going to work together more harmoniously because there's a little behind the scenes coordination going on. So, that's a very good point, Tom. I appreciate it.

TS: By all means. Like I said, we all have a little bit of egocentrism, we all have vanities, which is quite natural and normal. But at this stage in our history, and again I don't want to sound too pathetic. I certainly appreciate your noble effort, because I know you personally. You're not a guy who likes quarreling. We're not going to discuss about that. But I certainly like insisting among my friends and foes, folks, let's just unite our efforts.

You have certain things where you really excel, where you're the best and I've probably got certain things where I might be good. So, we certainly have to pull our efforts together. That's a good point.

Greg, let me ask you. What are your next projects now? I'm sure you've got some secrets now. Are you going to be publishing some more books? Are you translating something? And tell us a little more about your project. Are there any conferences that you might be setting up or something? Just feel free to tell a little bit, but try to intrigue a little bit, especially for my listeners here in Sweden and Norway. I did not even realize the other day that I got quite a few people listening to me here in Scandinavia.

GJ: Well, we've been looking at the countries from which we get the most traffic, and the Scandinavian countries are always in the top ten or top twenty countries from which we have readers, which I think is very interesting. The number one country is the United States. After that is Great Britain, Germany, Canada, but Sweden, which is a much smaller country than Great Britain or Germany, usually comes in around 5th or 6th in terms of readership. So, I think that's very interesting.

What are the projects that I'm working on now? I am working on the first volume of *North American New Right*, which is our print journal. The idea of *North American New Right* is basically based on *TYR*, which is this neo-pagan publication edited by friends of mine, and the idea is to bring out a print volume that's basically a book that contains interviews, essays, reviews, and translations. The goal is to have a thing that showcases the best work being done by the North American New Right and also brings in exemplary work from the European New Right in translation. The goal is basically to advance, year by year, this intellectual movement. The first volume has a lot of really good material in it. I'm really very pleased that we have something so good to begin with.

After that, I'm going to bring out Kerry Bolton's *Artists of the Right*, which I think is a wonderful book, and then down the road we're going to bring out a collection of Trevor Lynch's reviews. There is a collection of essays by Julius Evola called *East and West*, which are East–West comparative philosophy essays.

That's something we will bring out. And I'm searching for other things. Derek Hawthorne, who has been writing on the German mountain films, is going to publish a little monograph, a thin volume on the German mountain films with us and also a thicker book on D. H. Lawrence. A lot of the chapters of that have already been published on the Counter-Currents website. There's no shortage of material for us. We're going to publish another novel by Andy Nowicki in the fall called *Under the Nihil*. So, that is something that if you liked *The Columbine Pilgrim*, you'll enjoy it.

That's basically an outline of where we're going from here.

TS: I'm glad you mentioned D. H. Lawrence. My wife is a great fan of his. She knows every book of his. She knows all of his poems by heart.

But anyway, I'm glad indeed by what you are doing and I'm sure we'll catch up shortly when I'm over there.

Thank you, Greg, and thank you, folks! Until next time, this is Tom Sunić from VoR. Bye for now!

ETHNONATIONALISM FOR EVERYONE

INTERVIEW WITH ROBERT STARK[*]

ROBERT STARK: Good evening, everyone! I'm joined here with Greg Johnson. We're going to be discussing his essay called "New Right vs. Old Right." I think to start things off, what do you mean by the "Old Right"? There's this idea when people think of the New Right . . . We've talked extensively on this show about the New Right, but I guess some people think of neocons vs. paleocons or traditional conservatives. What we're talking about is completely different.

But I guess to start things off, what is your basic definition of what the Old Right is?

GREG JOHNSON: Well, first of all, Robert, thank you for having me on the show again. I really appreciate it.

The "New Right vs. Old Right" piece is my attempt to lay out the differences between what the North American New Right and the European New Right are all about and the Old Right.

First of all, by New Right and Old Right I'm actually talking about something very specific. The Right-wing in general as I want to define it is all about inequality, the philosophical and political doctrine of inequality. Human beings are not equal in any significant way, and what separates the Right from the Left is basically the attitude that people take towards egalitarianism. The Left is all egalitarian; the Right is inegalitarian.

Now, much of the Right today, however, pays lip-service to egalitarianism. As Jonathan Bowden would point out sometimes, even though people defend ideas and systems that lead to *de facto* inequality they will never defend it as such. They

---

* On June 22, 2012, this interview with Robert Stark for The Stark Truth first appeared on The Voice of Reason network, which is no longer online.

will always talk about freedom and opportunity and things like that, but they will never defend inequality as a good, whereas I think that inequality actually is a good thing for the simple reason that human beings are not equal; inequality is a fact of life, and, therefore, if you're going to have a system that is just, you're going to have to treat unequal people unequally.

The ancient Greeks had this notion—you see this in Aristotle's *Ethics*—of proportional inequality. Aristotle believed that people were not equal, and, therefore, it would be an injustice to treat unequal people in an equal way. However, he also believed in a notion of equity, so that it would be improper to treat unequal people in dramatically unequal ways. So, for instance, if someone is twice as meritorious as the next guy, proportionate inequality would be to give him twice as many rewards or twice as much honor, where it would be unproportional to give him one hundred times as much honor. So, the good life, politically speaking, has to be in accordance with nature, and if man is unequal then political, social inequality in some way has to be a good thing and has to be defended as a good thing.

I think the true Right plants its flag in the defense of inequality as a fact and as a norm whereas the phony Right and the Left are united in their egalitarianism. The New Right vs. the Old Right distinction has to be understood in that context.

So, for instance, when I talk about the Old Right I am specifically talking in the 20th century about explicitly inegalitarian Right-wing movements like Fascism and National Socialism in Europe and other kinds of Right-wing populist movements around the world, including in the United States. These movements were explicitly anti-egalitarian, and the New Right is explicitly anti-egalitarian as well, but what differs between the Old Right and the New Right in my view is simply this: the Old Right was very much caught up with totalitarianism, party politics, one-party politics in particular, and in that sense they were very much like the Old Left, the Communist Left. So, the Old Right and the Old Left in the Communist sense were united in their model of having a hierarchical, revolutionary political party that would seize power either electorally or by force of arms, and was organized to do both, and then the creation of a one-party state that would basically force people to do what is right according to their own definitions and would engage in tactics like terrorism and even genocide in dealing with their enemies.

I think that just as the New Left after the Second World War repudiated the Old Left's harshness, its totalitarianism, its genocides, its camps, its party politics, and so on and so forth, the New Right has repudiated the Old Right's totalitarianism, terrorism, party politics, and all of that kind of stuff, but it has maintained the focus of the Old Right which is the defense of inequality and the idea that a society that is in harmony with nature and that is just is therefore going to be in harmony with human inequality, and that's both racial and sexual and between individuals. People are all unequal, people are different, the races are different, the sexes are different, and if you're going to have justice you're going to have to take all of those differences into account.

The North American New Right is basically just taking up the politics of the European New Right and trying to apply it in the North American context. So, the basic distinction between New Right and Old Right is strictly analogous as the distinction between New Left and Old Left. The New Left repudiates the harshness, the slaughter, the genocide, the meanness, the one-party politics, the cults of personality, and things like that associated with the Old Left, but maintains its commitment to its ideals and tries to bring those ideals about in a new way. In the same way, the New Right maintains the inegalitarian ideals of the Old Right, but repudiates the means by which these things were realized in the earlier part of the 20th century and instead seeks to bring these about in a different way.

RS: Well, the thing about the present-day phony Right, as you described it, I wouldn't say they're egalitarian. They're politically correct, and they speak out in favor of racial egalitarianism and much of the agenda of the politically correct Left. But on economic issues they're far from being egalitarian.

GJ: Yeah, that's true. They're quite inegalitarian, and yet at the same time they will never defend inequality as such. They always defend instead things that lead inexorably to inequality like equal opportunity or capitalism, freedom, things like that. So, they will defend it on those grounds, but they won't defend it on the grounds of inequality. They'll defend it on the grounds of freedom and procedural notions of rights and things like that.

In that sense, I think that is a sign that they are morally cowed by the Left. So, they feel that they can only advance the Right-wing values that they hold dear by encoding them in the language of the Left and in terms of the values of the Left, squaring them with Left-wing values. Of course, that can only go so far, and of course they are always being hoist by their own petard when they start doing that because the Left is always calling their bluff and demanding that they live up to the values that they profess.

But they do have a strong egalitarian element to them though, but it's more in terms of their sentiments. They wax all gooey and sentimental about especially issues like racial equality. They've really gone completely over to the Left on matters of racial difference. I'm talking about the mainstream phony Right in America and the sort of center-Right parties that you have in Europe as well.

RS: So, you say that the true Right has three species: traditional society, the Old Right, and the New Right. How is traditional society different than the Old Right?

GJ: That's a good question. Every society in human history up until modernity has been Right-wing by modern standards. By Right-wing I mean inegalitarian and fairly openly so. This is just based on nature. It's based on the necessities of social evolution over time, that always give rise to inequality. Traditional society, however, has been under attack systematically all over the world since the 18th century, since the rise of the Enlightenment, and the reactionary defenders of traditional society have been in steady retreat since the 18th century.

What happened at the beginning of the 20th century is what I call the Old Right now, which was an attempt to resuscitate and restore pre-modern, traditional, inegalitarian social forms within the context of modernity. By that I mean modern technology, modern mass society, capitalism, and so forth. And really the template of that, the first successful form of that was Fascism in Italy.

Italian Fascism was inegalitarian in its aims, but it was remarkably modern in its means and the fact that it accepted things like universal suffrage, that it was a mobilization of the masses, and things like that. It was an attempt within the context of modern mass society to reassert certain pre-modern, traditional, inegalitarian, healthy, biologically harmonious, biologically-based social institutions.

Now, that of course went along with a certain number of totalitarian tendencies, and I do think it is important to understand that the genus totalitarianism is somewhat misleading. For instance, it is very misleading to say that National Socialism and Stalinism are totalitarian in the same way. Superficially, they might be totalitarian in the same way. You've got the same kind of art, same kind of cults of personality, and so forth. However, as a matter of fact, Fascism and National Socialism never interfered in private human life to the extent that something like Stalinism did or Maoism. They never went so far.

I was reading recently *Hitler's Table Talk*, and one of the most amusing parts of the table talk is a conversation between Hitler, I think Keitel, who was one of his generals, and Himmler where they were complaining about bureaucracy, and they were talking about how they needed to get rid of bureaucracy and streamline things, and Himmler was talking about how in the past the government was so arrogant with the citizens and how when the SS demanded people to appear before them, he redrafted these summonses. He was quoting them, and they were very, very gentle. "You are cordially invited to show up at the SS for some inquiries." That kind of thing, and then if they didn't show up he said, "We'd send them a reminder." And I was thinking, "This simply isn't the totalitarianism of something like the USSR. They're just in a completely different category.

However, still, the term totalitarianism comes out of Fascism: either Mussolini coined it, or certainly popularized it. So, the tendency of the Old Right though is to depend on one-party politics and state force to bring about its ends, and I think that there are other better ways of doing that, and that's really what differentiates the New Right and the Old Right. The New Right maintains the same values, the same ends, and a lot of the same analytical framework as the Old Right, and I'm quite open about the debts that we bear to figures like Hitler and Mussolini and Codreanu. People like that. I think that their deeds and their words were very useful and provide a lot of insight, a lot of guidance. Yet at the same time I think that the whole apparatus by which they tried to realize their ends is unnecessary and counter-productive in the world today, and so what separates us from them is really we embrace a different means of realizing the same values and the same social goals.

RS: So, you say that the Old Right means Fascism and National Socialism and other populist nationalist movements, and you say that their attempt was to restore traditional hierarchical social forms, which are the total antithesis of egalitarianism.

I think it's important to differentiate populism with egalitarianism. The perception of populism is the common good rather than the good of a few.

GJ: Right. There's a certain picture you have of populism. You think of William Jennings Bryan or someone like that. You think of the KKK, or you think of populist appeals by the Democrat Party whenever they want to hornswoggle white working class people into voting for them one more time.

Populism doesn't mean crude populism. It doesn't mean necessarily the anti-intellectual populism of America. I want to use that word in a completely different sense. Although I think that they are related in some way. Populism as I want to define it is simply this: it is this idea that the common good of a society should trump factional interests, and the individual good, wherever these things actually conflict. A populist society is a kind of norm for evaluating different social institutions and laws. Populism is a normative principle, and it allows you to eliminate forms of government that really are only conducive to the interests of one group, one class in society.

So, my definition of what populism is really comes from Aristotle's *Politics*. He doesn't use the term populism, but Aristotle says that lawful, just rule is always oriented towards the common good of the society whereas unlawful rule is oriented towards the good of an individual or the good of a particular social class or faction. I think that it is possible to be populist in that sense and also to realize that there is a real human inequality and that the interests of the whole are not necessarily served by, say, universal suffrage or just direct democracies.

I think that a certain amount of elitism is necessary to serve the interests of all. However, there need to be checks against the elites just serving their own interests.

RS: Yeah, elitism and inequality. Is it earned or is it just or is it unjust? Some people, based on their merits, will obviously do better, but then you have societies where there are injustices where some people . . . In our society, a lot of the people who have the most are obviously degenerate or parasitic individuals who are undeserving of what they have and there are people who obviously have good qualities who have faced disadvantages. There's just blanket egalitarianism where everyone deserves the same. Then you bring up the discussion of elitism and egalitarianism, about injustices and unearned elitism.

GJ: Right. Aristotle said that government by the few for the common good is aristocracy, government by the few for the interests of their own class is what he called oligarchy. What we have today is a largely oligarchical society where you do have people in power who are governing basically in the interests of people like them. And that's as true of the Democrats as it is of the Republicans. We have a tightly oligarchical society, I believe, and the solution to that form of oligarchy is to have a kind of society where talent can rise. Where there are no impediments to talented people from humble backgrounds. So, you have a way of recruiting the best people from all classes of society, from all walks of life.

But the other thing you have to have, and very few societies have ever institutionalized this, is a way of eliminating the people who are in positions of power who are unworthy. You have to have a way of allowing the wastrel children of the rich to fail.

My great objection to the first President George Bush was that in the end he loved his son more than he loved his country, because no man who really cared about the common good would have wanted George W. Bush to be president. He was a person who was raised far above his just station in life because of his connections, and that's the kind of thing that a good society needs to address. There has to be a way of allowing these people to be shuffled off the stage of history and neutralized. Certainly not to become leaders in and of themselves. As far as I know the only aristocracy that ever institutionalized that kind of selection was the Venetian Republic. They actually had ways of eliminating from the ranks of the aristocracy people who were found unworthy of it.

RS: Well, obviously we don't have that today. The thing about today is that people who have power or extreme wealth aren't necessarily the better people but they have the right connections or are born into it. That's an oligarchy or a plutocracy, but what you're advocating in the New Right . . . What are the New Right's solutions to these issues?

GJ: What I would advocate is something like this: one of the main ways that oligarchy or plutocracy perpetuates itself in the United States is through educational institutions. You have very expensive prep schools, and then you have Ivy League colleges that are prohibitively expensive and very, very difficult to get into unless you are already part of the elite.

These give the people who attend them a huge leg up socially that can compensate for their lack of objective merits often times. What I would do is have a system where you would basically abolish those kinds of exclusive educational institutions and simply have them open to everybody on the basis of objective merit.

So, at Harvard, the smartest home school children, the

smartest kids from trailer parks, and the smartest kids from Manhattan and so forth, from the moneyed elites, would all be able to go there if they're objectively the smartest. You would abolish the tuition, which they actually don't need to function, because they have massive endowments, and you would just turn this into a strict meritocracy. I think that would be an excellent way of dealing with that.

The National Socialists ultimately had that strict meritocracy. The SS was a strictly meritocratic organization, and they looked at it as the way they were going to create the elite that would run Germany in the future. That elite included the best people of the old aristocracy, but also the best of the peasantry, the best of the middle classes. Anybody who could get in and prove himself worthy was taken in. So they were replacing an old aristocracy of blood and also the bourgeois aristocracy of money with a new meritocratic system. I think that's a very reasonable reform.

RS: It's time for a break. Please stay with us.

Welcome back! I'm joined here with Greg Johnson. We're discussing his essay on Counter-Currents titled "New Right vs. Old Right."

Greg, before the break you were discussing the meritocracy that existed in National Socialist Germany.

GJ: Well, I think that the SS was an attempt to create a new kind of meritocratic elite that would run the society. That was their attempt. That was their aim. Similar meritocratic institutions existed in Italy.

I think military institutions and also the Catholic Church are models of meritocracies where obviously status is not inherited. If you're in the military and there is a war, there might be social prejudices that determine where you go, how high you can rise, and things like that. However, in the conditions of a war it is still possible based on sheer performance and sheer merit to rise very high.

The Catholic Church for a very long time was a meritocratic institution. They would recruit the brightest people from all castes of society and try to bring them into the Church. One of the models of the SS was the Jesuits. Hitler actually said that he believed that Himmler was the Ignatius Loyola of National Socialism.

So, the West has been served very well by both hereditary aristocracies throughout our history, but also by non-hereditary, meritocratic orders, and I think that is something that is deeply rooted in our traditions.

RS: It's important to emphasize meritocracy. So, a true meritocracy rejects both plutocracy and egalitarianism at the same time.

GJ: Exactly. And also to an extent it has to reject a hereditary caste system. I do think that heredity is very, very important. However, it is not an infallible way of determining quality.

There is this phenomenon that Philippe Rushton talks about called regression towards the mean, where you have extraordinary people, and if an extraordinary man meets an extraordinary woman, the law of averages will tend to dictate that their children will be less outstanding than they are. They might work very, very hard with all their connections and wealth to make sure their children have a leg up in the world, but chances are there are brighter kids out there from humbler backgrounds, and therefore you can't just have heredity as a factor either.

So, I think that meritocracy has to reject the aristocracy of blood, it has to reject the aristocracy of money, and it has to reject any kind of egalitarianism, the idea that we're all good enough in some way. If we're really going to mobilize the best people, then quality alone has to be the main criterion.

RS: Back to the North American New Right. The North American New Right is based upon the European New Right, but it's basically a very new and small movement. I would almost say a movement within a movement. The greater movement, I guess, being the Alternative Right. You're saying that the American New Right doesn't really have any thinkers of the caliber of Alain de Benoist and Guillaume Faye. Who would you consider to be the top thinkers of the North American New Right?

GJ: Well, it is kind of awkward what I'm doing. Basically, anybody today can go out on the internet and declare himself a journalist. Anybody on the internet can declare himself the leader of a movement. You create yourself as these things, and then you hope that it sticks.

I decided that one of the things that we truly need in the United States, or North America in general, including Canada — Mexico not so much — is something analogous to the European New Right. We need a metapolitical movement that will challenge the hegemony of egalitarian anti-white ideas and eventually work to replace it with a different hegemony, a counter-hegemony, whereby white self-assertion, white preservation, and a kind of relaxed and unapologetic inegalitarianism become the common sense of society.

We need that to happen. Nobody else was doing it, so I said, "OK. I'm going to run up the banner and declare myself the leader of the North American New Right until somebody better comes along to take the banner away from me."

The people I think who have done the most so far to contribute to this project are Michael O'Meara and Collin Cleary. They have written the highest level material, I think, the most intellectually sophisticated material. I think that I've done some pretty good work myself, but I don't think it measures up to what Collin Cleary or Michael O'Meara have done. They're the two guys that I look to the most. I think they've done the most to prepare the way for this.

But in all humility, we need to think of ourselves as just creating the space. We're creating an intellectual space. We're creating an intellectual infrastructure. We've got an online journal with the Counter-Currents website. That's counter-currents.com. We've got *North American New Right*, which is our print journal. The first volume of which is now being shipped to me. I got an email about that today. We've put out thirteen books so far.

The goal of this is to create a welcoming, intellectually exciting milieu in which we hope we will attract or cultivate talents like the ones we have in Europe. That's the goal. In all humility, that's what we're hoping to do.

Matt Parrott said something to me really profound a couple

years back. He said, "Sometimes you've just got to put aside your humility and lead." And I decided, yeah, that's what I need to do. I need to put aside my humility and just try to get this thing started. My real hope is that better people will come along and turn this into a large, vital, world-transforming intellectual movement just as the Left has transformed the world. We want to transform the world back, or we want to transform the world forward; we want to transform it forward and recoup some of the healthy things that traditional societies have always taken for granted and that have been under massive attack since the Enlightenment.

RS: But with the terminology "the New Right," isn't that a little confusing to people? I brought this up at the beginning of the show. People might get that confused with the neocons. It's different terminology and it gets kind of confusing. Some people use the terminology Third Positionist, Third Position. What's your take on that?

GJ: I think it's all well and good. I don't want to get caught up in terminology.

You know, the term "New Right" was not something that Alain de Benoist came up with. That was imposed upon him by the press in France in the '70s, but it stuck. We don't have the power, really, to call ourselves what we want to call ourselves and make it stick. That's just reality. And there is truth to the idea that we are a movement of the Right *if* you define the Right as anti-egalitarian. And that is definitely what we are. We are anti-egalitarian, and so I will accept that label: Right.

Now, there's a whole big mainstream Right: The libertarians, the Republicans, the neocons and there was this term the New Right which was talked about in the late '70s, early '80s that would embrace people like Ronald Reagan and Margaret Thatcher. They would also call them neoliberals in Europe. It was a kind of resurgence of classical liberalism within the center-Right parties. We don't stand for any of that.

RS: Yeah, it reminds me. For Third Position, the terminology was coopted and there was some political scientist who came up with the term Third Way to describe these establishment type globalists like Bill Clinton and Tony Blair.

GJ: Yeah, the thing is that there's never going to be a perfect definition or perfect term, so I don't worry about that too much. I want to be pragmatic about terminology and just be on call to clarify things if people are confused.

There's no way, for instance, that you can avoid terminology that's negative, that's stereotyping, that's loaded. Especially when our enemies basically have control of the press and academia and things like that. They can get away with calling us anything they want, and they can make it stick. We just have to accept that that is the reality. We have to define our goals. We can be very clear about our goals, and we just have to be pragmatic about the terms that we use to describe them, and we have to be available to defend ourselves from being misunderstood or being smeared, and that's really the best we can do.

But there's no magic term. There's no final magic term that we can use that will be immune to misunderstanding, immune to parody, immune to distortion.

RS: So, the North American New Right cultivates a much more frank and direct critical engagement with Fascism and National Socialism. You said before that it's founded on the rejection of Fascist and National Socialist parties. Those being totalitarianism, terrorism, imperialism, and genocide. So, you do agree that those are things that should be rejected?

GJ: Yeah. I think that those are all bad things. I mentioned earlier that I was reading *Hitler's Table Talk*. It pains me to read the comments in there that Hitler makes about the Russians and Ukrainians and how basically under the new order they'll just be taught the first ten numbers and how to read road signs, and they'll basically be helots in a new kind of serf system that he wanted to set up in Ukraine and Russia. I think that's very sad.

I think that the basic ethnonationalist principle is this: that every people needs a homeland or homelands in which they have political sovereignty and the freedom to develop according to their own natures, their own lights, their own culture. What makes every distinct people different should have the right to a room of their own, a country of their own where they can develop and perfect who they are. I think that is a universal principle that one can get behind no matter whether you're black or white or Asian, no matter what ethnicity you belong to, no matter what nation. I think that we can defend what we're doing on that universal basis. I think it's not unreasonable — it's kind of utopian to be reasonable, I realize — to aim and try to convince the people who matter, the people who make history, which is a minority, that everybody has an interest in that kind of future.

So, that's one of the things we want to do. We want to convince people that everyone has a stake in ethnonationalism and that the main source of trouble, quarrel and strife, enmity and hatred in the world is multiculturalism. Multiculturalism/multiracialism is the idea that different peoples have to share the same societies, the same political systems. We think that is inevitably a source of hatred and violence. If it doesn't flare up into hatred and violence, it at least is a kind of gentle friction that wears away any cultural differences that matter.

RS: The other thing is it leads to plutocracy or an inegalitarian system where one ethnic group is the plutocracy.

GJ: Yeah, that generally happens. Every multicultural society turns out to be some kind of empire in the end. By an empire I mean a society where one ethnic group rules over other ethnic groups. They can be kind of disguised and sneaky about that, or they can be quite open about it, but generally that is what happens. That's what happens in every one of these African societies that were cobbled together by the colonial powers where you had multiple tribal groups in the same country, and they're suddenly supposed to work together and have the same state. It's certainly the case everywhere in Asia where the Chinese are powerful. You have Chinese economic dominance in countries like Malaysia or Indonesia, so that is definitely the case. Wherever you have multiculturalism you end up with a lot of friction, and you also end up with the empire of one groups over other groups and nobody is happy with that.

RS: You say that this can be achieved through gradual and humane programs such as territorial partition, which an example of that would be the Singapore solution. The other way is population transfer. I don't know. Usually population transfer involves violence.

GJ: Yes and no. Look at America. Americans move constantly. America is a very unsettled society. Imagine the reimposition of some kind of racial segregation in America. You could do that over time. And I don't advocate for this. I don't want a segregated society. I want a homogeneous white society.

But what I would like is a system whereby people from other races are simply encouraged, the next time they move, to move outside the borders. People move around a lot.

RS: Yeah, but the thing about that is people tend to live where there's prosperity, and they're going to want to move to the areas that are the most prosperous, and you can't really expect them to voluntarily move to an area that's kind of shitty.

GJ: Well, that's true, which usually means returning home to wherever they came from in the Third World. But here's the thing. You don't have to make it entirely voluntary. You have to say, "Look, starting January 1st, 2013" — let's just say I became emperor of California — "non-whites do not have a future in California in the long-term." We're not going to take away your civil rights and take away your property, burn your houses down, or do anything crappy like that. But in the long-term you don't have a future here. What does that mean? It simply means that you are going to have fewer and fewer opportunities in the future, and, therefore, we will set up a dynamic which will encourage people to move way.

Now, is that an unfair thing or is that a violent thing? Well, I would say, in a way, no it is not, because that is really what whites have accepted when you get right down to it. Every white in America, consciously or unconsciously in the present system, if they don't change that system, has accepted living in a society where our kind does not have any future in the long run.

What I'm basically saying is this: if I were put in charge of a state or a region, I would simply say that that system would now have to be accepted by the other groups there. We're going to have a future. We are going to make sure that we have a long-term future where not only do we survive, but we flourish. But the other racial groups who are our competitors, whether they're cordial or violent, they don't have a long-term future. So, they need to start thinking of sending their kids to college in Singapore or getting them jobs with overseas Chinese communities. Things like that. They need to start thinking in terms of finding a place where they do have a future.

I think that within a generation you could quietly change things. You could simply restrict economic and educational opportunities within a white state such that non-white groups would voluntarily — and by voluntarily I mean of their own accord without having a gun stuck in their back — relocate themselves. What you would have in time is a situation where the only Asians or the only blacks in California would be really old people who can't really pursue opportunities anywhere else. I wouldn't have any objection to that, because when really old people get a little older and a little older they die off, and the problem has biologically solved itself. It's something that you can do gradually over time.

Whites are being subjected to genocidal conditions, but it's not fast, hot genocide. It's slow, cool genocide, which means that we do not have in the long-term a future in our own societies. We don't want to take away Chinese societies or Japanese societies or black societies. They have a whole host of societies of their own. But within our own societies, in order to get ourselves off this slow genocide treadmill, we're going to have to say, "We're going to impose a slow, gradual process whereby these people will absent themselves from our society, and in the end we will be the only people left in it." I don't think that is an impossible or utopian or unreasonable or inhumane thing. It's imposing conditions on people that we have allowed to be imposed upon ourselves without violence and without too much conflict except a bit of grousing on the internet.

RS: I think at first when people hear you say that, especially people who consider themselves to be humanitarians, maybe they are kind of shocked at first. Your basic response then is that it's what is happening today, but in reverse. For people out there who are concerned about doing this, ethically, you just make the point that what you're advocating is no different than what is happening today.

GJ: Yeah, but it is different in one sense. If we do nothing, we will cease to exist as a people. If I get my way, and I do this thing that I am describing, the Chinese are not going to cease to exist as a people. By no means. They have China. They've got Taiwan. They've got Singapore. They have their homelands, and they are in no threat of losing them, but we are in threat of losing our homelands. So, in a way, what I'm doing is different, but it's far more moral than what is being done to us, because what I believe is happening to whites is slow, cool genocide. I don't advocate for that against other ethnic groups, but I do think that you can use the same kind of slow, cool, gradual methods to basically recreate or create homogenous white societies. That's what I think should be done. In a generation or two, that's what you'd have.

You wouldn't have to have totalitarianism and camps and all this nasty, harsh stuff. You wouldn't have to have race wars like this sort of contemporary totalitarians of the White Nationalist movement that they fantasize about at night. You wouldn't have to have any of that horrible, harsh stuff. You would simply have to have whites asserting ourselves and saying, "We no longer consent to having no future in our homelands, and in fact we are going to turn the tables and the invaders, the people who demographically crowding us out, they're the ones who have no future here. But they have a bright future in China or Singapore or Nigeria or wherever else."

RS: We are out of time. One thing that you mentioned, put importance on, was metapolitics. Is there anything you can say briefly to wrap this up?

GJ: Well, metapolitics is basically the idea that there are certain pre-conditions that have to exist in a culture and in people's minds before political change can take place. People have to believe that a political system is basically just, and they have to believe that it's basically possible. If you don't think it's right or you don't think it's possible, it's off the table. It's simply inconceivable. It's a non-issue.

One of the reasons why white ethnostates don't exist today is that people have been taught to believe that it's amoral . . . Well, not amoral. At best it's amoral! It's immoral. It's evil, and it's impossible, and therefore one of the main practices of the North American New Right is simply to argue that we are a distinct people, that it is right for us to assert ourselves in ethnic conflicts with other people, that these conflicts are real and unavoidable, especially if we have to share the same systems, and that it is possible to get rid of this ethnic conflict by having homogeneous, sovereign ethnic states. That's what we want for everyone. Even the Jews. The last thing I want to see is Israel disappear. I want it to stay there so all the Jews can go there, and I want there to be a Palestine right next door to it so all the Palestinians who are here can go back home and live peacefully too.

Ethnonationalism for everyone—I think that's a completely moral, reasonable, and practical solution.

SOUND MONEY FOR THE BROWN PEOPLE

INTERVIEW WITH MATT PARROTT*

MATT PARROTT: Welcome to Radio Free Indiana! I'm Matt Parrott. Today we're going to have Dr. Greg Johnson, author of *Confessions of a Reluctant Hater*, on the line. Greg, welcome to the show.

GREG JOHNSON: Thanks, Matt, for having me on.

MP: Greg Johnson, Ph.D., is the editor of Counter-Currents Publishing and the journal of the *North American New Right*. He's a first-rate academic philosopher and writer. His www.counter-currents.com website translates the best ideas from Europe's thriving New Right movement and features articles from writers here in America who are part of his emergent North American New Right.

Greg Johnson recently took a break from translating, editing, and publishing other people's works to publish a work of his own: *Confessions of a Reluctant Hater*. It's a collection of some of the best articles he has written over the years aggregated from several websites and written under several pen names.

Greg, could you give us a brief sketch of *Confessions of a Reluctant Hater* and why you wrote it?

GJ: *Confessions of a Reluctant Hater* is a collection of 28 essays that I wrote beginning in 2001 going up to the end of 2010, and they represent a lot of different stages along the way in my intellectual development in my attempt to find a white voice. I don't pretend that they are all consistent with one another, but the goal of the book was basically this: I had a suggestion from one of the readers of Counter-Currents that I put together a collec-

---

* On June 3, 2011, Matt Parrott's interview with me appeared on Radio Free Indiana at The Voice of Reason network, which is now defunct. The audio is no longer available online.

tion of works that are sort of introductory works, that are not deep-end philosophical analyses of New Right thinkers and their predecessors but rather they are pieces that appeal to any intelligent layman who is puzzled about politics.

So, I have a section on finding a white voice. It deals with things like the question of race hate, immigration, books like Christian Landers' sequel to *Stuff that White People Like*, a documentary about the Tea Party, Craig Bodeker's *A Conversation About Race*, and so forth.

MP: Now, I have been reading through here, and I'm working on a review that should be posted here pretty soon probably at theoccidentalobservor.net. One of the articles I really liked, one of my favorites is "A Nation of Immigrants?" that really dissects the notion that America is a nation of immigrants and explores that notion and explores what it means in context for an ordinary white American in the 21st century.

GJ: Yeah, I hate the cliché that we're a nation of immigrants, therefore, we should welcome every other would be immigrant to our shores. I think that's a very, very bad argument. It doesn't follow.

What I basically do is explore the topic of immigration, and I end up by raising the question, "Should we have any immigration at all?" I think we should treat that as a legitimate question. America was founded by colonists. There were Dutch and some Germans and some Swedes, but it was primarily people from the British Isles who came here, and when the thirteen colonies became independent they were overwhelmingly Protestant and Anglo-Saxon and almost entirely Northern European, because the Swedes and the Dutch were from Northern Europe as well. The society, if it was smart, should have tried to do everything possible to preserve that homogeneity. Why? Because diversity of any kind is a weakness. Religious diversity, racial diversity, sub-racial, national, linguistic diversity . . . All forms of diversity like that are bad. Unfortunately, the United States didn't do that, and we started importing other groups, other national groups, other religious groups, and so forth, until we've got the sort of European tapestry of America where we've got Poles and Russians and Germans and Romanians and people from all over Europe now living in the United States.

That's all well and good, and I love a lot of those people who came in later. They are friends and so forth, and I think it's crazy to be moaning about the Irish in these contexts, for instance. But at the same time I just want to establish the principle that homogeneity is a strength and diversity is a bad thing, and any policy of immigration should try to up the homogeneity of the society and resist diversifying it.

I also just raise the question "should we have any immigration at all, whether it's the best people or the worst people of other countries?" We want to rob other countries of their best minds. And, of course, it's clear that we shouldn't want to import the worst people, the "wretched refuse" of other countries. That doesn't make America a better place.

MP: You raise an excellent point there about how the integration of all these parts of Europe, of all these other people from around Europe who weren't from the British Isles caused a lot of conflict too. And I speak as what you might call a "Euromutt" myself, but we did have the white immigrant gangs. White immigrant gangs were a major problem throughout a lot of the 19th and 20th centuries, and there was a lot of pain from that. There was a lot of economic pain where large corporations would use these immigrants to lower the wages for existing Americans, and for a lot of that time we were a frontier nation, and so there was an added value in filling our country up with people and so forth, but that's not really the current context, and we have integrated every nationality from Europe. It wasn't pain-free. It was difficult, like you said. Any introduction of differences like that results in conflict, but we worked it out and this notion that after having managed after several decades to get through that to just beset ourselves with a new problem, a far more severe problem, a really intractable problem of trying to integrate these completely alien people is just boggling.

GJ: Well, yes, I agree with that. I am the last person to go on today in this context trying to pick the old wounds of, say, 19th-century conflict between English-descended people and Irish immigrants in the United States. I love the Irish. I love the Italians. I like all the European stocks that are here. I have friends who come from all of those groups, and the last thing I am thinking of is that we should send them all back or some stupid ass thing like that. It's completely foreign to my outlook.

My tendency is to be a self-hating WASP. I look upon my ancestors who are all, as far as I know, from the British Isles — so, I'm pretty much a pure Anglo-Saxon, if that means anything — and I'm not terribly proud of that because I look at my WASP relatives, and they're the people who gave the country away. They're the people who gave the country away to Jews. They're the people who imported coolie labor from China. They're the people who imported blacks from Africa. They're the people who really made a mess of things. I am far more sympathetic on a personal level, and I have a lot more fun with people like Italian-Americans, who don't have any of that white guilt that WASPs carry around, and they take their own side in ethnic conflicts. They're not hamstrung in the ways that WASPs are. So, if anything, I'm a self-hating WASP.

But the point is that throughout the history of America every introduction of a new group has been not in the interests of the people who are already there. It's not in their economic interests to have to compete with a new influx of laborers who lower wages, who disrupt their communities, and so forth. The argument I make is that even with the frontier, America could have shut off immigration as soon as the ink was dry on the Constitution. We could have shut it off, and what would have happened is this: the necessity of the system's expansion would have created incentives for the stock that was already there to reproduce.

So, for instance, if the big factory and mill owners and mine owners couldn't import cheap labor from Europe they would have had to looked at the people who were there and thought, "Well, we have to invest in these people and increase their population so that we'll have more workers." Labor would have been scarce, and so it would have been expensive, so laborers could have afforded to have large families that way, and so the sheer necessity of the system's survival would have created incentives that would have filled up the country anyway.

Francis Parker Yockey in *Imperium* talks about this. He was the person that put me on to this idea. His view is that every immigrant who was brought into the United States basically suppressed the incentive for the native population to produce a new individual. I don't know if you can really turn that into a hard mathematical law, but I do think that there is a pattern there, and that's reasonable. So, immigration might have been completely unnecessary to populate America, and if we'd never done it we would have a very homogeneous society.

We didn't do that. We imported a lot of people from Europe. Fine. European peoples are basically the same. We have much more in common genetically and culturally and historically than what differentiates us. A lot of these national differences are fairly recent and superficial anyway. If we go back far enough in our history, we all thought of ourselves as Europeans. When Charles Martel fought the Moors at the Battle of Tours the chroniclers described him as the leader of the Europeans. There was a homogeneous, Latin-speaking, Catholic European Christian society at that time in the Middle Ages, and that slowly differentiated itself over time into the modern nation-states that we have. So, in a way, one positive thing that you can look at in the American colonial experience and also the colonial experience of countries like Canada, Australia, and New Zealand, which were similar, is that these are places that the original unity of the European people is being reconstituted after being divided up and pitted against one another for all these centuries. So, in a way, that can be looked at as a good thing.

But the fact that we've been able to assimilate other European stocks does not mean that we can assimilate blacks or Asians or Papuans or Pygmies or radically different people, and it's madness to try to do that. So, the idea that because all of our ancestors stepped off boats at one time in history that we have to welcome everybody that stepped off a boat today is just sheer madness.

MP: Right. I couldn't agree more. The current economic and social situation in America today, especially with how low our own birth rate is, any immigration is a threat to the survival of our people.

GJ: I agree, and I think that one of the things that causes the suppression of our birth rates is immigration, and it suppresses it in two ways. One is a very obvious financial thing. Mexicans are coming here and having four kids, and every one of these kids is born in an emergency room, and the bill is paid for by working and middle class whites who are responsible and civic-minded and pay their bills, and they sit down and balance their books and think, "We can't afford to have a second child." They can't afford to have a second child because they are subsidizing a Mexican baby boom. That's a very simple way.

There's another more subtle psychological thing that's going on here. Whites are kind of a nervous, finicky race. I remember when I was in grade school—I think I was a 4th grader—for whatever reason in my class there was a cage with some white mice in it. I don't know why they were in there. Some kind of biology lesson. I remember that the mother mouse had some babies, and the teacher said, "Stay away from the cage. Don't look in the cage. Don't do anything, because when the mother mouse has babies and you're around the cage it will cause her to eat the babies." I thought that was a bizarre notion, but apparently there are certain animals that are really, really finicky, and if they feel like their nest is being encroached upon they will basically kill their own children or not have them. I think whites are that kind of finicky, weird creature, and when we feel like our living spaces are in some way not safe—whether they're crime zones or whether we just don't feel quite at home in them—I think that suppresses fertility, which is why one of the major factors that causes whites who live in diverse areas to move to homogeneous areas is when they start having kids. Suddenly they look around, and they don't feel safe having their nest in a diverse area, and so they move to a suburb.

So, I think any kind of diversity in a very obvious way or in very subtle ways is one of the ways that causes our finicky whites to stop having kids.

MP: Hopefully, we won't eat our own babies.

GJ: Well, we abort our own children all the time. And then people say, "Why not use the stem cells for research?" I mean, we eat our own children in more subtle ways than just carving them up, but we do consume our children in this society, and we're a very sick people. I must say.

MP: I guess you do have a point there.

Now, Greg, in another article, "The Persecution of American Renaissance," you explain your perspective on the challenges that Jared Taylor's American Renaissance organization has recently had. This article was written before the more recent debacle. In America, things have reached the point where we are truly losing the freedom of speech and constitutional rights and all those WASPy things we sort of just took for granted like air. There's one section here I'd like to quote from you real quick.

> Within the White Nationalist community, American Renaissance stands for gentlemanly debate and strict legality. The underlying assumption of this approach is that White Nationalists can work within the American system. America was a *de facto* White Nationalist society. America became a multicultural society within the system and America can be reborn as an explicitly White Nationalist society within the system as well. The American system is not so broken that it cannot be fixed.

Now, that's quoting you, but you were paraphrasing what you essentially believe is the approach and attitude of American Renaissance, correct?

GJ: That's correct.

MP: Do you think in light of this more recent episode that that assumption has been further undermined, that we can get out of this through working within the system?

GJ: I don't think that we can fix this system, and I didn't believe it at the time that I wrote that. I was basically stating what I think is the American Renaissance position and its assumptions, but at the time I was writing that I did not believe that we could work within the system to fix it, and I believe it even less today. I think that this system is rigged, and it is very brittle. I don't think it is going to allow any fundamental change, and why should it? No sane society has a suicide clause built into it. The only people who believe in something like that are white people, high-minded white people who think that following their ideas off a cliff is the ultimate proof of their high-mindedness and their idealism. So, white societies can commit suicide out of high-mindedness, but we aren't a white society anymore.

The people who rule us are not whites. What is it? Well, it's a coalition primarily led by Jews. They're the ones who give all the direction. The coalition also includes a lot of deracinated, pluto-cratic white people—WASPs like my kin—and others. And there's this large group of minorities and disgruntled alienated groups that are held together in this coalition. But the real people who run it are Jews. They're not like us. They're not going to cede power like WASPs ceded power. They're not going to commit suicide on principle. They're just not going to do that.

My feeling is that America has been hijacked, and the people who are running it are not concerned with the long-term viabil-ity of the system. I had this epiphany one time when I was an undergraduate. I went to the local library, and I saw this shiny new CD on the shelf, and I checked it out, took it home thinking, "Oh boy, I'm going to be able to hear this without having to buy it, and I'll decide whether I want to buy it." I opened the case and this apparently brand new CD was all scratched up and un-playable. I was horrified by that, but the reason why these sort of things happen with library books and library CDs is that it wasn't the property of the person who checked it out, and so he treated it badly. Well, the people who run America today are basically just borrowing the country or, to use something from Alex Linder, basically they've stolen America, and they're joy-riding in America. America's like a stolen car, and they're taking it for a joy-ride, and when the thing crashes into a ditch they're just going to be pumping on the gas and spinning the wheels and cursing at the car for failing them. Then they'll get out, and they'll go somewhere else and hijack somebody else's car.

So, the people who are running this society are running it into the ground because ultimately it's not their society. They're act-ing like it. The idea that these people are going to maintain freedom of speech and not shred the Constitution and not destroy the system is ludicrous. It's not their system. They're not concerned with its long-term viability. So, I really don't think it's going to be possible for us to restore a sane racial hierarchy in this society within the system that we have today.

Fortunately, to extend the joy-riding metaphor, the people who are running the society are running it without brakes, and it will crash. When it crashes, then I think that we can do something about this situation. I think that a lot of the people who are running things into the ground will decamp for safer climes once things crash. I think that if the federal government defaults, a lot of functions will revert back to the state level. And if we have fifty state governments running things rather than one federal government that gives our enemies a lot less leverage. I think that in 42 out of the 50 states we might be able to actually get things going in the right direction.

So, my feeling is that (a) we cannot reform the system and (b) we don't need to reform the system because the system is going to self-destruct. My only fear is that it's going to self-destruct too soon, and sane white people are not going to have the infrastructure, the movement, the media that we need in order to get our message out and become the people who have a voice in setting things right once things crack up. My fear is that what will happen in America is very much like what happened in the former Soviet bloc countries where after the Communists were thrown out, who ends up running things? Well, rebranded Communists in a lot of cases, because they're the people who had the organization, the money, the networks, the access. So, they just rebranded themselves and got back into positions of power.

I think it's very important for our movement today to do everything we can to get our acts together and get prepared so that if suddenly events break our way—and they can break our way very suddenly and unexpectedly (nobody expected that Communism would fall apart in Eastern Europe) . . .

MP: Especially those right in the middle of it.

GJ: Yes, exactly. If you polled all the experts at the beginning of 1989 and asked them, "Will Communism be around in 10 years?" every one of them would have probably said, "Oh yes, of course." And if you said it's going to be gone in less than a year all over Eastern Europe, they would have thought you were a crank and a kook. It was a very brittle system running on lies, founded on lies, and kept in place by intimidation and conformism.

Our system is just as brittle. It's based on the same lies. A different version of the same lie: the lie of human equality. And it is just as brittle.

Let me back up and say this: what Communism did to destroy itself is that it was a school for cynicism. It made people cynical. What the whole diversity system is doing in the United States is similar. It's making people cynical. I really do think that pushing diversity all the time, pushing integration, pushing Affirmative Action, all these fictional black computer geniuses and all these dumb blondes in the movies, all that kind of stuff is making our case for us. The people I know who are the most Jew-wise and race-wise are people who live in New York City. Why? Because they have been exposed to those sorts of issues; it's been rubbed in their faces all their lives, and they're finally getting the message. So, integration and diversity are making our arguments for us, and that's one of the things I argue for in the title essay, "Confessions of a Reluctant Hater."

What I say there is the main cause of racial hatred is having to compete with other racial groups in the same living space, and the more that people of different races are thrown together, the more they learn that there are differences, and differences matter and the more they come to wish that they didn't have to deal with this. So, I think our system is creating the conditions of its own collapse just like Communism did. As more and more people become cynical about this, eventually there will come a point when the system's ability to enforce conformity out of fear will waver just for a moment. There will be a glitch in the Matrix or whatever. There will be a person who comes out and speaks his mind and doesn't then retreat and apologize. Imagine if just one politician stood up and said, "It's all bullshit!" and they don't back down. Or one movie director or one prominent business-man or ten prominent philosophy or political science professors or whatever. If they just stood up and said, "It's bullshit!" and stood their ground. (You can hear my academic bias, my egghead bias.) Or better yet, what if Rush Limbaugh called bullshit to his tens of millions of listeners and didn't back down. I think the system could start falling apart very, very fast if something like that happened.

So, again, my great fear is that it will collapse, and we won't be in a position to really put things back together in a sane way. It would probably still be better, but it won't be ideal.

MP: Right. When they have ears to hear, we won't be there with the message.

GJ: Exactly.

MP: That's my own fear, too. I know a lot of people have this idea that voting isn't going to accomplish the job, therefore I have to hide in my basement with my guns and dehydrated food. I don't think you have to go to that extreme that because the system is integrally against you . . . Like I like to say, the system's not broken. It's working fine. It's just not working for you. We have to be refining our message and practicing the art of leadership if we expect to lead if and when that time comes to be able to lead.

GJ: Yes, I agree with that, and this is where I do believe that it is important for those of us who are so inclined and talented for actual political activity, we need to get involved in politics. Now, I do not believe that we are going to vote our way out of this situation. I do not believe that there is a politician on a white horse who is going to get elected into office and change the system. I don't think that's going to happen. I don't think there's a single politician in the mainstream who believes in what we believe. I do not believe in libertarianism. I do not think that Ron Paul is on our side. He is a libertarian ideologue who, basically, would be quite happy if in 100 years the brown people who inherit America have a sound functioning economy. And I just think that's craziness.

MP: Gold standard currency.

GJ: Yeah, they'll have sound money for the brown people. That's what he stands for, and I think that's madness. It irritates me to no end, and I'll say it right now. I'm going to write something about this someday, but I'll just get it out there on the air now. I am going to socially shun any White Nationalist I know from now on if I find out he donates another dime to Ron Paul.

MP: So, are you telling me right here on the air to tear off my Ron Paul bumper sticker from my car?

GJ: Well, if I catch you paying $1,500 to sit down to a dinner with Ron Paul I promise you I will shun you. I will not invite you to any of my glittering dinner parties or anything like that. I'm going to socially shun you, and I think that we should all have that attitude, because there's just something crazy about White Nationalists getting so excited about this guy who doesn't share our philosophy but is happy to take our money, because that's his philosophy. It's money. It spends all the same. He doesn't care if it comes from dirty racists. But he's not going to listen to us, he's not going to respect us, and just because he pisses off some of the right people doesn't mean that he's our friend.

MP: Recently, on the immigration issue he's really come out ideologically. That was one of the things I really did like about Ron Paul was that he was for a relatively strict immigration policy, and he's recently flip-flopped on that to a more libertarian ideologically consistent "borders interfere with optimal trade" perspective. When an ideologue has an ideology it's just a matter of time before you, as a people, are betrayed by the abstractions he's a slave to.

GJ: Yeah. The market is a global thing. If you worship the market, you are committed to globalism, and that means that you are committed to the breakdown of all national borders and all national identities, and it's just a matter of time before people follow that logic out. It was just a tactical, temporary compromise that Ron Paul had to have any kind of sensible immigration views at all probably based on his assessment of what he needed in order to keep getting reelected in Texas. Now that he has his eyes on the national stage he's realizing that a more consistently libertarian position—which happens to be the same position as the liberals and the mainstream Republicans, namely break down the borders, and let them all in—he thinks that is a politically expedient thing to do, and so expediency and principle are beautifully aligned now for Ron Paul, and so, of course, he's for open borders.

I remember one time, years ago, a libertarian said, "having borders is just another form of racism." Yep. OK. You're right about that. Exactly. It's just like racism. Why? Because you have a preference for your own over aliens, and that's what racism is.

But anyway, back to political engagement. I do think that people who have the talent for getting involved in politics and the interest in that who are our people should get involved in it to that extent. Why? Because it's a really good school.

MP: It's practice.

GJ: Yeah, it's practice. They learn a lot about how the system works and how to communicate with people, and all those skills will become necessary. We want to have people who know how to do political campaigning and fundraising and all these sorts of things when suddenly people have ears to hear and we want to get our message out. That is very important experience, and if people temperamentally inclined to do that and if they've got the talent, I say more power to them.

Personally, it's not for me. It's not my temperament. It's not my talent. But I'm a pluralist about these things. I want to get as many people involved in White Nationalism as possible with as many different talents and interests and we need to find a place for them all. We need to encourage people with all these different talents and interests to work for the cause in the way that feels best for them, that's most authentic for them, that is most harmonious with who they are and what makes them tick. But it's not for me, personally.

I'm not one of these guys who thinks that everybody's got to be publishing little essays on Nietzsche and Spengler, and that's the only way we're going to get things done. Little essays on Nietzsche and Spengler are what float my boat. I absolutely, totally understand that that is not the only thing that we need, and we're not going to win if we're the best Nietzsche scholars in the world. We're going to win if we have the ability to beat our enemies in the field of political struggle.

MP: Guided by the lodestar of solid philosophy.

GJ: Yeah, we need to have the right orientation. We need to have the right foundations in place, but ultimately we're not going to win by who has the best Nietzsche scholars, but by how many divisions we can mobilize. That, I think, is an important thing, and I definitely get that, so I don't want to be misrepresented as somebody who thinks that by some strange occult power ideas alone are going to change things.

But ideas ultimately are the things that shape how people fight, what they fight for, how far they're going to go and things like that. So, I think that metapolitics, which is what Counter-Currents is about, is an important thing, but it's not the only thing.

The essays in this book, *Confessions of a Reluctant Hater*, are more political essays than metapolitical essays. They are engaged with political issues and cultural issues. I have a section in here on finding a white voice, which is where I try to learn how to speak as a white person and take my own side as a white person in all these issues. Then there's a section called *Polarizing Moments* which are just commentaries on political events that I think will be very exciting because they are signs of racial polarization and racial awakening. Then I have a section on white lifestyle politics which deals with a lot of things. It deals with miscegenation, lawyers, sex crimes, drug legalization, Jim Goad, Christmas shopping and, one of my favorite writers, Alan Watts. It's kind of all over the place.

I just want to stress that although I am all about metapolitics this book is more about politics and culture than the sort of higher order ivory tower things that I am going to be talking about in later books.

MP: Well, I would consider it a good gateway, a good primer for somebody who's interested in Counter-Currents and thinking about these things on the next level.

But we are completely out of time. What I can guarantee to you, I've thought about it, I am going to take the Ron Paul bumper sticker off my car tomorrow morning. I don't know why it's still there. I do want to thank you for visiting the show. There are several things I'm thinking of here that I want to ask you about, but we're out of time. Hopefully, you'll come back and we can discuss West Coast White Nationalism. If you could come back soon that would be great.

GJ: I'd love to. "West Coast White Nationalism" is one of the essays in that third section on lifestyle politics. So, yeah, I'd love to come back, and I'm glad to hear that you're going to get rid of the Ron Paul bumper sticker. I have a sticker that says "Spengler was right," and since I don't have a car, I could pop that in the mail to you, if you'd like, and you could put that one its place.

POPULISM, ELITISM, &
ECONOMICS

INTERVIEW WITH ROBERT STARK*

ROBERT STARK: Hello, everyone! This is *The Stark Truth* with Robert Stark. I'm joined here with Greg Johnson. Hey, Greg! It's nice having you on.

GREG JOHNSON: Thanks for having me on, Robert.

RS: So, what we're going to be discussing is the issue of economics and how it relates to class struggle and class warfare. Whatever term you want to use to describe our political and ideological circle, there are these two conflicting views and concerns about economics and class that have to be addressed.

One of them is that there's this fear—and you really see this fear among the Tea Party crowd, and it exists within our ideological circle, but also it exists among mainline conservatives—of a growing underclass. They have this fear of socialism and the underclass demanding wealth redistribution from the middle class, and this fear has been exploited by a parasitic elite, by the plutocracy, to get the middle class to align itself with the plutocracy. That's basically why you've seen the middle class aligning itself with the Republicans.

Greg, you're also familiar with the sort of Rothbard meme, which is the foundation of paleo-libertarianism.

GJ: Yeah, that's right. As I understand it, the paleo-libertarian approach really was created as a reaction to David Duke's emergence as a national political figure. Based on his performance, it was decided there was a great deal of potential for racially-aware, white-interest ethnic politics, and so Rothbard and Lew

---

* On May 18, 2013, this interview with Robert Stark appeared on The Stark Truth on Counter-Currents Radio. The audio is available online here http://www.counter-currents.com/2013/05/robert-stark-and-greg-johnson-on-wealth-redistribution/

Rockwell and others associated with him tried to fuse libertarianism—classical liberalism—with certain populist Right-wing elements. I think the best synthesis of that was those Ron Paul newsletters that Ron Paul claims he never read, where he's addressing concerns about things like Affirmative Action. It's an attempt to co-opt racial anxiety and channel it into a race-blind, race-neutral free market ideology.

RS: And the thing is it is a legitimate concern about a growing underclass making more economic demands, but the problem is we have so much wealth and power concentrated in the plutocracy. That's actually a far bigger threat, because, even though the underclass is growing in numbers, wealth basically translates into power, and power triumphs over the number of people in regard to political power.

Greg, one of the things you proposed in one of your articles—I forget what it was called, but it was something about the failure of conservatives or why the GOP must perish, it was one of those articles—an income cap at one million a year, because that's really the problem. Having so much money concentrated in the hands of a few is what has led to the corruption of our political system.

GJ: Yeah, I would agree with that. There are two problems. There is a problem of a growing underclass of net tax-consumers—parasites if you will—and of course immigration from low-IQ countries is contributing to that dramatically. But even Asian immigrants are actually a big problem because they bring their elderly relatives over, and they're very, very savvy about getting people enrolled in all kinds of public benefits programs. So, it's not even the low-IQ people who are a problem. It's the high-IQ people who are cynical and manipulate the system, and so we really do have a serious problem, and there's no question that you cannot have a functioning Western, First World society if you have too many people who are basically unwilling or incapable of producing enough value to sustain that kind of lifestyle. If you give these people the vote, and you give these people social welfare programs, they will take more than they contribute until basically they ruin the system.

So, that is a definite problem, but by the same token I think the overclass, if you want to put it that way, is equally problematic, and it's the overclass who are bringing in the underclass and afflicting the middle class with this immigration. The overclass, the super-rich, really are benefiting tremendously by exporting American jobs overseas and importing coolie labor into America to undercut the gains of the labor movement, basically.

I used to be a kind of conservative, a kind of patriot; I was something of a libertarian, so I looked upon American history as something that was glorious and wonderful, but I have come around to thinking that really the only glorious chapter in American history is the history of the labor movement and the populist movement and what they did to try to rein in the kind of predatory capitalism that we had in this country and give working people the breaks they needed to produce the extremely large and powerful and prosperous American middle class, which the plutocracy is now dismantling again by outsourcing jobs or shipping jobs overseas and by bringing in low-IQ, low-tech stoop labor from the Third World.

So, we do need to address the problem of the overclass, and I think that in those terms libertarianism is a completely worthless ideology. It's completely worthless, because basically their only objection to Goldman-Sachs or Time-Warner or any of the big companies and the agendas that they push would be if the checks didn't clear. If certain people want to buy up huge chunks of the economy and pump filth and depravity and propaganda into people's homes, well, if the checks cleared then libertarians have no problems that, and I just think that's a form of self-induced stupidity, politically speaking.

What you need to look to is a non-free market, Right-wing critique of contemporary society, and there are a lot of resources for that. There's a whole tradition of Third Way economic thinking, including classical republicanism, populism, social credit, distributism, and the like that can mount a critique of the kinds of plutocratic system that we have today. So, I think one of the most important things for the agenda of the North American New Right is the complete destruction or a deconstruction of the free market orthodoxy that reigns in Right-wing circles. I think market economics is bad science. Well, what it is really is classical liberal politics presenting itself as science.

RS: Yeah, the thing is the capitalist, free market propaganda is so ingrained in the American Right. On the one hand, you get these libertarians—and the Tea Party movement is basically run by the Koch brothers—so they're very apologetic for the plutocracy. But then you get these people who are kind of pseudo-populist or paleoconservative types like the Alex Jones crowd. If you listen to Alex Jones and those people, they do have a visceral hatred for these globalist elites beyond what you get among the Tea Party types, but they still have this capitalist, conservative orthodoxy where they have the sphere of government and socialism that they would be opposed to any kind of tax increases on the ultra-wealthy.

If you look at the issue of campaign finance reform. Campaign finance reform is meaningless. Canada has fairly strict campaign finance reform, but their politicians are just as corrupt and reprehensible as ours. But really the way you have to deal with the concentration of power in the hands of a few is to limit their wealth.

One solution that's been put out—I think it was in my interview I did with James Bowery—is there needs to be an asset tax. Instead of an income tax where you tax income there needs to be an asset tax on corporations and banks. That's probably the best way to start and then there's your idea of putting a cap on income at $1 million a year, but you would make an exception for people who invent stuff.

GJ: Yeah, I think that would be a legitimate kind of exception, and I chose that figure just arbitrarily, basically to get the idea circulating out there that part of the problem could be solved simply by capping incomes. There are a lot of people who would up stakes and leave America if we capped their incomes, and my attitude towards people like that is: let them go. Good riddance! We don't want people like that. If a person just can't make ends meet on a million dollars a year, then I hope they do what Denise Rich did, which is up stakes, renounce her citizenship, and leave.

We would eliminate I'd say 70 or 80% of the 500 top wealthiest people in the country, who would simply up stakes and
leave because they have no connection to the United States anyway. It doesn't matter to them one bit, and the reason I believe
that is because their policies indicate that this country doesn't
matter to them one bit. They're enriching themselves by dismantling the American economy and the American way of life by
corrupting the American system of government. Good riddance
to them. I'd like to see them all go.

I think the only thing I would regret is if we didn't make the
people who have profited from dismantling the country give
back a lot of their gains before they leave. I think that they definitely should have their gains expropriated, and they should be
able to leave with whatever legitimate wealth that they have ac-
cumulated.

I think that populism in a broad sense is a really legitimate
outlook. But if you're a real populist then what you would want
is basically a classical republican model. What do I mean by
that? It's a society where the common good of the people is the
law. It's the highest law. It's the aim of politics. If you look at the
classical republican tradition really starting with Aristotle's *Politics*, there's a strong argument there for maintaining the middle
class. Meaning a large number of people who are independent
enough intellectually and especially economically to participate
in politics. If you have a large enough middle class, that is the
bulwark against the tyranny of the elites, and so the only way
that you can really have a society that's free and a society that's
just—meaning a society that looks out for the interests of the
whole—is to maintain a balance against the tyranny of the elites.
The elites are richer and smarter than the average, and unless
there is some kind of balance or check against their power they
will basically turn the system into some kind of oligarchy or plutocracy. The only way to stop that is to have the many, the majority, to be propertied, independent, and leisured enough to
participate in politics to counter-balance that, and that is the argument for middle-class society.

If you look at the populist tradition in America—you look at
somebody like Thomas Jefferson, you look at the 19th century—

the great concern of populists was to prevent the middle class from being disenfranchised, disempowered by losing their property and their independence, and the main mechanism by which independent farmers and business people lose their property and become more dependent on the wealthy is basically foreclosure. It's borrowing at interest and losing their property through foreclosure. That is the main cause of downward mobility for middle-class people, and that brings us to a critique of interest-bearing banking and things like that. I think that is absolutely crucial element in a populist, Right-wing critique of capitalism.

RS: I'd like to get into detail about those two issues—the issue of foreclosure and the issue of banking—but what I want to say is the first step in educating people in metapolitics is we have to kind of wean the middle class off of capitalism. The core reason these middle-class conservatives are capitalists is because they have this fear that any kind of redistribution of wealth at the top is a sort of slippery slope to full-blown socialism, and they're afraid that their money will be confiscated and given to the underclass. So, I think the very first step is to educate those people and to address their fears and concerns which are causing them to be exploited by the elites.

GJ: Yeah, I would agree with that. I am very critical of just pure redistributionism as a political strategy. The idea that you're going to have as a regular day-to-day function in government taking money from productive people and giving it to people who aren't productive is a very bad thing. There's no question about it.

I would, however, be in favor of certain quick and massive redistributions of wealth from people who have gotten it through dismantling the American economy. I don't know if I'd just give it away to anybody who wants it or anybody who's needy, but I think it would be a very appropriate thing to basically take away ill-gotten gains and use that to fund some kind of government programs.

But the most appropriate thing to do with expropriating ill-gotten wealth of the plutocracy would be to use it to capitalize new American manufacturing industries. I think that would be a very, very useful thing, and so instead of just handing it to people you would use it strategically to recapitalize and reindustrialize America. I think that would be a good thing.

RS: So, this is basically the key of what you were getting at. Redistribution of wealth in itself isn't necessarily a bad thing. It just has to be done the right way. The wealth has to be taken from the people who are basically engaged in destructive behavior and redistributed to people who have potential to be productive.

We reject egalitarianism, but just because we reject egalitarianism doesn't mean . . . I mean, the real problem with capitalism is that capitalism doesn't necessarily reward the very best behavior. The people who thrive the most in a capitalistic system are those with sociopathic tendencies.

GJ: I would agree with that, and you're exactly right. The most important thing that we just have to get out there is that we are not egalitarians. We do not think that the bedrock, default moral prejudice should be for equality across the board. That's simply not true. People are not equal, and they should not be made to be equal.

However, I think that a broad middle class is different from numerical equality. Radical egalitarians cannot help but have the people of lowest quality and least potential be the moral benchmarks. I've heard liberals gushing and drooling about how "The measure of a society is how it treats the most needy and vulnerable," and I just think if that's really true then you have basically set your moral compass in a way that will lead to the destruction of the strong, the productive, the creative, and so forth, and I think that's a terrible idea.

I think that really the criterion for justice in a society is not how it treats the least talented and least productive but rather how it pursues the common good, and I think that reorients politics tremendously, because if you think in terms of how to pursue the common good one of the things that we do know is that a society where people who are creative and virtuous, if those people are rewarded for that, they will be productive, they create wealth, they create inventions, they create an atmosphere of social trust, which I think is enormously important, and that kind of society where you reward real excellence measured in terms of creating real things of value and also moral excellence, character, I think that kind of society is good for everybody.

Therefore, a kind of elitism is appropriate, and it's actually best for the people as a whole. So, I'm a populist in the moral sense, but I think if you actually look in causal terms, if you look at what is actually conducive to the good of the whole, then what you have to be is resolutely, inflexibly an elitist. You have to be an elitist on principle. You have to reward people for excellence, and you can't put your thumb on the scale, and you can't reward people for mediocrity or need. I think that even the needy and mediocre actually benefit from a truly aristocratic, elitist society. Of course, the way to prevent that kind of elitism turning into the selfish rule of elites like we have today is to have a large and empowered middle class that's politically capable of preventing that from happening.

But the other thing you need to ensure is the circulation of the elites. What do I mean by that? I just mean that if you have a real elitist system you're going to be having things like public education where you give people access to excellent education as just a baseline condition of citizenship and you resolutely promote the best people from all classes of society, and you do not have this kind of elite that we have in America today which is increasingly hereditary, where you have wealthy people sending their kids to exclusive schools, getting them into Ivy League universities, and you get this self-perpetuating, somewhat impervious elite. I think that if you have an elite that's genuinely elitist you're going to be constantly pulling in people from all different ranks of society based on their worth, and you're also going to have mechanisms whereby the mediocre children of the wealthy and powerful are allowed to descend to a lifestyle and amount of power that are appropriate to them.

I think that a system like we have in America, where you have manifestly mediocre people like Albert Gore, Jr. or George W. Bush aspiring to become president or actually becoming president, is a bad system. I am sure that there are 10,000 Iowa farm boys or 10,000 people from Appalachia in the coal region or 10,000 people from any part of the country from humble backgrounds who are probably smarter and better than a lot of the people who are going to Harvard and circulating from government to board rooms in the current corrupt system. So, if you're really an elitist, you're going to have an elite that circulates a lot. People will rise from all areas of society because of their genuine merit, and people who are descended from the best people but are not as good as their parents are not going to enjoy the same level of power and influence and wealth that their parents have. I think that's a very just system.

RS: The thing about implementing it is that's basically how it's always been throughout history even going back to the European aristocracies. Wealth and power was usually passed down from one generation to another. I think this idea that anyone can become successful, which is what people call the American Dream, it's happened in some situations, but I think it's really a fantasy. It's never really been the case, but if you want that to be the case the question is how do you implement that.

GJ: Right. I think that upward mobility is a very nice thing. You do not want a society where you've got sort of fossilized, impervious castes. I think that is an injustice, and it makes a society weaker, because there are people of genuine greatness who come from humble backgrounds, and if they can rise to positions where they can give more to the world, then the world is enriched because of that. So, I think that's very important. I think that upward mobility is an important thing, and I am all for that.

I think that one has to enshrine that, and one of the ways to do that is to have an elitist system, a meritocracy, if you will. Lots of libertarians love to talk about meritocracy, but honestly what they're really talking about is plutocracy, because merit is really measured in their eyes in terms of wealth when you get right down to it. I think that if you had a genuine meritocracy, genuine ability for people to rise and fall according to their merits, that is actually the best kind of system for the people as a whole.

So, again, I'm a populist in terms of my overall moral foundational outlook and in terms of what I think the proper goal of society is, but I'm an elitist because I believe that having a real meritocracy is the best way of assuring that the common good is taken care of.

RS: The other thing about the economic system is that the economic system is set up to keep down political dissidents. If you want to rise up in a big corporation or a financial institution, you do have to be basically apolitical or you have to adopt the political ideology of the ruling class. Basically, if you're a political dissident it does limit your economic opportunities. If you look at the top 1% I can't think of a single person with dissident views.

GJ: Right. I would agree with that, and that's, again, really the populist principle.

Let's define middle class, too. By middle class I don't just mean middle income people, because there are lots of middle and upper income people who are not middle class in the sense that I mean. By middle class I mean economically independent. In some sense self-employed as a small businessman or a large businessman, farmer, things like that. If you are self-employed as opposed to employed by another person you have greater freedom of thought and action in the political realm, and there's just no question about that. There are a lot of people with middle and high incomes who still work for other people, and they have very, very little real freedom of thought, and I think that's very bad.

We have to define what dissident ideas are too, because . . . Was it Charles Koch, one of the Koch brothers, I think the senior one? I think he's the fifth or sixth richest man in the world.

RS: Yeah, Kevin MacDonald wrote an article about the Koch brothers buying up the *LA Times*.

GJ: Right.

RS: He's not a huge fan of him, but I think he's a little less cynical about them than we are. They haven't taken an official stand on an issue like immigration, but if I had to guess they're probably for open borders. But their main political issues are basically less taxes on the wealthy, less regulations on business, and less environmental regulation. I think for some people who are focused solely on ethnicity they may look the other way, but those issues by themselves are reprehensible positions to take, and they definitely should be viewed as despicable individuals.

GJ: Oh, I would agree with that. Libertarians are open borders enthusiasts. The Koch brothers are libertarians. They are the main bankrollers of libertarianism in the United States in the 20th and 21st centuries, and it is just astonishing how much money they have put over the years into these various libertarian organizations.

Years and years ago, when I was on the sort of fringes of libertarianism, people would talk about "the Kochtopus," all the different arms of the Koch machine. They've been investing millions and millions of dollars into promoting libertarian ideas for decades now, and they are a wonderful example of metapolitics. If the North American New Right had people with anything like the money of the Koch brothers, or one thousandth of the money that the Koch brothers have, we could still do so much to promote better ideas. They have created think tanks, they have endowed professorships at universities, they have wormed their way into various institutions, and they are very, very successful at promoting their version of extremely bad ideas, their Right-wing, classical liberal version of bad ideas.

And yes, I am 100% on the side of the progressives when it comes to things like environmental regulation, for instance, so I think the Koch brothers are pretty bad. I think they're worse than your average Republican in many ways, because they are very, very ideologically purist. They're purists. They're ideologues. They're not these compromising and corrupt Republican politicians. In some ways, I would prefer a corrupt politician who has bad ideas, but betrays his bad ideas all the time, to somebody who is incorruptibly wrong and has a personal fortune of $34 billion to back it up and is willing to actually write checks. That is a very dangerous person.

George Soros is a bad guy in a different way, but the Koch brothers are bad as well.

RS: I think it was Chesterton who said this, but this goes back to your definition of the middle class: "The problem with capitalism is that there's too few capitalists."

GJ: Exactly. I think that's really well put. What we stand for is private property and free enterprise broadly distributed, and that is the key issue. You can pretty much deduce everything from the necessity of maintaining the broad distribution of free enterprise and private property. You can deduce regulations on the amount of wealth people can have. You can deduce things like protectionism. You can deduce getting rid of interest-bearing currency and getting rid of the banking system. You can pretty much arrive at social credit. If you just ask yourself what is necessary to maintain a private property, private enterprise society with a huge prosperous powerful middle class, the whole range of third way economic things follows, and they are all very consistent with one another. Distributism and social credit, all of these things can be fit together, because they're all working towards the same end, and they share a lot of the same basic premises.

I think that Chesterton is very, very good on that sort of issue.

RS: So, earlier on you touched on the foreclosure crisis. I'd like to get into that issue more in detail.

GJ: Well, foreclosure just happens when you pledge your property for security on a loan. We've gotten into this system where the primary asset that most middle class people can aspire to have is a home, and there's this built-in idea that it's this wonderful thing if home prices are going up 10% a year, which I think is catastrophic. If orange juice went up 10% a year or cars or clothes went up 10% a year people would be screaming bloody murder. College educations are going up 10% a year, and people are screaming bloody murder about that, but somehow we've got this idea that it's wonderful if home prices keep going up, and, of course, the reason that some people think that is because they have a home, and they want to sell it, whereas most people don't have orange juice or college educations to sell.

RS: Yeah, that's why the home prices are going up. I think part of it is just supply and demand. In California, we have a rapidly growing population due to immigration, but the housing supply is not growing to keep up with that.

But the other side of the reason why housing prices are going up is because of the banking system.

GJ: Well, right. Exactly. There's a lot of speculation going on, and frankly if you have things like deductibility of mortgage interests . . . Mortgage interest deductibility is a giant redistribution mechanism to the banks. Let's just face it. House prices are higher because of mortgage interest deductibility, and, of course, banks benefit from that tremendously. Of course, middle-class people want to hold on to that because they think they benefit from it, and as individuals they do, but the system as a whole doesn't benefit from things like that. I think it just creates high prices.

What I would do with housing is simply have interest-free loans that are underwritten by the government or private enterprises that just have a fee. A fee for writing the loan and administering it. You pay that maybe once, right? It's not calculated as a growing, compounded interest payment on the amount that you borrow. It's simply a fee, and it would allow people to get started in life, buy homes and things like that.

I would actually limit the number of houses and housing units that individuals can own.

RS: You know, Steve Sailer had an article about that. He said that in places like Los Angeles or I'm sure the Bay Area part of the reason why there's a growing gap between the rich and the poor is because of real estate. You have some people who are monopolizing large amounts of the best real estate or who own several homes. So, you're right. There does have to be a cap on how much real estate one person should own.

GJ: Yeah, why not have one house and a vacation house or something like that and have a limit? Basically, what that would mean is you would have people who have lots of capital not going around and buying homes and flipping them and contributing to these bubble-speculative mentalities in real estate, which of course we should have learned how disastrous that was, but now people are all excited, "Maybe the bubble is coming back!" We don't want the damn real estate bubble to come back! In fact, I would like to see housing prices deflate a great deal.

And let's face it, when I was living in Berkeley in 2003 I saw a two-bedroom bungalow up for sale for $1 million. That's absurd! The fact of the matter is that most of the people living in Berkeley never paid those kinds of rates for their houses, and so you had a town where the vast majority of the people living there could never afford to live there if they had to purchase their homes at the going market prices. Now, they're all delirious because they think they're going to retire and sell that house at $1 million or $2 million or whatever, and they'll have lots of money to play with, but what will happen eventually is that Berkeley will be nothing but a town full of rich pretend hippies. I've seen this happening in San Francisco. You go to the Haight-Ashbury district, and it's a pretty disgusting place really. There are bums all over the streets and mangy dogs and panhandlers and drunks and druggies, and then scurrying between them are people who want to hang out in the Bohemian district who bought a three-bedroom flat a couple blocks off Haight Street for $1 million.

RS: Yeah, it's basically what James O'Meara talks about in his *Gilmore Girls* series.

GJ: Exactly! Exactly. You've got this situation where you've got certain communities that are basically just becoming hollowed out simulacra of communities where rich people go to pretend that they're New England villagers in Martha's Vineyard or hippies in Haight-Ashbury, things like that. It's basically the equivalent of when Marie Antoinette pretended like she was a milkmaid in the gardens of Versailles. It's a completely debased, hollowed out, globalized, false simulacrum of communities. And meanwhile real people who work in these towns, who teach school, who are the postmen, who are small business owners, clerks, hairdressers, you know, the people who actually work in the town can't afford to live there. They have to recruit 60 miles. Ridiculous situations. Towns like Aspen where people commute 60 miles to work there, and then they go back to a trailer that they live in, which is massively overpriced because it's 60 miles from Aspen.

It's a ridiculous situation. It's unjust, it's artificial, and it's driven largely by all this easy money flowing into housing. People say, "Oh, our interest rates are low!" Whenever I hear that I panic. I want to reach for my revolver. Low interest is one of the worst things for an economy. If we're going to have interest, I'd rather have high interest than low interest. Why? Because low interest is the crack that powers these stupid, destructive, speculative economic bubbles. So, if you're going to have interest I'd rather have it high than low. There are countries that have enjoyed sustained, slow economic growth and prosperity with high interest. It's a totally doable system, but America, I think, is too addicted to fast growth and Ponzi economics all fueled by low interest, and I think that's one of our great economic follies, and it's creeping back. People want to have the stock markets going higher and higher. Housing prices are up.

I feel like I'm back in 2007 and 2008. That wasn't so long ago, but people don't seem to have learned anything.

RS: I'd like to talk a little bit more about political strategies. I think there are two political strategies. We've talked about the conservative middle class. There's the underclass and then there's also people who are on the Left. One thing is conservatives are really obsessed with selling capitalism to the underclass and to poor minorities. I think the key is I see a trend where you have an alliance . . . The underclass is basically being exploited politically by the elite, so I think it's important actually to encourage the underclass to really turn against the elite like you've seen in places like Venezuela.

GJ: Well, yeah, I would like to see that happen. My attitude about the underclass is basically that we should try to reduce it in size, and the best way to reduce it in size is, first of all, let's send all of the recently arrived underclass members home and get rid of incentives for idleness and parasitism.

Let's just say I'm running America as it is today, America the multicultural society afflicted with the millions and millions of non-whites that we have. I would actually much rather just pay welfare to anybody with an IQ of 85 or under for the rest of their lives, because I think one of the worst things we do in America is actually put these people in jobs where they pretend to work. They pretend to work, and they gum up the economy.

I used to live in Atlanta. Atlanta, I think, was 60% black, and the city government was like 96% black, and the people in that city government consisted of large numbers of useless eaters who basically went to their offices and pretended to work. Anybody who actually had to deal with the city government or the county government getting their business going or buying and selling property, doing anything that was economically necessary, had to go through this bureaucracy that was full of morons who are just loafing, chatting on their cell phones, letting the office phone ring or go to voice mail, then the mail box was always full. Your heart would sink through the floor when you would hear a black woman's voice wishing you a "blessed day," because you would just know that there was absolutely no hope. People who lived and did business outside Atlanta in some of the further ex-urban counties that were predominately white would go into the city hall, and people would just rush them through. They'd be really helpful. None of this passive aggressive stuff, none of the laziness, none of the craziness that the people in Atlanta have to deal with.

So, my attitude about the underclass really would be: why not just put them on welfare for the rest of their lives, get them out of jobs that they can only pretend to do, and if they're of child-bearing age give them incentives to be sterilized? I think that if you would just do that we would actually be a richer society than we are today, a richer and more efficient society than we are today.

So, my attitude about the underclass is that it should be reduced, and the best way to reduce it, ultimately, is to have a kind of gentle, slow-functioning eugenics program in place. What we should have is a safety net—I believe in that kind of social welfare—but you do not want to have these communities which generation after generation are basically lounging around in the social safety net like it's a permanent hammock. That's not the way to do things.

Practically every time you hear idiots talking about moral up-lift programs, economic uplift programs, minority uplift pro-grams, it's always wealthy white liberals like the people who live in the Marina District in San Francisco trying to ally them-selves with mestizo day-laborers and blacks, and who ends up getting screwed? It's the middle class. They're the ones who al-ways foot the bills for these things. So, I do see middle class people as right in their fear of any kind of discussion of these kinds of egalitarian schemes: redistribution, minority uplift, and things like that.

RS: California is run by a coalition of basically three groups: the very wealthy, the public employee unions, and the under-class, and they run the California Democratic Party. So, the key is to break up the alliance between the very poor and the very rich. The underclass just basically despises the rich.

GJ: Yeah, they despise the rich, but the fact of the matter is that they generally do not have leaders who will lead them to confront the rich. I remember when I lived in Atlanta there was this Negro minister and businessman, the Reverend Hosea Wil-liams, and Hosea Williams was just one of these vaguely ridicu-lous, Southern black, poverty pimp, Civil Rights politicians. But Hosea Williams was a cut above a lot of the others, and one of the things he said about himself was that he actually believed in the interests of blacks, whereas he believed that people like Coretta Scott King and Jesse Jackson and people like that had basically sold out to the ultra-rich and to the Jews. He actually referred to himself as a "nigger's nigger" whereas he said that Coretta Scott King was a "Jew's nigger." Now, that's pretty salty language, but that's the way a lot of minorities see things. But there are very, very few of them that will actually stand up and occupy a leadership role within their community that could gal-vanize them against the plutocracy.

Instead, anybody who looks like they have the potential to rise in their community is co-opted very quickly. Look at Barack Obama. There were people who spotted him as an up-and-coming potential person and mentored him, and basically a lot of them were Jews. A lot of them were Left-wing Jews who looked at Obama, saw this up-and-coming black, and they stepped in and played this mentoring role. They are constantly looking for talent in different communities that they can mentor and harmonize with their interests, and that's the way that the plutocracy works.

RS: Yeah, you saw that with Cesar Chavez, who was against the big corporate agriculture, and now the so-called "Chicano" movement is aligned with corporate agriculture.

GJ: Oh yeah, of course. They're keeping corporate agriculture rich by being so poor, right? Exactly.

RS: I would say those corporate farms should be shut down and sold to people who want to start up small family farms.

GJ: I wouldn't even say sell them. I'd just say homestead them out like we did in the past.

RS: Yeah. I don't mean sell them and give them the revenue. You could sell them and the revenue could go back to the public and be invested.

As you know, I do a TV show up in the Central Valley and I drive through that area. That agriculture industry generates billions or even trillions of dollars. That whole area is one of the poorest areas in the whole country.

GJ: Most definitely. It's horrific. A generation or two ago it was a prosperous area. It was kind of boring. San Franciscans would make jokes about Fresno being kind of dull. But the fact of the matter is that there was a large white middle class in that area, and the white middle class is gone in a lot of these towns; property values are very, very low because of the massive number of mestizos who live there now; crime and corruption is terrible; poverty is terrible. It really is becoming a kind of Third World plantation economy, and that is one of the things you have to guard against.

Again, small farms with independent farmers = a prosperous, middle class society. But what you get with the concentration of property is you get the *über*-rich plantation, which is worked by landless peasants.

RS: I know a lot of people who call themselves neo-Con-federates, but that's one of the reasons I'm not a big fan of the Confederacy because it was a feudalist system like that.

GJ: Calling it feudal is an underserved compliment, because on feudal estates the lords actually had obligations to their ten-ants. They were not chattel slaves. Even serfs in Russia had more rights than chattel slaves. What it was—and this is the truth with America and Anglo-American capitalism as a whole—is nothing but a cut-throat, inhuman form of capitalism where the people who got really, really rich from it cashed in all of their blood money and bought houses that looked like the estates of the Eu-ropean aristocrats, but it was only aristocratic on the surface be-cause there was none of the morality that goes along with genu-ine feudal aristocratic society. It was just the manners and the accoutrements. It was the furniture, it was the airs that these people put on, but they had absolutely no mutual feudal moral obligations.

Slavery is just capitalism at its worst, and that's why I can't really pine for the South either. If I lived in the South, frankly I would have been a white populist revolutionary who would be burning down the big houses.

RS: Yeah, I heard a video of Tom Metzger speaking to a group of Black Nationalists and he said that if he was alive back then he would have been pointing a cannon at the plantation owners.

GJ: I've always liked Tom Metzger. I hadn't heard that one, but he's a man after my own heart. One of the best things Tom Metzger ever said, which I thought was really, really funny but profound, was basically directed at the kind of White Nationalist types who think, "Well, we should just surrender some of our territory to the invaders." And Tom Metzger said, "I support the idea of reuniting Baja California with Alta California. We need to reunite Baja California and drive out all the Mexicans." I thought, "Yeah!" OK, it's not a serious proposal, but he's mak-ing a point. The mestizo nationalists are talking about basically driving white people out of power and just physically out of large parts of this country and taking it over, and what's the most radical position in opposition to that? "Well, we'll just cede some of this territory to you." It's appalling. That's the most radical position, whereas a really radical position would be, instead of having this idea that "What's yours is yours, and what's ours is negotiable . . ."

RS: Yeah, and you have a lot of those Northwest migration people who talk about a country in the Northwest. I think California is one of the most remarkable places in the world, and they're telling people to just leave California and abandon it.

GJ: Yeah, and I think that's really too bad. California is really worth fighting for. That's why I love California. It's just too nice to give up.

But yeah, instead of having this attitude that "what's theirs is theirs and what's ours is negotiable," we need to have the exact opposite attitude towards the Mexicans. It's like, "Folks, we're going to keep this country of ours, and if you're really quiet and good and all go home, we won't take a few slices out of Mexico for our growing population." That would be really radical. That would go beyond even the position that I think I would legitimately defend. But it makes it clear just how defensive a posture white Americans are in when even the most radical ones are just basically saying to the aliens, "OK, let's just make a deal: you can take *part* of our country from us."

I like Metzger because he has a fighting spirit, and when he made that proposal that really, really shows how defensive we are, and it's a position of weakness that we have cast ourselves into and that we are arguing from. We have to psychologically emancipate ourselves from that position of weakness, or we are going to be weak, and we're going to lose everything.

RS: We kind of went off on a little bit of a tangent, and that's OK, but I think before we wrap it up let's get to the topic of social credit.

You have that article "Money for Nothing" and you can talk a little bit about that and your correspondence with Dick Eastman, who's a big advocate of social credit.

GJ: Well, thanks for mentioning that. There are a few articles that I've written on economic topics that I really want to recommend to people who haven't read those articles, because I'm rather proud of them. These are all at the Counter-Currents website: counter-currents.com.[1]

One is called "The End of Globalization," which simply makes the point that if you're serious about opposing globalization then the natural boundary where globalization stops is the nation, and therefore nationalism is the only really viable alternative to globalization.

Another article I wrote is "Some Thoughts on Debt Repudiation," which I think has to be a feature of setting up any new system.

RS: About a third of our debt is to China, but most of it is actually to private bankers.

GJ: Yeah, and I think they can go without a new pair of shoes. My attitude is we'll just say to the Chinese, "Look, we're not going to pay you this, but all the capitalists who built companies, built factories in your country? You can keep those for domestic production."

RS: Yeah, let the Chinese confiscate the property of the Western factories in their country.

GJ: Exactly. And we'll just build new factories in our country for domestic production, and they can produce their cheap crap with lead paint for domestic consumption over there. I think that would be great.

So, the debt repudiation piece is another one, and the third one I want to recommend is called "Money for Nothing," and that's basically my attempt, in as naïve a tone as possible, to lay out the best ideas in the whole social credit theory that's associated with Clifford Hugh Douglas, Alfred Richard Orage, and Ezra Pound. I really recommend that, and I was just really flattered, just profoundly flattered, when Dick Eastman, who knows

---

[1] These articles are also reprinted in Greg Johnson, *Truth, Justice, & a Nice White Country* (San Francisco: Counter-Currents, 2015).

a hell of a lot more about social credit than I do, sent me a long email where he basically cut and pasted my entire article and went through it and commented on it line by line. I really benefited from that, and I feel like, "Yeah, my take on this was substantially correct," and I had the testimony of a guy who knows a lot more about social credit than I do. So, anyway, I do recommend that piece. It's a starting point.

I really do want to write more about this in the future, but I'm just so thinly spread. I've got so many different projects. I might just take a month in the Fall, maybe the month of October, and just sit down and grind out several more social credit pieces, because I've always been pretty good at explaining difficult ideas. I use to teach Heidegger, and I used to teach Kant. If I can teach Heidegger, and I can teach Kant to undergraduates, then I can teach social credit to the world at large. There are certain ideas at the core of social credit that are actually kind of difficult, and I think that I've found ways of making them easy for me to understand and I think easy for the rest of the world.

But yeah, so I don't want to go into that so much right now. I'll just issue that sort of promissory note that there's more to come at Counter-Currents on social credit, and if there are social credit writers who are comfortable associating with people like me at Counter-Currents and want to write for us and review books or try to popularize some of these ideas I would be really, really eager to hear from you. So, if you're out there contact me. I want to hear more from the social credit people.

RS: Alright, Greg. Thanks for being on *The Stark Truth*.

GJ: Well, thank you, Robert. I really, really enjoyed this, and so I look forward to our next conversation.

THE BOOMERANG GENERATION

INTERVIEW WITH ROBERT STARK*

ROBERT STARK: Hello everyone, this is Robert Stark. I'm joined here today with Greg Johnson, and we're going to be discussing his article on the Boomerang Generation.[1] You touched on this lightly, but this is a major issue going on. Basically, the Boomerang Generation is all of these young people, basically part of the Millennial Generation, people who I would say are roughly under the age of 35, and they're going to universities, and many of them have almost $100,000 worth in debt. Basically, they're graduating from universities, and they can't even find a job, and they're moving back in with their parents and their family. These are not your stereotypical losers. These are people who are very intelligent, hard-working people. So, Greg, I will let you introduce what you had to say in your article on this topic.

GREG JOHNSON: Thanks, Robert, for having me on again. I appreciate this.

The Boomerang Generation piece is something that I wrote at the end of August, I believe, and in it I talk about how White Nationalists tend to complain about the lack of young, educated people who are attracted to our movement. I think that today we have a golden opportunity to try to connect to this so-called Boomerang Generation. They're boomerangs, of course, because their parents throw them out into the world, and they come boomeranging back after college because they can't find a job or a place to live, or they can't afford to live on their own. So, they end up in the rec room in the basement sitting on the computer all day.

---

* On December 5, 2013, this interview with Robert Stark appeared on The Stark Truth on Counter-Currents Radio. The audio is available online here http://www.counter-currents.com/2013/12/robert-stark-interviews-greg-johnson-on-the-boomerang-generation/
[1] Reprinted in *Truth, Justice, & a Nice White Country*.

RS: You said it's a white issue, but I don't think it exclusively applies to whites.

GJ: I think it applies to whites more for the simple reason that they are unfairly targeted because of their race in two ways.

RS: Disproportionately, but not exclusively.

GJ: Yes, but a lot of whites go to college, and even if they get scholarships they have to take on student loan debt. A lot of non-whites go to college, especially the less college-bound, the less college-fit populations, the blacks and so forth. A black who can go through college is such a rare commodity that they are often given full-ride scholarships to universities that they can't really prosper in. If they do graduate, they generally graduate without any student debts at all, whereas a comparable white student going to the same school end up with $100,000 or more in debt.

RS: So, you're saying they get total debt repudiation because of Affirmative Action. I did not know that until you brought that up in your article.

GJ: Yeah, there are a lot of non-whites because of Affirmative Action in the universities who will end up coming out of the universities debt-free. You know, $100,000 in debt is not just $100,000 you have to pay off. You have to pay off the interest as well, and that can be a crippling debt burden for somebody starting out. Then when white students who have this huge debt burden go into the marketplace they are systematically discriminated against as well, because not only are there lots of non-whites in America who are competing with them for jobs. But because of globalization, because of open borders and things like that, white Americans are competing with positions for the cream of non-white countries around the world.

Countries like India have hundreds of millions of high quality people, and many, many of the best of them are coming to the United States and other European countries and competing for technical, professional, business positions with the native populations now. They are not worthless people who are being given a hand up through Affirmative Action. They are highly competent, intelligent people.

RS: They're not eligible for Affirmative Action.

GJ: They are in a way, because there's official and unofficial Affirmative Action. The unofficial form of Affirmative Action is just the worship of diversity, diversity, diversity. And when you get South Asians and East Asians who are highly competent and also non-white circulating around in the job market, they have so many things in their favor even though they're not officially, necessarily being favored in the United States. And if they're a woman on top of that, then they're really highly valued.

RS: That is the other thing.
Did you see that interview that Matt Heimbach did with . . . I forget the guy's name. He's a black man. I think it was the black guy that pointed out that actually the biggest beneficiaries of Affirmative Action have been white women.

GJ: Well, I don't think it's white women who are the greatest beneficiaries of Affirmative Action, because black women, for instance, rank higher than them on the food chain. Black women, I think, are in some ways the best people for diversity jobs in the sort of lower end skill set of jobs, for the simple reason that they have both their blackness and their femaleness counting for them. Also, unlike black men, their testosterone is lower, they tend to be more docile, and they tend to be more responsible. They tend to have kids at home and no husband, so they tend to be very, very focused on keeping their jobs. They might not be the best worker for the job if there were fair competition for the job, but they tend to be steady dray horses that employers can count upon, and I think that they're actually the most desirable group in terms of the Affirmative Action racket in America today. Again, to fill the lower end positions.

RS: Yeah, at the lower end. I was talking specifically about the higher end.

GJ: Yeah. In the higher end . . . I don't know. Maybe that guy's right. Maybe it's white women.

In any case, white men are the great losers in the diversity thing, and that's by design. I really do think that diversity, Affirmative Action, and other forms of anti-white discrimination primarily discriminate against white males and that white men are the one group that were indispensable for building our civilization. The women could have stayed at home. We didn't need blacks. We didn't need browns. We didn't need Asians. You look at the rise of an entirely white country like Sweden, which didn't have colonies overseas or anything like that, they show you what white people can do on their own. The essential population group for creating white civilization has been white men.

The one essential group for creating white civilization, in terms of building the infrastructure, the science, the technology, and all the things that are distinctive about white civilization have been white men. White women, of course, had to be there. They had to be wives and mothers. But they could have been entirely wives and mothers and history would have basically unfolded pretty much the same way. So, I don't want to denigrate women. I just want to say that the essential group that had to participate in the creation of our civilization is white men, and they are the primary group that is being discriminated against, and that cannot have good consequences for our civilization.

I was walking my dog the other day, and I was trying to think of an analogy that would explain how Affirmative Action could hollow out a system, and everything could be sort of OK for a while, but then it would collapse suddenly if there was a shock given to it. I walked by a firehouse, and I thought what would happen if basically the fire department just started hiring people who *pretended* to be firemen. They *looked* like firemen; they could put on the firemen's uniforms, all the external stuff that firemen do that has nothing to do with fighting fires. They could go through the motions of it, right? There could be women firemen and black firemen, and as long as they could look like firemen and go through the motions of it, well, that could go on for a very long time—until there's actually a fire.

Until there's actually an emergency. And then suddenly you discover that you've hollowed out the fire department, that there's nobody left who can actually do the job of firemen.

I really think that's what is going on with our civilization. Our civilization can go along on inertia for a long time where the old forms are just preserved even though the people who created them are replaced. Why? Because they're there, and even the people who had nothing to do with their creation can still enjoy them. There's an Irish pub on my corner that is owned now by Chinese. Most of their customers are now Chinese. And Chinese like to go bars. They like to drink. They like to listen to certain kinds of music. It's an experience for them. But after a certain point, there's going to be a tipping point where there are not enough of the original people around to maintain the institution, and then suddenly if there's a shock to it it's just going to disappear. Let's say that there is a bit of an economic crunch. Let's say things get more competitive. Eventually, the Chinese owners are going to ask if it makes any sense to keep going through the motions of running an Irish pub. Then it will change to something very different. Something more familiar to and comfortable to the owners and their clientele. And that is to be expected.

So, I think that the general tendency of Affirmative Action is one way — along with multiculturalism and immigration and things like that — that the distinctive institutions of white civilization are being hollowed out. And after a while there will be a shock or two or three, and we're going to discover that it's simply not working anymore. It will come apart at the seams.

RS: Basically, there are these movements that came about. There's Occupy Wall Street, and there's the Tea Party. They're different in some ways, but they have some overlap. The Tea Party is primarily older white people, older white males of the Baby Boomer Generation, and they're people who see the middle class declining, but they blame it all on socialism and the government taxing them. But then the other movement is Occupy Wall Street and it's primarily fueled by the Boomerang Generation.

GJ: Yeah and Occupy, I think, sopped up a bit of the discontent of the Boomerang Generation. But it didn't really last, and one of the reasons it didn't last, I think, is because Marxism and the progressive stack and all this Leftoid nonsense that it degenerated into really was not ultimately addressing the concerns of these people. So, they sort of drifted away from it. And I think this is an opportunity for White Nationalists.

In what sense could White Nationalists connect better with these people than the Left? Well, first of all, we have a better understanding of the dynamics of the system that is dispossessing them. It is not "capitalism." It is not some personal, aracial logic of capitalism. That's nonsense. That's bullshit.

RS: Well, I think it is. I disagree with you. I think capitalism and greed is the driving force behind most of these problems. Look at Mitt Romney, for instance. Mitt Romney is obviously a white male, but look at what he did at Bain Capital. He laid off large amounts of workers and you see that as typical of white capitalists going back and it's not a recent phenomenon. Look at someone like Henry Ford who did the same thing where he laid off workers.

GJ: I think capitalism in and of itself is a nation-wrecking phenomenon. It's an inherently global, anti-national, nation-wrecking phenomenon. But what you're talking about more is the dispossession of the working class and the middle class, and I'm talking about these college-educated people who tended to be towards the upper middle class and professional areas. A lot of them are being displaced not just by outsourcing and offshoring or things like that. They're being displaced by Affirmative Action primarily, and I think that we can therefore put in a much more explicitly racial angle here.

RS: These are kids from well-educated, upper middle class backgrounds. These aren't like your stereotypical redneck hicks.

GJ: Yeah. They're well-educated, and they're intelligent, and they're the kind of people who used to think that the rising tide of color would float their boats rather than swamp them.

They're the kind of people that chuckle at Christian Lander and showed up when I saw him speak a few years ago in San Francisco. These people feel themselves immune to dispossession. They feel like they're always going to be on top of the system, and already, just in the last few years, it has become apparent that no, they are being displaced too, and I think that we can explain to them the specifically racial angle of this.

I think also that we have a great critique of debt and banking and that whole economic dimension as well. I think that we should say, "Look, we will end Affirmative Action, and we will cancel all of your college debts. We will reinstitute protectionism and recapitalize the American economy. We're going to rebuild it for the working class, and we'll rebuild it for the middle and professional classes as well, because they are now being dispossessed, too. We're going to create a society where white people are going to feel at home and they have a sense of real hope for the future. We're going to make it possible for people, when they grow up and get a college education, to know that they can get a job, buy a house, and start a family. We're going to make affordable family formation for our people one of the corner stones of national policy."

Those are the priorities that White Nationalists have. Those are not things that are being addressed by the Left, especially the far Left, the Occupy crowd, and they're not being addressed by any of the mainstream political parties. So, that's the sense in which I think that we can better connect with these people, and we should.

Fellow White Nationalists tend to complain that the system is very good at co-opting people by giving them jobs and getting them mortgages and getting them started in life and so they feel like at a certain point they can't afford to rock the boat. They have to keep their views to themselves. They can't get involved in anything edgy or oppositional. They have to be really mainstream and play it safe. Well, the system isn't co-opting people anymore. It's lost its ability or interest in co-opting the former "leaders of the future," and I think that's an enormous opportunity for us. We need to exploit that. They're not being co-opted. They don't have jobs. They don't have mortgages. They don't have families, yet. They have crushing burdens of debt. They're living at home with their parents. Their parents are worried and wondering why the upward mobility that they enjoyed is no longing being enjoyed by their children. This is a golden opportunity for us to connect with a new constituency, and I would like to be able to do that.

Now, I can't do everything, and I'm already sort of stretched thin, but I would love to find a blogger, a single person, who can focus with laser-like persistence on this issue. Somebody who is a Millennial Boomerang kid who's got all this leisure time. Because that's another thing we always lament, that once people get jobs and have families they don't have the leisure time to engage in any kind of political activity. Well, these people have nothing but leisure. They might be working 20 hours a week at Starbuck's, but they have a lot of leisure time. I want to find the blogger with the leisure and the writing skills and the desire to connect with this generation and show systematically—commenting on stuff in the news, doing broader studies of things, but keeping the message out there—that we have a message for these people, that we can represent their interests, that we understand their plight better than the mainstream and better than the Left. I think that would be an enormous advantage that White Nationalists need to exploit, and we haven't done it yet. We haven't found that person yet. I'm still looking.

RS: Well, it appeals to the Left and the Right, because as you were talking about there are two halves of this issue. One issue is the issue of demographic dispossession. That's one half of it. But the other half is that the one-percenters that Occupy Wall Street rants about are basically looting the middle class. They are sucking all the wealth out of the middle class for themselves, and they do it for things like obviously the banks and mortgages, foreclosure, insurance. Insurance is another example of that.

GJ: Exactly. And believe me, most of the one percent are not our constituency. They're not our people whether they are white or not. They certainly don't think of themselves as white or think of themselves as Americans. They think of themselves as a member of some kind of rootless, global elite. Fine. I would like to cut them loose and get their suckers, their tentacles, their fangs out of the flesh of America.

RS: We may get called Commies for saying this, but I say just confiscate all their wealth and give it back to the middle class.

GJ: My view is similar. I believe that we should find those people who have been making billions by dismantling the American economy, bringing in non-white immigrants to undermine the wages of American workers, or just firing American workers and shipping their jobs overseas. We need to find those people who have made their billions by dismantling the American economy, and we need to take their billions away from them and use it to recapitalize the American economy.

I don't necessarily think that everybody who's grown rich in the present system is guilty of any sort of malfeasance. We can sort the ones out who are and the ones who aren't.

RS: So, you're not a full-blown Commie?

GJ: I'm not a full-blown Commie, but sometimes I am actually brought up short by the realization that we might have to contemplate Pol Pot methods to create a middle class capitalist society, and that's a pretty horrifying prospect.

RS: Yeah. Pol Pot is politically correct to say. Don't ever say Hitler, because that would be a hate crime, but I think it's safe to say a Pol Pot or a Mao Zedong.

GJ: Oh yes. They were torturers and murderers and liars and butchers, but they were morally unimpeachable because they were egalitarians. That's the insane attitude of your typical college-educated person today. But we can ween them away from that nonsense. I've weened a lot of them away from that nonsense in the years that I've been doing this, and I haven't been doing it all that long, but I keep meeting people who are 22, 23, 24 and who know so much, and I say to them, "I wish I knew at your age what you know." And they'll say, "Well, we were reading Counter-Currents when we were in college." It's helped.

So, we are reaching people, and I would like to reach more people, and I'd like to have more writers who can target these people better. I tend to have writers who are a bit older than that and so when we write about music it's music that was more current in the '80s, for instance, than things that are going on today, and that's true in a lot of areas. But I do think that our great growth market is going to be with this Boomerang Generation, with the Millennials. I think it was a very good idea when Richard Spencer offered deep discounts for Millennials to go to the recent NPI conference. I thought that was quite smart.

So, we need to focus on this, and if there are people listening to this who want to get started writing who are good writers—I can't re-write everything for people, you know; you've got to be good, produce clear copy, be witty, be incisive, and want to communicate these ideas to your constituency—I'll give you a platform that's getting 80 to 100,000 unique visitors a month. That's my promise.

RS: The other thing I want to touch on is I want to personalize it and talk about some of the stories of these people and what their future is in the current system. What is the future of these people? And I guess I'm of this generation myself and I admit it applies to me to a degree. But what is the future of these people in like 10 to 20 years under the current *status quo*.

GJ: Well, I hope they're not living at home in 10 to 20 years. I think that if this continues for another decade there is going to be revolution in this country. I guarantee that. The system needs to start thinking about co-opting the white, college-educated former middle class again or there will be revolution.

Unfortunately for them, fortunately for us, Obama is all about giving cell phones to brown people. He's completely uninterested in this kind of thing. I think there's a great deal of lack of realism in the current regime, and I think that's working in our favor. These people, they don't know how wealth is created, they don't know how societies are run, they don't know the difference between being a fireman and pretending to be a fireman. Your average black, and I taught a lot of black students over the years, including cream of the crop, bright black students, but even those students didn't understand the difference between *seeming* and *really being* something. They thought that to be a businessman you dressed in a business suit and you bullshitted with other people, and that's what a businessman was. Being a lawyer was dressing up like a lawyer and going through the motions.

RS: I think that's true to a degree. That a lot of it is bullshitting.

GJ: Yeah, a lot of it is bullshitting, and, of course, with Affirmative Action and so forth they're allowed to bullshit their way through life.

Because a lot of people don't really fundamentally understand the difference between being and seeming. Again, once you have a lot of people who are just going through the motions of being a fireman and don't actually know how to do it in positions of responsibility, when the fire breaks out we're going to see a breakdown. I really do think that's playing into our hands.

So, I don't think this can last for another 10-20 years. There's got to be a change, and the people who want the system to continue for a while longer before it breaks down, they have to be thinking, "We have to get this mulatto newsreader out of the White House and get somebody else in there who actually knows the difference between being a president and looking presidential." And, believe me, that attitude starts at the top of the administration and works its way down. It's working its way through the whole society. We can't have a society that works if people persist in this, but that's the logic of the system today. So, I don't think it can last for that long.

What are people going to do, though, before the revolution breaks out? Well, I think there's a tendency now towards people dropping out, and by dropping out I mean finding alternative ways of living in America that do not require mortgages and debts and things like that, that do not require lots of cash in your pocket. There's a whole movement now of people who want to have houses without mortgages. How do you do that? Well, you build your own house. You get pre-fab materials, you get bales of straw, you do dug-outs, you get scraps, and you build a small house for $5,000 or $10,000 or $20,000 in cash, and that's your home. There's a whole universe now of magazines and blogs and things like that dealing with just this little area. Who's primarily going into this? It's primarily whites.

So, people who want to have houses without mortgages, people who want to be more self-sufficient by growing more food, by adopting voluntary simplicity, by living in group homes, and things like that these are primarily whites. They're primarily Millennials, and a little bit older, and I think that they are showing the direction that a lot of these people are going to have to take. Because if the system isn't going to let them back in, eventually they're going to have to rally themselves and create a new system, or we're going to rally them and create a new system. That's my goal, at least. In the meantime, they've got to find a way to live, and that I think is the direction it's going to go. They're going to be an army of agrarian Hobbits that we're going to rally someday to storm the system to take it over. But that's the direction I think it's moving in. So, those are some of the thoughts that I have.

For instance, let me just toss out something. In 2001 I visited William Pierce's National Alliance headquarters up in the mountains of West Virginia, and he had a lot of acreage, he had a lot of buildings, but he was never able to keep people living there. They didn't want to live in the mountains of West Virginia. Now I think that property has been let go. It's been sold or will be sold. It's being abandoned, basically, by the National Alliance. And I just think that's a crying shame, because with a little bit of leadership in the present-day circumstances that'd be a great place. There are people who have nothing today. The system gives them nothing. They're smart, they're focused, they're hardworking. They could homestead that place and turn it into a little commune, and you could put them to work doing the former work that was done when the National Alliance was a thriving organization.

I think that kind of direction is something that the movement needs to look to as well, because we're not getting rich doing this kind of stuff, and if you want to be a full-time White Nationalist activist, let me tell you, you've got to find ways of living way cheaply, and this is one of the reasons why I'm so interested in all of this, because my standard of living is comfortable, but I don't have a lot of cash. Figuring out how to live comfortably and securely without a lot of cash is a problem that a lot of people are facing, including a lot of people who are younger than myself. So, I'm looking at these blogs like John Robb's *Sustainable Communities*. I'm looking into gardening. I don't grow vegetables yet, but I'm planning to do that starting next year. So, that's the direction I think a lot of our people are going to have to go.

Eventually, though, they're going to have to stop adapting to this system, and they're going to have to break it.

ECO-FASCISM

INTERVIEW WITH ROBERT STARK*

ROBERT STARK: Hello, everyone! I'm joined here with Greg Johnson. The subject for tonight is going to be the idea of eco-fascism.

Greg, you told me you're thinking of working on a book about the subject, but the very first thing I want to get to is the idea of kind of giving ammo to enemies, because, on the one hand, on the Left you have the SPLC, who has their whole essay called "The Greening of Hate," and on the Right you have the conservative capitalists, who will want to smear environmentalism and ecology. They actually like to use the term eco-fascism. So, are you concerned that if you do write a book on this topic and discuss this that you might give ammo to those certain enemies?

GREG JOHNSON: Well, I'm not really particularly concerned with what the SPLC or the Rush Limbaugh crowd think about this. I'm really more concerned with issues of truth.

I am very much a pro-ecology person myself. My outlook is very much nature-centered. Interestingly enough, it turns out that, although today ecology is considered a preserve of the Left, the truth of the matter is that if you go back far enough, ecology was actually something that was pioneered by a lot of figures that today would be considered figures on the Right.

One of the projects that I would like to write some day when I get enough time is a book on eco-fascism, and it would focus on a lot of different thinkers from the late 19th and early 20th centuries who were both pioneers of ecology and pioneers of, for lack of a better term, fascism or National Socialism.

RS: What's your definition of fascism? It's kind of one of

---

* On April 2, 2012, this interview with Robert Stark appeared on The Stark Truth on The Voice of Reason network. The audio is no longer available online.

those words people just like to throw out against someone and a lot of people who throw that terminology around can't even define it. What is your personal definition of fascism?

GJ: For me, fascism just represents a tendency in modern political practice, political theory. First of all, it's anti-liberal. It's defined by rejection of liberal egalitarianism and the sort of liberal model that the purpose of the state is to ensure the maximum amount of individual liberty or the kind of Communist egalitarian model, which basically says we're all equal and the purpose of the state is to ensure maximum comfort and access to physical goods.

The fascist outlook is perforce hierarchical for the simple reason that if people aren't equal, then when the problem of how to have political order is raised, obviously you want the best people to rule. You want to be ruled by people who are on average better than you rather than people who are on average worse than you. So, that's one of the essential characteristics. Fascism is a hierarchical, anti-liberal political philosophy.

If you go back far enough in time, of course, every political philosophy was hierarchical and anti-liberal. Fascism represents a return of perennial ideas that were really the core ideas of all the serious thinking about politics as far back as human history records. However, it's a recurrence of those ideas within the context of modernity where you have the rise of mass civilization. The rise of the masses and the empowerment of the masses creates a problem, and so the fascist outlook is basically an attempt to resuscitate and restore a classical, hierarchical, healthy, and holistic form of society within the context of a world where the masses have been emancipated and enfranchised and empowered.

And so it's also, by its nature, populist. I don't think there's any real contradiction though between elitism and populism if you understand those terms properly. The core of fascist populism is basically the idea that society should be organized as an organism, as a body politic. Meaning that it's organic, but within every organism there's a hierarchy of functions. The goal is to make sure that the best rule, the most far-sighted and dispassionate and also the most public-spirited rule over the body politic, and yet the criterion for just rule has to be rule for the interest of all. This is a notion that you get in classical political philosophy going back to Plato and Aristotle.

Aristotle in his *Politics* defines the difference between just and unjust rule in terms of the common good. You can have a society that is ruled by one man. If he rules for the common good, you call it monarchy. If he rules for his own private interests, you call it tyranny. He said that if you have a society where the few rule, if the few rule for the common good, that's aristocracy. If they rule for their own private interests, he called that oligarchy. And the same with popular rule. You can have a society that's ruled by the many for their own factional interests, and he defines that as democracy. Democracy is a bad form of government by definition in Aristotle, but he said it's possible to have popular government for the common good and he calls that "polity."

In my view, the core meaningful notion of populism is basically the idea that a system is not just if it is ruled for the factional interests of the ruling class rather than the common interests of the whole body politic. That populist principle, I think, is consistent with having a hierarchical society, and Aristotle lays that out very nicely. You can have one guy in charge, but if he rules for the common good that's justice.

Fascism in some ways represents a return to that kind of classical political philosophy within modernity.

So, let's go into eco-fascism. What's the connection, if you will, between fascism in a generic sense, which would include things like National Socialism in Germany, and ecology? How did these things get connected in the 20th century?

I think that the basic thing that connects these two bodies of thought and really makes them one is the centrality of nature. Modern egalitarianism is very much man-centered and anti-natural in its outlook, and so we need to define some terminology here. I think that the best and simplest way of defining the distinction is to look at Savitri Devi's book *Impeachment of Man*.

Impeachment of Man was written in 1946. It's one of the most far-sighted and radical books on deep ecology that's ever been written. In there, she makes the distinction between man-centered outlooks and nature-centered outlooks. Throughout most of history, most traditional societies have been nature-centered. So, the idea is that the most important thing is not the individual or the human society, but that they're part of a larger whole. There are things in this world more important than man.

With the rise of modernity, you get an increasing anthropocentrism, and Savitri Devi says that really goes back to the Old Testament. She thinks that Judaism is the beginning of anthropocentrism, because the Jews in the Old Testament believe that man has a higher nature than all the other animals. Man is made in the image of God, and God gives man dominion over nature. That dominion is not necessarily understood in terms of stewardship or positive obligations. Nature is there for us to use.

RS: Yeah, it sounds like that in the Bible where it says that animals and plants were put on Earth for the use of humans.

GJ: Exactly. Basically, modernity is somewhat anthropocentric even if it rejects biblical religion. So, what you have with the classic modern thinkers like Descartes and Hobbes is this egocentric and rationalistic point of view. You have these people who basically are very reason-focused and very ego-focused and self-interest-focused. That presupposes a certain alienation and lack of connection with a larger social whole and also with the larger natural whole, and once you get that alienation, if you will, from nature and from society that's sort of built in the foundations of modern philosophy, the working out of that leads to a sort of violent attitude towards nature.

We don't come out of the world. We're thrown into this world. We're alienated from it, and we look around, and we see that the world consists of raw material for our use. We don't have a sense that we're part of the flesh and blood of some sort of larger natural organism, and so with that modern idea comes an extraordinarily exploitative and destructive relationship with the natural world. It just doesn't occur to somebody to hack off his own limbs. Yet, in a very subtle way, we are as much a part of a larger organic whole as our own limbs are part of us.

But if you get rid of that underlying assumption that we're embedded within a larger whole, and it's just man against everything else, then you get modernity, then you get capitalism, then you get modern technology, you get burgeoning populations, and you get the on-going environmental crisis.

The reason why I think the fascist and National Socialist outlooks reject that is because they're more nature-centered. There's a sense that, "No, wait a second here. We're not isolated individuals defined by our reason, who have purely technical and instrumental relationships with the world. What we are, first and foremost, is organisms. And we're members of a larger extended family, namely our peoples. And we're organisms within an environment." And so, there's a sense that there's a return to a kind of holistic, organic relationship with the world. But that's completely consistent with being highly aware of things like natural differences, including racial differences, and it's very consistent with wanting to put limits on exploitative relationships between man and man, and man and nature, because modern capitalism and modern science and the way that it's used is seen as a product of a deep error, a kind of deep alienation that's entered into the world with modernity, and once we heal that rift we will, in a way, de-escalate the assault on nature and also really the assault on one another.

This is another issue that I would like to throw out there. There is no reason to think a fundamentally ethnocentric worldview implies an exploitative relationship to other ethnic groups. Now, historically speaking, of course, human groups have struggled with one another for domination, but if you take an ecological standpoint and affirm there's a basic biodiversity in the world, including human biodiversity, it might lead you to the attitude that it's very important to preserve human biodiversity as well as natural biodiversity, and you get the outlook of somebody like Savitri Devi, for instance, who said that her dream is of a world where you have many races and each race has its own place in the world where it can live according to its own lights. So, she was a National Socialist, she was in some ways to the Right of Hitler, and yet her dream, because she was a fundamentally ecological thinker, is of a world where every race and every people has its own place and could live according to its own nature.

I think that's an important fact to throw out there, because if you start thinking in terms of biological concepts sometimes you can be led to the sort of "nature, red in tooth and claw" idea and think history is all about different groups slugging it out for global domination. But that's not the only outlook that is consistent with that.

There's also the possibility of taking a more enlarged outlook and saying, "Well, look, that's primate behavior, and we're primates, but we're more than primates because we have a sense of the ecological whole and our place in it, and that produces new responsibilities for us. Chimpanzees can slug it out and behave like animals because, well, they don't know any better, but it's possible for us to have a more enlarged perspective on things and to, in a sense, step above nature while remaining part of it. But we step above nature in order to be stewards of nature and stewards of biodiversity." I think that's an outlook that is very consistent with a lot of these eco-fascist thinkers, even though a popular view about fascists is that they're all about dominating other people and exterminating other people and things like that. That's not necessarily true.

A lot of German National Socialists had this idea that there were different peoples in the world, and they needed their own places, and they were actually somewhat supportive of the aspirations of colonized peoples for independence, and I don't think that was necessarily just political expediency at work. Although you have to ask yourself how consistent that was with their plans for, say, Ukraine.

RS: You mentioned Savitri Devi. Tell us more about her life and how she got involved with National Socialism. She was also a Hindu. I think she lived in India and converted to Hinduism.

GJ: Right. Savitri Devi is a person that I'm very interested in, and I've done a lot of research on her over the years. She was born in France on September 30, 1905. She was not of French descent. Her mother was English and her father was basically Italian and Greek. Her father was a quarter Greek and three-quarters Italian, but he had a Greek surname which was Portaz. Because she was 1/8th Greek but she carried that Greek surname the young Savitri Devi—her name was Maximiani

Portaz — identified very strongly with the Greeks.

She was a child prodigy. She was quite brilliant and showed this from a very young age. She started learning Greek from the local Greek community in Lyons, France where she was born, and she became very interested in politics and Greek history. She was intensely nationalistic from a Greek point of view. She just fell into that outlook. She was also a pagan, an instinctive pagan, from a very early age. She didn't like Christianity. She was drawn to ancient Greek . . .

RS: Was that her main reason for disliking Christianity? The Judeo-Christian view towards nature? Was that the main reason at first?

GJ: Well, yes. She was a big animal lover, and she had an aunt who made her read one chapter of the Old Testament and one chapter of the New Testament every week. She started these lessons early, and she did not like the anthropocentric attitude that you find in both the Old and New Testaments, and so that was one problem that she had. Although because she was so nationalistically Greek — the Greeks, of course, are very nationalistic people, yet at the same time their Greek Orthodox church is very much caught up with their national identity — she became a communicant of the Greek Orthodox church, and she only really rejected Christianity when she was in her 20s. But she was sort of always attracted to pagan ideas from a very early age, but she didn't sever her ties to Christianity until she was in her 20s.

She went on a Greek Orthodox pilgrimage to Palestine, and there she saw all these proud, nationalistic Greeks crawling in the dust and prostrating themselves before shrines to a foreign people, basically, and she also saw the Jewish settlers in Palestine. She sort of had a revulsion to the whole spectacle and said, "Why can't the Greeks worship their own gods, and the Jews can worship their gods, and everybody can have their own gods and be proud?" So, anyway, that was one thing that happened with her.

In 1935, when she was about 30 years old, she decided she was going to go to India. She got a Ph.D. in philosophy, and she also got an M.A. in physics and chemistry from the University of

Lyons. She spent a lot of her time when she was working on her dissertations in Greece. She traveled back and forth. She took Greek citizenship. She spoke fluent modern Greek. She worked with a woman in Greece who was attempting to revive classical Greek paganism, and she threw in her lot with this project, and she made no headway. And the reason she made no headway is that Greece, and all of Europe really, had had its roots to its ancient pagan religion severed violently by Christianity. Christianity came in and did as much as it could to break any kind of living tradition.

So, she started thinking in terms of going to the East and going to India, because in India there was an unbroken tradition of Indo-European religion. It had been fused with native cults in India, and they worshipped gods with elephant heads and things like that. Obviously the original Aryans didn't do this.

RS: So, was she kind of into the pan-Aryan philosophy?

GJ: Yeah. Exactly.

RS: Explain pan-Aryanism to the audience.

GJ: Well, pan-Aryanism, may not be the right word. But she was very interested in the idea that there was a unity of civilization between the Indians and the Europeans. It was this vast Indo-European diffusion of language and culture and civilization that was discovered really starting in the 18th century by comparative linguistics and then comparative mythology, and people are still working on this project of trying to figure out what the proto-Indo-European homeland was, what the proto-Indo-European language was, and its pantheon and so forth by looking at archeology and also clues based on linguistics and comparative religion.

She was very attracted to getting back to the spiritual roots of European civilization, and since European civilization had been cut off from a living religious tradition she thought, "That tradition is still alive in a very different guise in India," and so she thought she would go there.

The person who I believe influenced her thinking on this most fundamentally was the French esotericist, René Guénon.

Guénon, in his book *The Crisis of the Modern World*, actually addresses the problem of European pagans, and he basically says, "If you want to get in touch with this tradition you can't really get in touch with it outside the Christian church, because that took up certain elements of pre-Christian religion, but you can't really get in touch with it in any fundamental way, because the Church took care to basically sever anything important, and it just held on to certain symbols. So, the only real living tradition that gets you back to this primordial Indo-European tradition is in India." Guénon was early on a Hindu scholar.

I believe Savitri Devi read *The Crisis of the Modern World*. I know she read many other Guénon books. I believe that was one of the factors that influenced her to go to India.

When she got to India she fell in with the Hindu nationalist movement, the people who wanted to give India independence and return India to its Hindu roots. India, of course, had been conquered in an incredibly savage and still psychologically destructive and traumatic way by Muslims, and then it had been colonized by the British, who brought Christianity. Hinduism, though, was still the dominant religion.

She took up with this group called the Hindu Mission, which was an organization to try to bring Hindus who had left Hinduism for either Islam or Christianity and convert them back to Hinduism and reintegrate them into the Hindu caste system. Then she married a Brahmin from Bengal named Asit Krishna Mukherji. Mukherji got a Ph.D. in London, and basically he was a scholar of Russian history.

RS: Are the Brahmins an ethnic group?

GJ: The Brahmins are a caste. They're the priestly caste. He was a Brahmin from Bengal. He was very much a supporter of the Axis powers starting in the mid-'30s. He was an open supporter of Mussolini, Hitler, and, later, the Japanese. He published a publication called *The New Mercury* in Calcutta, which started out as a pro-Italian periodical, and as Italy allied itself with Germany it became pro-German, and then finally the British government shut it down. Then he opened up a new publication called *The Eastern Economist*, which was a pro-Japanese publication.

They married and were close collaborators. She claimed that it was a purely celibate marriage, that it wasn't by her standards or by her husband's standards a permissible marriage, because he was an Indian and she was European.

RS: It's time for a break. Please stay with us.

Welcome back. I'm joined here with Greg Johnson and we are discussing Savitri Devi.

So, you were talking about the marriage to her husband, who was an Indian Brahmin, the highest caste in India, and her reason for being celibate through the marriage. Was it that she viewed it as race-mixing?

GJ: Right, and so did her husband really. The Brahmins have very strict rules about endogamy, and she was not an appropriate mother for his children. He didn't really want to have kids, and neither did she. They were both caught up in their projects. So, anyway, they had this celibate marriage.

During the Second World War, she worked with him in Calcutta doing some espionage work on the behalf of Japan, and after the war she went back to England and France, and she spent some time in prison. She got herself thrown in prison in occupied Germany for passing out National Socialist propaganda leaflets.

She had a very colorful life. She wrote a number of books, and one of her most interesting books for the purposes of our conversation here is *Impeachment of Man*, which she wrote in 1946 right after the end of the Second World War. She published it in 1959. It's dated 1959 and came out in early 1960. It took her a long time to raise the money to publish it.

But *Impeachment of Man* is a very radical book on deep ecology. She talks about, first of all, the root of the problem of the environmental crisis and the crisis of civilization that had enveloped the West, which was anthropocentrism, which for her is rooted in Biblical religion.

She also talks about non-anthropocentric religious outlooks like Hinduism. She has a chapter on the Pharaoh Akhenaton, who had a kind of biocentric or life-centered solar monotheism.

This was in ancient Egypt.

So, she was exploring a lot of religious alternatives to Biblical monotheism, because she thought really that was the root of our problems. She has chapters in there about the rights of trees, vegetarianism, animal cruelty, circuses and farms, and things like that. Every form of exploitation of animals and nature she writes about in a very radical way, and yet she talks about man having a steward's role in the natural world. She doesn't deny that man has a special status in the world, but to the extent that we have a special status she believes that our status is to be stewards of nature rather than exploiters of nature.

She ends the book with her vision on an ideal world. It's called "Race, Economics, and Kindness: The Ideal World," which I've reprinted at Counter-Currents, by the way, which is counter-currents.com. We sell *Impeachment of Man* there, and we also have that final chapter there.

So, she continued to witness for her ideas for the rest of her life. She spent all of her time, basically, caring for abused animals and stray cats and also bearing witness for National Socialism. She lived in a great deal of poverty and hardship, and the people who knew her regarded her as a saint. She was like a Hindu ascetic. She divided her time between Europe and India on and off for the rest of her life, and she died in England in 1982 at the age of 77.

So, in my opinion, she's really one of the great eccentrics of the 20th century. But she's only eccentric from the point of view of sort of your average person who would think, "How could a person who's all lovey-dovey about animals be a Nazi?" When you actually get inside of her head, it's very clear that it's all very consistent, but it's consistent in a way that's so surprising it can kind of shock people into a completely different outlook on the world.

So, she is definitely somebody who I think is worth looking at. She didn't really have a lot of influence in terms of ecological thinking. In fact, I'd say she had virtually none. Certainly in terms of the mainstream of ecology.

RS: Yeah, I had no idea even who she was until I discovered her from your site.

GJ: Yeah. The book *Impeachment of Man* is uncanny, because it anticipates a lot of views that other people have had, and yet it didn't really influence those views. She was drawing on a common set of assumptions and therefore she was coming to common conclusions that other writers who have worked independently of her have arrived at.

Somebody like Pentti Linkola, who calls himself an eco-fascist, is not a National Socialist, but he shares a lot of Savitri Devi's assumptions about man and nature and he arrives at very similar political conclusions. Linkola, who is still alive—he's a Finnish fellow; he's in his late 70s now—is the author of a book that's available now in English called *Can Life Prevail?* Arktos published that, and you can order it from the Counter-Currents website, which is counter-currents.com.

Linkola underscores some of the differences that you find within this broad movement or current of thought that I'll call eco-fascism. Two of the main differences, I would say, are these: some of them are basically just "nature, red in tooth and claw" Darwinists. It's the idea that nature's all about struggling for survival, and some groups exterminate other groups and dominate them, and they don't see any reason why since human societies and human interactions can't be modeled on that. Whereas others—and I would say most people who take this ecological perspective, don't look at it that way—think that man is able to have a higher calling in the world. The idea that the fact that we exterminated all these species and we should pat ourselves on the back for our Darwinian superiority is grotesque to a lot of people like this. They think that we are highly fit—there's no question we could exterminate all the life on Earth if we want to—but that's not really the measure of success. We are called to exercise stewardship in the natural world and preserve nature, which is really preserving ourselves if you have an enlightened view of the self.

The other big issue that divides what I'll call eco-fascists is vegetarianism. Some are vegetarians like Savitri Devi. Others like Pentti Linkola are not vegetarians. They look at vegetarianism as not natural. The question then becomes, how unnatural does man want to be? It's not natural for other species to preserve other forms of life either, so vegetarianism could be considered just another aspect of a sort of higher spiritual obligation towards preserving the natural world, whereas some people like Linkola will eat meat and say, "Well, that's going too far. That's hyperbolic to not eat meat. It's part of our nature to do that."

The real question for Linkola, and think this is really very important, is that the question is not about preventing animals from dying, which of course you have to do to eat them, and because everything dies. The real issue is the quality of their lives. If you are just concerned about animals not dying, and if your main concern is with their death, then all you need to do is be very humane about how they die. But that leaves it wide open to have the most brutal and monstrous forms of factory farms. So, Linkola basically wants to focus on the quality of animal life rather than just preventing them from dying, and so he is not a vegetarian but he is a radical opponent of factory farms and all this kind of really monstrous forms of agriculture.

RS: The thing about it is that most meat comes from those sources, so you kind of do have to become a vegetarian. It's very difficult to avoid that.

GJ: Well, yeah, exactly. Either you have to become a vegetarian or you have to go catch your own fish, which is what Pentti Linkola does. He fishes. And then he at least knows he's catching it and killing it in an honest way. So, that's an important consideration. From a practical point of view, you practically do have to become a vegetarian not to participate in this monstrous factory farming system. You practically have to stop drinking milk and eating cheese too, because dairies are remarkably inhumane as well when they're on the giant agribusiness scale.

So, it is a problem trying to get produce from people that I know, including eggs. But that's very hard when you live in a city. It's very, very expensive in this world to eat simply. It's one of the grotesque ironies. You have to pay more to have food that's not adulterated. You have to pay more to get less crap in your diet. It is a great difficulty from a practical point of view.

RS: Yeah, it's become a luxury item.

GJ: Right. There's a hilarious interview that Truman Capote did years ago. He had all these rich New York socialite friends, and somebody said, "Mr. Capote, what's the difference between the rich and the rest of us?" And he said, "The vegetables." He's just being flippant. But no, seriously, rich people have the best vegetables. They're fresh. And he's right. You have to be rich, or you just have to grow it yourself, right? You can be a peasant and have your own little garden, and you can eat like a king. But the vast majority of Americans today can't afford to eat decent food. It's something that only the rich or the people who grow it for themselves can do.

RS: So, some of the other names you put out . . . Let's see. I guess we can talk about Martin Heidegger, and there's Henry Williamson and Jorian Jenks. That's three of them, so I guess we can touch on each one briefly.

GJ: Heidegger is a very interesting figure. He was a National Socialist. He was also not necessarily an ecologist himself, although his interests certainly were in that direction, but I don't know if he was particularly informed about these things. His instincts were certainly ecological. But what is really important about Heidegger is that he tries to really get to the root of the modern alienation with nature. He tries to get to its metaphysical root and also tries to find a way out of it.

For Heidegger, modernity is defined by this deep assumption about the way the world is and about our relationship to it. It's the assumption that nature is transparent to our understanding—that we can get to the bottom of things, we can figure it out, we can explain it—and it is available for our use. So, this dual assumption of *transparency* and *availability* is really the foundation of modern science and industry and modern technology and therefore the foundation of man's amazing assault on nature.

For Heidegger, the way out of that is a meditation on its historical roots. How did this idea that we can understand nature come about? And how did this idea that we can control nature, that it is available for our use, come about?

His ultimate answer to that sounds like a cop out, but in a

subtle way it's not. It really is the solution. The answer is this: He said: We can't understand where this idea that everything is understandable came from. Well, if you can't understand why we think that everything is understandable, then you've got a counter-example to that whole assumption. If you believe in principle that nothing is mysterious, but yet when you try to get to the bottom of that attitude you discover that you can't really figure out where you got that notion . . . It just came upon us and grabbed us and enthralled us. It happened. It caught us up. It's operating us. That assumption is operating us and modern society, but we don't know how it came about. Well, if there's one giant mystery there, then that restores all the mysteries to the world.

For him, one of the most therapeutic things is to recognize that there is a kind of mysterious withdrawl in the world, that things are not just available and open for our understanding, but that things are mysterious and close themselves off to our understanding. He thinks that if we can wrap our minds around the mystery and sort of follow its tug, it might pull us out of this modern mindset.

The allied sort of therapy, if you will, is this: we have this notion that we can make everything available, and we can control it. But can we control history? No. The very idea of man's conquest of nature is not something that we've conquered for ourselves or set for ourselves. Again, it just came upon us. It was this eruption of titanic arrogance and aspiration that mankind suddenly was taken by. And so, again, we don't control history. We are enthralled by this idea.

So, for Heidegger, if you can just wrap your mind around the fact that modernity is in itself mysterious and uncontrollable, once you've wrapped your mind around that, the spell is broken and what that does is clear open the possibility for another, radically different form of life.

Now, early on in his life, during the 1920s and 1930s, Heidegger looked at National Socialism as a movement that was trying to escape from modern technology. He thought that the National Socialist movement was the only form of politics in the offing that was an alternative to the fundamental materialism of

Anglo-American capitalism or Soviet Communism, which are both materialist, and he thought that National Socialism could be understood as a response to the challenge of modern technological civilization.

Later on, as the war happened, he came to think that promise never really came to fruition because of the simple necessity of fighting a war. Nazi Germany had to fight against materialist, technological enemies, and therefore it became by necessity more and more materialist and technological, and it might have won the war if it had gone further down that path of materialism and technology. He felt that National Socialism really hadn't lived up to the promise that he had hoped for it, and he spent the rest of his life waiting for another historical dispensation to arrive. So, he ultimately ended up adopting a mystical—I that think would be a good way to describe it—attitude towards nature and history, because he thought that if you could cultivate this sort of mystical as opposed to scientific, technological attitude that could break the spell of technology.

Henry Williamson is an extraordinary 20th-century English novelist. He was a very frank, very idealistic National Socialist. He was also a friend of Sir Oswald Mosley, the leader of the British Union of Fascists. He was not so prominent in the British Union of Fascists that he was interned during the war like Mosley and many other British Union people were.

Williamson liked country life, and he was a nature writer. His most famous book is called *Tarka the Otter*, which is a children's book. It's written so even children can appreciate it, although it offers enormous pleasures to adults. And it's about the relationship that he had with an otter cub that he found and named Tarka. He also wrote other nature books that were oriented towards the imagination of children, but he also wrote very many, very adult novels and also memoirs and essays where he lays out, in his view, the connections between politics and his love of nature.

Again, it just goes back to the idea of seeing man as a natural being within the natural world. From that follows an organic, hierarchical view of society, the rejection of egalitarianism, the rejection of modern technology and capitalism and a search for some kind of third way between communism and capitalism.

For that, he was attracted to Fascism and National Socialism.

You mentioned Jorian Jenks. Jenks is somebody I am reading about right now actually. I think he's a really remarkable thinker. I had heard about him years ago, but I never really looked into him, and then the Historical Review Press in England republished his book, *Spring Comes Again*, which we have for sale at the Counter-Currents site. That's counter-currents.com.

Anyway, Jenks was a member of the British Union of Fascists. He was a very trusted senior member of the BUF, and he was a personal friend of Oswald Mosley, and he was a farmer. Mosley had Jenks work on economic and specifically agricultural economic policies, and he really defined the policies of the British Union of Fascists.

Again, the concerns were nationalistic. They wanted to basically restore England to being independent of foreign food imports, and that involved also protection for the English farmer. But it went beyond that. There was also protection of the countryside.

After the Second World War, Jenks maintained cordial ties with Mosley and his new Union Movement, which he created after the war. But he somewhat retired from politics. He wasn't openly political, but he was very much involved in the Soil Association and pioneering in countryside and wilderness preservation. There's not much wilderness, actually, left in England, but the countryside is still rich with beauty and biodiversity. He was very important in working for that. Also, he was very important in British organic farming and agriculture.

Again, if you scratch the surface and ask, "What's the coherence between his fascist politics and his ecological sensibility?" both of those ideas follow from the idea that man is a being who is part of the natural world; it's a nature- and life-centered outlook as opposed to the anthropocentric view, which is that we are the crown of creation, we're in it for ourselves, and we can basically have a destructive and exploitative relationship with the natural world without worrying about it coming around to bite us.

RS: Well, we're out of time, so I would like to thank you for being on.

GJ: Well, thank you for inviting me, Robert. I really have enjoyed this. I was a little anxious about talking about this because I hadn't talked about it with anybody for a while, but once I got going I think it went pretty well. I really encourage people to visit Counter-Currents. We have a number of projects underway, reviews and translations and things like that, of literature that deals with some of these questions. So, it's counter-currents.com. Thanks for having me on.

RS: That's all that we have for tonight. Take care, and we'll be back with you next time.

EXPANDING THE POLITICAL IMAGINATION

INTERVIEW WITH DENNIS FETCHO*

DENNIS FETCHO: Good morning, everybody! From Amman, Jordan and streaming globally across the World Wide Web this is the Fetch, and you are live *Inside the Eye!* Today's date is Saturday, September 8, 2012.

Our guest today, Greg Johnson, holds a Ph.D. in philosophy. He is the editor-in-chief of Counter-Currents Publishing. That's Counter-Currents with a hyphen. He is also the editor of the journal *North American New Right* which appears online and as a printed volume.

He is the author of *Confessions of a Reluctant Hater*. He is the editor of Alain de Benoist's *On Being a Pagan*, Michael O'Meara's *Towards the White Republic*, Michael Polignano's *Taking Our Own Side*, and Collin Cleary's *Summoning the Gods* among other books. His fields of interest are intellectual history, philosophy, religion, and the European New Right.

Greg, welcome to *Inside the Eye Live!*

GREG JOHNSON: Thanks, Dennis, for having me on!

DF: Well, thanks for coming! I think you were recommended to me by one of our listeners, but you're probably one of the few who actually contacted me. I think the last guy who contacted me to be on was Harley Schlanger from the Lyndon LaRouche people.

GJ: Well, I guess that puts me in dubious company, maybe, but I have been trying to do more interviews and reach out, so I took my friend Roger's advice, and I got in touch with you, and I

---

* On September 8, 2012, this interview with Dennis Fetcho appeared on Inside the Eye on The Oracle Broadcasting Network. I removed transitions into and out of breaks, as well as chit chat on such topics as the weather.

also got in touch with Deanna Spingola, and we had a really good conversation.

DF: Yeah, indeed, you appeared recently with Deanna Spingola, and for those of you out there who have not heard that interview it's really quite an entertaining interview. I probably caught about 60% of it, and it sounded very entertaining. And Deanna, of course, is very focused on what she does, so I thought the two of you hit it off very well, Greg.

GJ: Yeah, I did, too, and I'm going to be back on her show next week, actually on September 10th, so I imagine we're going to be talking about September 11th.

DF: Ah, very good. I actually didn't prepare anything for September 11th for you . . . Greg, I figured we would just skip that. There's enough of that in the alternative media and main-stream media this week. We'll focus on you and your work. Now, you're the editor-in-chief of *The Occidental Observer*?

GJ: Actually, *The Occidental Quarterly*. *The Occidental Observer* is something that Kevin MacDonald runs.

DF: OK. He runs it, but you were editor-in-chief for quite some time.

GJ: Of *The Occidental Quarterly*, yeah. I ran *The Occidental Quarterly* from 2007 to 2010. A little more than two-and-a-half years, and I also created their online presence, which I edited for a year. That's toqonline.com which is basically now mothballed. It's kind of an archive of old issues and previously published work.

DF: And then now you have counter-currents.com?

GJ: Yeah, Counter-Currents Publishing is something that Michael Polignano, who's my business partner, and I started in June of 2010. It went online June 11th 2010. We are a publishing company, and we also have a strong online presence. The Counter-Currents website has a webzine associated with it, it's all on the front page there, called *North American New Right*. Five days a week we have new material going online, sometimes multiple new items.

Our goal is to create an intellectual movement in North America that is analogous to and influenced by the European New Right and that includes people like Alain de Benoist and Guillaume Faye. Mostly French writers, some German and Italian writers. But what they're trying to do is revive elements of what I call the Old Right, by which I mean basically fascism, in a new context, in a post-war context to show that their critique of modernity, democracy, and so forth has continuing relevance, and it's even better founded in facts and history and science than ever before and that it provides a lot of solutions to a lot of the quandaries of contemporary politics. So, they're trying to expand people's political imaginations in Europe, and we think that we really need to expand their imaginations in North America as well. So, that's our goal.

DF: OK. Now, counter-currents.com, you're reaching, I think I saw some stats out there, Alexa ranks you at 164,000 worldwide, which is very healthy. You had 110,000 visits in April, which is the last stats I could find. Over 421,000 page views. You're reaching a pretty strong audience there, Greg.

GJ: Yeah, we have about 50,000 unique visitors come to us every month. I can't really calculate the number of people who are hardcore, but 50% of the people who come to us come to us from some kind of bookmark as opposed to a Google search. So, let's say we have 20 some thousand people who follow us regularly. Not necessarily every day, but we have people who come multiple times a day, too. But we do have a hardcore following out there as well as a large number of people who come to us through Google searches.

Google, however, in the last month started monkeying with our search output, our search algorithms, however they do that. And suddenly some pieces of ours that were very popular and had been top ten articles for years suddenly disappeared from the search rankings, and that pushed our traffic down 20% in one month. However, it's bouncing back up. So, they've delayed us a bit, but they can't really deny us getting our message out there because people want it enough to actually search for it and not just to be satisfied with what pops up on the first page of their Google search results. So, that's heartening news.

DF: Yeah, it is. Now, your subject matter, for somebody who doesn't really know what you do, and quite frankly I didn't know what you do until I got introduced to you, what is your subject matter? I hear the term White Nationalism brought up. People might cringe at that, but I see this term. If you were to give yourself a tagline, what would it be?

GJ: Well, I am a White Nationalist. That is a term that I use. Basically, the situation is this: We believe that race is absolutely fundamental for understanding politics and ethnicity. We don't think that the abstractions like capitalism and communism and free enterprise and things like that are adequate for understanding what's really happening in politics. If you look at politics in Europe and America, however, through a racial lens, what you see is the struggles of different peoples for dominance, and we believe that the white countries of the world, and that means Europe but also the colonies like America and Canada and New Zealand, Australia, the Whiter countries in South America excluded for these purposes.

[Break]

GJ: We were talking about White Nationalism before the break, and what I basically believe is that you can't really understand politics without understanding that race is the primary factor in politics. It's the primary cause of a lot of wars and revolutions and upheavals around the world, and specifically in the white countries what I see happening is this: white countries are under attack. Whites are under attack through affirmative action, through non-white immigration, through the media that denigrates white people and white values and promotes non-whites and non-white values. I believe that ultimately what's going on here is that non-whites are really being used proxies for Jews.

I think that Jews have engineered in the United States and to a lesser extent, but to a real extent still, in practically every other white country the opening of the floodgates to Third World, non-white immigration, and they are at the forefront of combatting white efforts to restrict immigration. They are basically following a divide and conquer strategy. They are most powerful when they are middlemen in a disorganized, pluralistic, fractious kind of society, a kind of Middle Eastern bazaar society, a sort of *Star Wars* cantina society. They're the guys who know everybody and know a few words in every language and can broker deals, and they end up on the top. They stick out like sore thumbs, however, in homogeneous societies, and so wherever they show up in societies like that they try to engineer diversity. They're not engineering diversity because they think it's good for us. They're engineering diversity because they think it's good for them as a tool to gain power over us, and they've been very, very successful so far.

So, that's basically what I mean by White Nationalism. It looks at politics primarily in terms of racial and ethnic struggles, and it looks at the Jewish Question, in particular, as really the key to understanding what's going on in politics in the White countries today.

DF: I saw some latest census figures out of England. 64% of people born in England are considered white English. Only 64% White British people! I mean, 35% people born in England are not considered white British English. This is probably what you mean by this war.

Now, I heard you on Deanna. I like the concept of how really this is conquering in a very subtle way, a form of conquering a society or a country but in a very inverse, long-term strategy. It's covert, not overt.

GJ: Well, yeah, a lot of conquests throughout history have been slow. The Roman Empire: they didn't know that they were falling at the time. They thought they were very cleverly playing a game of inviting in these Germanic tribes because they would do work that the Romans wouldn't do. Specifically, they were putting them in their military and things like that. It took a very, very long time for the Roman Empire to collapse as a result of policies that were predictably ruinous. You and I would have predicted these policies as ruinous, but in the short run they looked like a good deal.

So, conquest doesn't necessarily have to be fast, and genocide doesn't have to be fast. The United Nations defines genocide not just as a quick, hot slaughter of a whole group of people, but rather as creating conditions that over the long-run will make it impossible for a people to preserve its distinct identity. That would include things like swamping them with immigrants, promoting miscegenation so they blend themselves out of existence, bombarding them with propaganda that makes them feel self-hatred and guilt for being who they are. All those are forms of genocide because if they are applied long enough to any people that people will cease to exist.

I believe that not only are we being conquered, but we are being exterminated or obliterated because if we don't get a handle on these trends there will simply be no white people left anymore. We will be blended out of existence.

DF: Question. I agree with everything that you're saying in this regard. I agree for the most part with what you're saying, I should say. But me, I'm German/Irish. I married a long time ago a Chinese gal. We had a son, who is now Chinese-American, but Chinese, Anglo-Saxon, German, and Irish. Why should people who are not of a pure ethnic white race or ethnicity care about White Nationalist ideas and interests?

GJ: Well, in a way, they shouldn't. Because we're really not trying to represent their interests. But, in a larger way, though, I think that they can look at it as something that's of interest to them in this sense: we think that nationalism is good for everyone, for all peoples. We think that every people should have its own place where it can go and live according to its own life, develop according to its own inner genius, have its own destiny and so forth.

Now, as a white person, I am particularly interested in this for my own group, but I recognize that this is also true for every other group, that we're all better off if we have a place of our own.

People who are of mixed race, I don't quite know how to fit those in. There will have to be some places, large cities . . .

Throughout history, commercial ports have always been places where people of mixed race would be born or would gravitate because they feel more comfortable there.

This is the vision of what I call the New Right has: Envision a world where there are thousands and thousands of flags, thousands and thousands of nationalities, places where people can go to live according to their own nature.

One thing I do want to get away from, though, is this very destructive white grandiosity which goes from believing that it's alright for other people to have their own homelands to saying that it's the white man's burden to go out and make sure that everyone's living the right way and doing the right thing. I think that's been a very bad thing for us in the long run. Our empires have turned around and are now colonizing us, for instance, so that was not a good thing to do from the point of view of the present.

So, I want to say everybody has a stake in nationalism. I would like to have the most cordial relations with other peoples. I don't see any reason to hate other peoples. In my book, *Confessions of a Reluctant Hater*, I really argue that hatred between groups is an inevitable consequence of forcing them to live together and compete in the same system, and therefore the solution to racial hatred and strife is to allow people to form their own independent states. I'm the last person in the world to have negative feelings towards other groups, but I found that when I was living in California I started having negative feelings towards other groups because I was forced to live with them and there was constant everyday friction.

[Break]

DF: Welcome back, everybody! This is the Fetch and you're listening to *Inside the Eye Live* here on the Oracle Broadcasting Network. [. . .] Really, Greg, I think the main issue that a lot of people have . . . Now, White Nationalism, you're looking at, it sounds almost like the segregation of races.

GJ: Yeah, most definitely.

DF: You believe that's a viable plan?

GJ: I think that in the long run it's the best way to preserve the distinctness of different groups, racially and culturally, and also to lower the amount of unnecessary and tragic strife and conflict in the world.

If you look at the end of Communism in Eastern Europe. What was the USSR? It was a multinational, multi-ethnic empire, and when that empire fell apart all these constituent units left and formed their own countries. Where do you have strife in the Russian Federation today? You have it in the Caucasus. And why is there strife? It's strife between Muslims and Russians, the Chechens and people like that. Those people were not allowed to leave, they were not allowed to form their own Republics or their own governments, and they're fighting to this day.

Or you look at Yugoslavia. Yugoslavia fractured pretty neatly on ethnic lines. The Slovenes and the Croatians went their own way fairly quickly. There was war, however, in Bosnia. Why? Because Bosnia was a multi-ethnic area. There were Croatians and there were Serbs and there were Muslims in Bosnia. Especially the Serb minority, which was about 40% of the population, just could not see themselves being ruled in a Muslim state, and so there was civil war there.

So, generally where you find ethnic and racial diversity you find conflict. The solution to that is to as peacefully and in as orderly a way as possible divide things up so that people have their own ethnostates.

And the best model of that, I think, was the very peaceful, amicable divorce that happened between the Czechs and the Slovaks. Czechoslovakia was an artificial nation that was put together after the First World War. When it reemerged after the Second World War, it was held together by Communism, but when Communism disappeared after a while these people said, "Well, there's no need for us to be in the same system." And so now they're just good neighbors.

DF: The case of Czechoslovakia is actually a great case, but this is an intellectual, amicable split. Now, where I see a danger, just to give you some insights here into the politics of the Middle East: I'm here in Amman. We have Shia, we have Sunni, we have Christians, we have many different ethnicities. They, quite frankly, do live together in peace, and everybody enjoys everybody. The same would be said of Syria. So, what you're talking about in some respects mirrors the neocon balkanization strategy. Aren't you kind of worried that you're following a strategy that is seen somewhat as a neocon strategy if you're going to apply it to places like here in the Middle East?

GJ: I guess the neocons can't be wrong about everything. But seriously now, the neocon strategy is basically divide and conquer, and they have absolutely no interest in creating a Kurdistan for the Kurds or a Shi'ite Iraq for the Shi'ites and a Sunni Iraq for the Sunnis. All they're concerned with is keeping these people corralled together in the same country and getting them fighting and hating each other. Why? Because that's to their advantage.

The Israelis are afraid of strong neighbors. Iraq was a strong neighbor, but Iraq had internal tensions and problems, and once the strong leader at the center was removed it was very, very easy — it was child's play — for these people to get all the Iraqis of different groups fighting with each other and killing one another, and once that gets started, well, it just takes on a life of its own.

DF: That's a good answer. You gave a great answer.

GJ: Well, thank you.

DF: That's a very strong answer. OK. Very good. Because yeah, you could have some people trying to say, "Well, we're trying to create what Greg is talking about by balkanizing all of these parts." But you're right, it is more of a divide and conquer and just keep people warring, where Czechoslovakia was an amicable split, and something that they've actually tried to do in North and South Sudan is create this amicable split even though it's not quite working.

But, Greg, is it the real problem isn't so much the ethnicities that we have among places, but it's the forced cultural diversity plan that's coming out of the Israeli group or the Jewish groups. Isn't this the real problem?

GJ: Well, it is true that in more traditional societies you

would have the possibility of, and this is especially true in the Near and Middle East, where you have these intensely ethnocentric, closed groups living together. In the past, they had reached a kind of *modus vivendi*. They could live together in a comfortable way. But they could only live together because they in effect practiced a kind of strong ethnic nationalism. They would only marry within their own groups, they would live in their own quarters, and things like that. I know somebody whose family lived in the Armenian quarter of Jerusalem for hundreds and hundreds of years, and they managed to live peacefully with the other Christian groups and the Muslims in Jerusalem for centuries. So, that is possible.

But what that requires is a kind of nationalism block by block, and the other thing that it requires is it requires a certain amount of self-assertion, a certain amount of pride in who you are and so forth. The trouble with the white countries today is we can't really live with other groups because we have been so bombarded with white guilt and self-hatred. We are so afraid of asserting our own standards that we simply can't have other groups around us without coming into conflict with them, because we're not the kind of people that can maintain proper boundaries anymore, if that makes any sense.

You're right that in a sense part of what causes a lot of conflict is that whites have been so bombarded with anti-white propaganda, and non-whites have been so bombarded with anti-white propaganda too, and they don't have any trouble asserting themselves. So, what you have is steady encroachment on our standards, on our boundaries, and it's causing a great deal of psychological turmoil and upset, and eventually it causes strife. So, if you got rid of that it, might be easier for people of different ethnicities to live in the same system or, what the United States used to have, we used to have minority groups living in the United States, but we maintained white standards. That would make all the difference in the world if we could get that back again.

[Break]

DENNIS FETCHO: Welcome back! It's the Fetch, and this is *In-*

side the Eye Live right here on the Oracle Broadcasting Network. Our guest today is Greg Johnson, Editor-in-Chief of Counter-Currents Publishing found at counter-currents.com, and he is also the editor of the journal *North American New Right* and the author of *Confessions of a Reluctant Hater*. Welcome back!

GREG JOHNSON: Hey, thanks for having me on, Dennis.

DF: Yeah, so, we were just going into the break there and just sort of tie up any loose ends you had there if you don't mind.

GJ: Well, I was talking about basically white guilt, white self-hatred. Whites today are just bombarded with the idea that we have to be guilty for every crime and misdemeanor and bit of bad taste from other white people throughout history. Yet, at the same time, we're told that we're not entitled to take any pride in anything other white people have done, which is a completely self-contradictory notion if you think about it. If we should feel guilt for the bad things white people have done, shouldn't we feel pride for the great things that white people have done? And if we can start balancing the books and looking at causes for pride in our people as opposed to causes for guilt or shame . . .

I think shame is the best word. I don't feel guilt for things that other people do, because I didn't do them myself, but if somebody does something bad in my name, or if somebody does something bad and they look like me and talk like me, I do feel ashamed of them. And the closer they are to me the more shame I feel. I feel shame if my relatives do stupid things, for instance, and that includes my extended family, my racial family. So, I do feel ashamed when white people do bad things, but I feel a great deal of pride in the achievements of our people, and I think that if you do the books, so to speak, on balance we have a lot to be proud of as a people. We should try to maintain who we are. We've given a lot to the world, and we need to make sure that we are in a position to give more to the world in the future.

In the present circumstances, though, white people are being bombarded with this white guilt, not a sense of pride. They go around with this nihilistic, hang-dog kind of attitude, and I think a lot of self-destructive behaviors can be attributed to this kind of bombarding of white kids, and it starts very young. It's child abuse when you get right down to it.

DF: When you're sending children, Greg, at 6 years old to holocaust museums of tolerance with the explicit point of trying to tell people how bad white people are in a very indirect way, but you're actually doing it, yeah, that's pretty child abusive to me.

GJ: That is definite child abuse, and that should be stopped. Why aren't parents raising holy hell about this? Because they themselves are intimidated, and if they could overcome this intimidation, this unwillingness to take their own side in ethnic conflicts, and that's what's going on here, it's an ethnic conflict between Jews and whites . . . Even countries that fought the Germans and ended the holocaust, ended the Second World War . . . Jews believe that we are more likely to be an aggressor people.

DF: It's projection, Greg. Come on. They're projecting their culture onto whites and everybody else, and that really is the issue.

You know, your website is doing great and so are your articles. You are a prolific writer! How many articles have you written?

GJ: I've lost count. I've written hundreds of articles and reviews just under my own name, and then I write under a couple pen names, too.

DF: And then I see that you're getting some of these translated into German.

GJ: Oh yeah, a lot of our articles from the website are being translated into languages like French, German, Portuguese (we have a large Portuguese readership), Czech, Ukrainian, Russian, Finnish, Swedish. It's really an international thing, and it's kind of ironic that we're really focused on building a movement in North America, but because we are translating a lot of material from French and German into English, we find that people all over the world can read that, because English is the second language all over the world. So, people who can't read French are reading Alain de Benoist and Guillaume Faye in English on our website, and then they'll translate those English translations into Czech or Portuguese or their own native tongues. So, it's really produced good effects for the European New Right, too. A lot more people are now having access to their writings as well.

DF: Interesting. Now, I'm not a nationalist like you are, but I do believe that we must preserve the ethnic integrity of what is the white culture, and the reason why I say that is because if Jews are so interested in destroying it then there must be so much good value in it, because otherwise, being a culture of destruction, they would not try to destroy it. And we see them trying to destroy it really throughout the world whether it's England, America, Canada, Australia, Germany. It's not English, but you know what I mean; it's white.

Now, when you go back to the holocaust idea, which I don't believe it even happened, especially as it has been advertised . . . I saw this from Thomas Dalton, I think he's someone who you've associated with in the past, he wrote, and it's a very apropos thing: "in the period of just 6 years from 1933 to 1939 and amidst a global depression Germany rose from a ruined bankrupt nation to the strongest on Earth. The holocaust, a real event, is a nationalist success story: reign in Jewish-controlled banks and capitalist enterprises, restore national integrity to the media, expel Jews from the seat of governmental power and your nation will flourish. What better lesson could be learned from revisionism?"

GJ: Well, I think that all of that is true. What I disagree about that is calling *that* the holocaust. Most people who accept the conventional holocaust narrative believe that the holocaust started somewhere around 1942, and so the period of 1933 to 1939, basically between when Hitler took power and when the British started the Second World War, there's no question that that is a period of great and in ways miraculous economic and cultural revival. And yes, it had to do with, in part, breaking Jewish power over the German economy, the German press, German culture, and really German destiny. The Germans were very successful in that, and there are a lot of lessons to be learned about how they did that that can be applied to this day.

Ellen Brown's book *Web of Debt* has some really interesting in-formation on what Hitler did to produce his economic miracle, how very simple it was, how it can be replicated in countries like Greece today if they just had the political will to do it. So, there's a lot to be learned. There are a lot of lessons from the Third Reich that are positive lessons, not just the lessons that the main-stream media want us to learn, which is that white people should always feel guilty and that we better not think about try-ing to separate ourselves from Jews or basically try to take con-trol of our own countries and our own destiny again, because if we do that, horrible things are going to inevitably happen to us. And that's simply not true. That doesn't follow.

I think there's a lot of room for historical revisionism about the Third Reich, about the causes of the Second World War, about the consequences of the Second World War. I think that putting that all in context it's truly astonishing what you learn. So, I'm all for going back and looking at that with fresh eyes, be-cause there's definitely a lot of lessons to learn.

DF: How many people are in the White Nationalist move-ment, Greg?

GJ: I would say, within the United States, very loosely de-fined, there are probably hundreds of thousands of people who would think of themselves as White Nationalists, more or less without apology. Now, those people include people who just log in to Stormfront and other online chat sites and read the material there but don't do anything more — all the way up to people who are intensely engaged in it, are activists who are reading and re-searching a lot. And then there are just a few, a handful of peo-ple really, who are full-time White Nationalists, meaning that they're devoting their lives to that. I can think of 5 or 6 people off the top of my head who are doing this full-time, and I am one of them. It's a big movement, but it doesn't have a lot of institu-tions that are well-funded and well-established yet.

DF: So, to say the least, you are no match for Jewish organiza-tions right now.

GJ: Oh, absolutely not. When you look at the number of Jewish organizations and the hundreds of millions, if not billions, of dollars—if they really needed billions of dollars, they could make a few phone calls and have billions of dollars to play with overnight. These organizations are massively well-funded.

There's a wonderful documentary called *Defamation* by Yoav Shamir. One of the things that Yoav Shamir does in *Defamation* is go to the Anti-Defamation League in New York City, and there's this lavishly funded organization with big comfortable offices. They have 14 regional offices. I think they have an $80 million per year budget, and of course we're told frankly that's not enough to fight anti-Semitism.

But the guy tries to find some actual anti-Semitic incidents that they're fighting with their $80 million dollar a year annual budget, and so he goes to the secretary, and the secretary just runs off a list of things, and most of the things on the list consist of Jews calling in complaining of anti-Semitism because they're not allowed to take off the Jewish holidays, which basically boils down to the fact that their employer—the school system, or a private company, whatever—is not going to give them special treatment for holidays. The very idea that there is this multi-million dollar a year organization that's basically a snitch line to complain about things like that is pretty ludicrous.

Yet, with White Nationalist organizations, we have hundreds of millions of white people in the United States whose interests are being vitally threatened—not just not being able to take off special holidays—but vitally threatened. We don't have a future in America if present trends continue, and it's almost impossible to scrape together a few thousand dollars, much less $80 million dollars to fight that. It's something that will change though. It's not changing fast enough, but it will change.

DF: Now, the way it's going to change is in a concept, correct me if I'm wrong, I don't know if you've coined it, but it's what people call metapolitics. Laying the foundation to allow this change to happen, and you're telling me, through your article that is, that Jews have done a great job in metapolitics, and really any community that wants to fight Jewish power has to start focusing on it.

GJ: Yeah. Metapolitics is not my coinage. Basically, it just means what comes before the political, what's above the political, before the political, what creates the conditions of politics. People sometimes say that politics is the art of the possible, and metapolitics would deal with what people think is possible, for instance, what's conceivable in the political realm. Metapolitics deals with people's sense of what's morally right in the political realm. People will not support a political agenda if they think it is not moral, if they think that it is not feasible, if it's not possible. So, metapolitics really deals with the desirability and the feasibility of political alternatives.

Jews have played this game very well. They think way ahead. They're chess players. They're thinking many, many moves ahead. They think in terms of centuries and generations, unfolding their plans over very long periods of time.

Whites really don't think that way. We used to have elites that ruled white countries that thought in terms of long games in hundreds and thousands of years. Those are the old aristocracies of Europe, those are things like the Vatican and the Papacy. They could think long-term. Democracies don't think that way, and just ordinary people don't think that way, and so we're really being outfoxed by the organized Jewish community.

They were very, very careful about laying the foundations decades ago. For instance, they realized that the idea that race is a biological concept was harmful to them. They wanted to push the idea that race is a social construct that's malleable through social engineering. And so how did they do that? Well, they slowly prepared a putsch, basically, where they took over the academic teaching of anthropology in America, and they ran the Darwinists out. Physical anthropology was shoved aside by cultural anthropology, and now in recent decades the cultural anthropologists—basically they're Marxists, Boasians, whatever you want to call it—have actually been trying to drive the very idea of physical anthropology out of academia altogether.

So, they think in terms of decades and centuries, and we don't think at all, generally. So metapolitics is really our attempt to get into the long game strategy of laying the foundations for creating a new white political order.

Basically, we need some sort of racial sovereignty, that's why we call it White Nationalism, if we're going to prevent our race from simply disappearing over time.

DF: White Nationalism, of course, is for whites, but this thing that is after whites, they just hate everybody. I think that's a key point for everybody to remember. This Jewish element hates everybody. They will go after everybody, and whites just happen to be the one thing that stands in their way.

GJ: Well, they rule our countries very effectively now. They don't really rule other countries effectively. They realized at a certain point that whites would be the people to latch onto, the break-out people, when they saw us spilling out of Europe after we had defended Europe for thousands of years against Asians pounding at the gates, the Huns and the Mongols and people like that. After the Europeans broke out of Europe, beginning in the 15th century, and started conquering the globe, Jews hopped on our backs, and they traveled around the world. We pacified the world. We gave them access to huge areas of the world that they did not have previous access to. That was a very good deal.

Revilo Oliver has a really nice analogy. He said whites in the past were like the Texas longhorns. We were tough cattle. We were somewhat hard to tame, though, but we were the kind of animals you needed to tame the West. But now that the West is tamed, they want us gelded. They want us replaced with more tractable cows, and so they have tightened up cultural control, and basically they have made us into a much more passive race, and they're trying to blend us out of existence now, because they haven't forgotten what happened in Germany and other countries in Europe in the 1930s.

DF: But the German thing is more myth than anything, but they believe in this myth and that's the key point. Do you agree with that or do you disagree with that?

GJ: Well, what the Germans really did, what they will never be forgiven for, is they explicitly identified Jewish power as the main problem for whites controlling their own destinies, and they took steps to extricate themselves from Jewish power, and they also unplugged from the international banking system. Now, what happened during the war with concentration camps and cattle cars and things like that, that all came later. But the stuff that they will never be forgiven for is the stuff from 1933 to 1939, which set a pattern that other countries started to follow or wanted to follow and that Jews are deathly afraid of other countries following.

The thing is that the basic pattern is applicable everywhere in the world. Nationalism, unplugging from international finance, resisting globalization, promoting your own indigenous elites, things like that work for every people, and Jews, of course, feel threatened by any nationalism that is not their own. Why? Because they want to live among other nations. They don't want to live on their own. They have their own country, but they don't all live there.

DF: They want it there just in case.

[Break]

DF: Greg, we've talked about there's not really a whole lot of people in the White Nationalist movement, but when we look at "white power," it's still quite substantial. Presbyterians, we know the Presbyterians are very strong, the Methodists are strong in those subcultures of white culture.

GJ: Well, yeah.

DF: And whites aren't going to go away any time soon, but I would tend to agree with the line that with the way with the Jewish political structures and their culture and society taking over America that this is perhaps one of the biggest capitulations we have seen on the historical scale. Do you have any thoughts about that?

GJ: Oh yeah, I think it's extraordinary. Whites basically behave like a conquered people, and a conquered people has to give up whatever they have whenever somebody demands that they do it. We are giving up, but we don't seem to know it. We are constantly preached at that we have these terrible white privileges that we should feel guilty for, and yet the reality of the situation is that whites live in fear.

DF: The reality is, Greg, I don't feel any white privilege, and I'm sure you don't feel too much either. And I'm sure most of the listening audience don't feel that way either. We don't feel this white privilege, but people keep telling us we have it. It's like, you know, I'm not so sure of that, guys.

GJ: Right, right. We have the privilege of backing down, saying, "Yes, sir," "No, sir," and packing up every ten years and moving one subdivision down the highway to get away from diversity, but we always do that in search of "better schools" and other euphemisms. We're desperately seeking a safe, comfortable, homogeneous white community for our children so we can sleep at night without the sound of gunshots and sirens and loud music and so forth, but we dare not say what we really want. We are the race that dare not speak its name. We can't talk about our standards, our interests, our future, or anything like that without an apology. We can always apologize for who we are, but we can never be proud of who we are.

Well, those are the traits of a conquered race, and if you look even 100 years ago, whites basically controlled the globe. We didn't control Bhutan and Tibet and Japan and Ethiopia. There were a few little outposts in Asia and Africa that we did not run, but pretty much everything else was under our control. To go from a race that basically controlled the world to a race that is losing control of its own homelands in a century has to be the greatest reversal of fortunes ever.

But it's not just fortune; it was engineered. And that's the thing that we have to understand. Our decline is being engineered by our enemies, and they're doing a very good job of it because they know what causes the decline and fall of empires. They've seen these empires come and go many times. They've been around for a very long time, and they know where to apply a little bit of pressure at the very weakest point and see that multiply into civilizational collapse, which they ride to the top, and then they hop off and latch onto another civilization. It's an extraordinary story, and I just don't want us to follow the Hittites and the Romans and the other people who have disappeared. I want our people to be around in the future and continue giving our gifts to the world and to the universe at large.

DF: What's the status of White Nationalism in white societies like Germany, Scandinavia, Sweden, etc.? What's the state of the movement right now?

GJ: Well, it's interesting. In Europe, they don't have the First Amendment, but oddly enough they are making better use of their limited freedoms in Europe than Americans are making use of our much broader freedoms in America. I don't know why that is, but it is true. They are stigmatized, they are spied on and suppressed in ways that we are not yet, and yet they have functioning political parties. In countries where they have proportional representation they actually have people in office, and they are, in countries like Denmark, actually influencing the direction of political debate.

So, I have high hopes for Europe, and the reason I have high hopes for Europe is simply this: Scandinavia, England, France, all these countries, the people who live there are pretty much the indigenous people. I am descended from English and Scottish people. Most of my DNA is the DNA of the people who were there when the last ice age receded 10,000 years ago. The English are the indigenous people of England; the Swedes are the indigenous people of Sweden, and so forth. They don't have any rivals that they need to feel guilty about displacing, whereas in the colonies we have the Indians and the Maoris and people like that who are used to guilt trip us. They don't have that weight, and they also have very strong national and regional identities that we don't have in the colonies. So, I think that they have greater resources for eventually saving themselves, and I believe that Europe will save itself before America does.

My feeling is that Europe will especially be able to save itself the more American power declines in the world. So, I hate to say this, as someone who used to be an American patriot, but I really think that the future of our race is contingent, and the good of the globe in general is contingent, on the decline of American power, and I am hoping that American power declines precipitously in the future.

DF: Yeah, I hate to agree with you on that point, being an American, being an expatriate, knowing how much America is loved by people around the world. It really is. Everybody out there would be surprised. But the America we have today is Talmudic. It's not the Anglo-Saxon America that we had 20, 30, 40 years ago. It's almost completely Talmudic now, and that's a problem.

GJ: It's amazing how they've managed to hollow out America. They keep the form, but they hollowed out the substance, and they've replaced it with something very different and very ugly.

DF: And people see it. People around the world are seeing it, and they're just feeling sad for America, because basically it's now this Jewish-run country. I believe America is almost the way of Weimar, that you're going to need a Weimar Republic type of upheaval to bring America back and that means throwing out much of Jewish influence.

GJ: I would agree. I was in India in 2004, and I spent some time with some young Brahmins from Sikkim. This was in Calcutta. They were studying there, and they were college students. They were very young. We were sort of hanging out together showing me the town, and they talked to me like I was a child about politics, and I was really intensely irritated about that, because I didn't know where they were getting this attitude, and finally it became clear that they just think that all Americans are completely brainwashed about what's going on in the Middle East. When I said to them, "Look, you don't understand. American foreign policy is controlled by Jews" suddenly they warmed up to me, because they realized that I wasn't just another hopelessly brainwashed American idiot. So, even young people around the globe are much more aware of how the world works than your average American, and I think they look at us like most Americans are these hopelessly brainwashed, but dangerously well-armed, children.

DF: Yeah, you're right, Greg. You go around the world, and if you want to make a friend just talk about how Jews run American foreign policy. People will smile on you much faster than if you try to defend the *status quo*.

GJ: One of the things that I noticed when I was in India is that wherever in Hindu society the caste system doesn't exclude foreign-born people, and that would include ashrams and things like that, wherever they are not excluded, Jews have wormed their ways into positions of power. The Hare Krishna movement is full of Jews. Jews like to travel in South Asia because it's cheap, especially Israelis. After military service, they bum around a lot. Well, anyway, I used to think that Indian merchants were the biggest, most formidable hagglers in the world but this English fellow that I met said, "Oh no, I was at a hotel in Kathmandu, and printed right on the menu was 'Israelis pay half price.'" And that wasn't because they loved Israelis. It was because they were so sick of haggling with them over their bills that they just had a flat policy that Israelis pay half price. So, if you can flash your Israeli passport they'll cut your bill in half just so they don't have to haggle with you. I thought that was a really interesting story. I almost wanted to fly to Kathmandu and take a photo of that.

DF: That's some privilege all by itself.

GJ: Oh yeah, that's definitely a privilege. Membership has its privileges.

DF: Yeah, the Jew 50% discount. I heard there's websites out there that because Jews make such terrible travel partners, there's a website out there that will actually monitor when Jewish groups are coming, especially in Thailand, to warn you not to come to these areas so they don't ruin your vacation.

GJ: That's really fascinating.

DF: Really, no, really that's a true story. Just to kind of tie this show up, it's been a great show, fun show. Again, Greg Johnson, editor-in-chief of counter-currents.com. The real lesson here is that you're a White Nationalist, and I believe that you have much to offer in this way. I do have many affinities with the movement, although I certainly could not be considered one. But certainly I agree. There's much to be preserved and saved and needs to be saved through white culture, white civilization has given to the world.

To tie things up very nicely is one to recognize that the main problem we have is this Jewish problem, this Jewish question that really is using their control of media assets and cultural assets to instill guilt that is undeserved and is something that they themselves would never subject themselves to.

GJ: That's right. I remember after the Bernie Madoff scandal was broken there was a Frenchman, I think, who had invested all of his money or his clients' money with Madoff, and he committed suicide, and I just chuckled and thought, "Whatever is happening right now, I know one thing for sure. Bernie Madoff is not under suicide watch. Bernie Madoff feels no shame." He might be ashamed that he got caught, but he's not in any danger of killing himself out of shame over failing his clients. I just think that that kind of self-assertion and shamelessness, that brazenness—they call it *chutzpah*—is one of the traits that really sets Jews apart. I don't like imitating them or counseling whites to imitate them in any way, but I do think that one of the things that we do need to do—because this is just a healthy animal instinct, and we need to get in touch with our animal instincts in this case, we're a little to over-civilized—is self-assertion, non-apologetic self-assertion. No animal, no beast goes around apologizing for its existence. They just go around eating and sleeping and being who they are. They live according to their natures, and they don't apologize for their existence, and whites need to stop apologizing for our existence. It's a sick thing to do. We're sick puppies, and we've been injected with this guilt virus, although I think we have a predisposition towards it, and it's being manipulated. But we need to get over that. We need to have a kind of unapologetic self-assertion. We are who we are, we are the only people who can be who we are, we have a right to exist, and damn it we've given a lot to the world, we are proud of what we've given to the world, and we need to take steps to ensure that we don't go out of existence.

Jews have this ludicrous pretense that they are a light unto the nations. I think that is almost the exact opposite of the truth.

I think that they are generally a force of disintegration and death in the world, and I think, like you, I have an inclination to want to reach for metaphysical explanations for that. But that aside, I think whites really are a light unto the world: our technology, our art, our political systems.

DF: Even our metaphysical reasoning, Greg, is being usurped by Jewish interests and culture. I got a call here. I want to go to the telephones, Greg, here quick.

Hi there! You are live *Inside the Eye*. Welcome!

CALLER: Hello, gentlemen! How are you doing?

DF: Doing fine. Welcome to *Inside the Eye Live*.

CALLER: I just wanted to throw out to your guest regarding White Nationalism. I myself am white, but my observation/question is that in order to get me on board with his idea my question to him would be, if we go all the way back to Alexander the Great and if we go today to Washington, D.C., City of London, the Vatican, and Israel, how can you not obviously take responsibility that all these individuals are white, which come from white aristocracies in Europe? So, my question is how do you explain these White Nationalists throughout history that have been basically using secretly Judaism, which I see them as crypto-Jews? Because it works for them legally, and it controls all these people and nations. That's my question.

GJ: So, the question is exactly how do I explain this?

CALLER: No, how do I, as a white man, take responsibility for the existing White Nationalists, the politicians, the judges, the police, all of these individuals . . . All of these people are whites. They basically are using your standard, but they are using the ecumenical system going all the way back to control nationalities. Therefore, they are crypto-Jews. Our legal system is crypto-Judaism, our political system is crypto-Judaism. The Queen of England and the aristocracy has always secretly used the crypto-Jews for their power because it's a military asset. So, how would you explain to me to get on board with you unless you and I to-gether wake up to tell these people who are, basically, defeating our purpose because they are using Judaism?

GJ: I would agree that a lot of whites are a problem. But here's the thing: A lot of these people are not thinking about the good of the race as a whole. They don't have this notion that our race is our nation, that we have to have a kind of organic community, and that the common good should be the standard for politics. They're in it for their own self-interest, their own group interests, and because of that they have been very, very easily penetrated and coopted by Jewish influence. So, white people like that, they are white in name only. They look white, they sound white, they talk white, but they don't function as members of our community, and my view is that they need to be deposed from power. They need to have their goodies taken away from them, and they need to be re-educated as much as possible to be made into good little white citizens.

The people who have made millions of dollars dismantling white countries, selling out their own people, these people need to be disempowered, disenfranchised, dispossessed, and sent away so they can reflect on their crimes. I am all very pro-white, but I don't have any illusions about the fact that we are ruled by an evil, rotten, mostly white elite, and that Jews cannot have done what they have done to us without white traitors. There's no question about that in my mind.

So, yeah, I want you on board, and I want you to realize that just because it's got white skin doesn't mean that it's got a white soul or white goals.

SET ASIDE YOUR HUMILITY
& LEAD

INTERVIEW WITH RUUBEN KAALEP[*]

RUUBEN KAALEP: Good evening, my name is Ruuben Kaalep, and I am from Estonia. Tonight I am here with Dr. Greg Johnson, who is an American White Nationalist, an intellectual, a philosopher, and in my opinion one of the wisest and most inspiring figures that we nationalists have on our side. Dr. Johnson has a Ph.D. in philosophy. He is the founder and Editor of Counter-Currents Publishing which has a really great and intellectually rich website (www.counter-currents.com). He is the author of three books. A new one is coming out this year. I really recommend his books and writings to anyone who is interested in our nationalist cause. I am making this interview especially for Estonian readers and listeners. We will talk generally about the situation of Europeans in Europe and world-wide, and a bit about liberal and post-Communist Europe, and what is the role of Estonia and Estonian nationalists in all this.

So Greg, you have been a nationalist and White advocate in the USA for around 15 years. Can you freely express your opinions in the USA, or do you have to fear repercussions?

GREG JOHNSON: Well, Ruuben, first of all thank you for doing this interview and for your very kind introduction. There are no laws against expressing nationalist ideas in the United States, since freedom of opinion is expressly protected by the First Amendment to the US Constitution. However, that does not protect nationalists from persecution and censorship by private organizations and individuals.

The mainstream media, both Leftist and Right wing, are en-

* On October 26, 2015, this interview with Ruuben Kaalep appeared at Counter-Currents/*North American New Right* in audio and print versions, http://www.counter-currents.com/2015/10/set-aside-your-humility/

tirely hostile to racial nationalist ideas and seldom bother with even the pretense of objectivity. Left-wing agitators have led many universities, businesses, and NGOs to adopt codes of conduct and mission statements that make adherence to multiculturalism and diversity conditions of employment, which furnish pretexts to fire dissidents. But even these pretexts are unnecessary, as Americans can be fired at will if they have controversial beliefs.

In Europe, freedom of speech does not have the same constitutional protection as in the US, but in many European societies, it is not possible for employers to terminate people arbitrarily, based on their political beliefs. Thus I believe that in the end, constitutional guarantees of free speech mean very little if dissidents can be subjected to private censorship and persecution with impunity. This may be why in Europe, nationalists who have less legal freedom of speech actually speak more, and more effectively, in favor of nationalist policies.

RK: Europe has been lately struck by a migration crisis of unprecedented scale. What kind of results do you foresee for both Europe and the whole world?

GJ: All European nations have shrinking native populations. If non-white immigration continues unabated, there are really only three possible outcomes.

First, Europe will cease to exist, culturally and racially, once its populations are replaced by fast-breeding non-whites. Once Europeans no longer exist, I fully expect the other races will breed recklessly and despoil the planet, leaving nothing but a blackened cinder in space. Thus, I believe that the welfare of Europe is ultimately identical with the welfare of the world. Want to save the world? Then save the white race. We are the part that cares the most about the whole.

Second, there will be civil wars, in which the European populations either unite to expel the invaders and secure their borders, or they will fail, and Europe will be extinguished.

Third, nationalist parties will come to power, secure their borders, and repatriate non-whites in an orderly and humane fashion.

I hope that Europe takes the third path, but if the existing political establishments do not cede power to nationalist parties,
then revolution and civil war will be the only other route to Europe's salvation. Under no circumstances, however, will Europe
"go gentle" into the night of extinction.

Of course non-white immigration into Europe is nothing
new, and nationalists have been warning Europeans about demographic displacement for decades. Thus the sudden massive
influx of migrants from Africa and the Near East is actually a
good thing, because the startling scope and speed of the chang-
es are awakening people who were sleeping through their slow
demographic displacement and galvanizing new levels of European resistance. This crisis is like a fever. Sometimes a body
needs to raise its temperature to ward off or kill an infection.
The temperature is going way up, and I think that is perhaps a
sign of health.

RK: What are the differences and similarities in the demographic trends of Europe and USA?

GJ: The main trends are quite similar: white Americans, like
white Europeans, are a shrinking population, who will be replaced by fast-breeding native and immigrant non-whites. The
only real difference is that the process is far more advanced in
the United States than in Europe. The United States has declined
from 90% white in 1965 to about 65% white today, and in a few
decades, whites will be less than 50% of the population. Para-
doxically, though, even though the demographic problem is far
less pronounced in Europe, the level of nationalist sentiment and
organization is far higher. I take this as a sign of greater racial
and cultural health in Europe.

RK: You have been staying in Budapest for a while. How
would you compare Western and Eastern (post-communist) Europe (taking into account politics, demographics, and culture)?

GJ: Unlike some Western nationalists, I do not hate liberalism
enough to praise Communism, except in a backhanded way: de-
spite its efforts, Communism was not capable of destroying ethnic consciousness and European high culture quite so effectively

as Western liberalism and popular culture. Therefore, there is a healthier national consciousness and a more vivid sense of a common European history and high cultural heritage in the former Communist bloc nations than in the West. That is particularly true of Hungary, which is the European country I have spent the most time in. The amount of European high culture that you see in Hungary is remarkable.

Western Europe is much more culturally deracinated and debased than the East, largely because of the post-war hegemony of the United States. Western Europe, however, is still far healthier than the United States, which is the vanguard of world nihilism. Eastern Europe needs to get over its inferiority complex toward the West and America. Eastern Europe should not be following the vanguard of nihilism. It should instead become the vanguard of European rebirth.

RK: How would you comment on Hungarian policies on immigration?

GJ: Viktor Orbán's policies and statements on the migrant crisis have been the best of all European leaders, and he has encouraged resistance around Europe to the arrogant demands of Merkel and Brussels to impose "refugee" quotas. Hungary has its political factions, like all nations, but the Hungarian people are overall highly patriotic and feel great solidarity with one another in resisting the invaders. It is a sign of health. I hope other European nations follow their example. There are already signs of that happening with the Czech Republic, Poland, and Slovakia, so we'll see.

RK: What kind of differences do you see between nationalist movements in Western and Eastern Europe?

GJ: Eastern countries tend to be genetically threatened more by emigration of young people than immigration by non-whites, but Mrs. Merkel is changing that quickly. The biggest difference is that delusional views about Russia increase among nationalists the further west one goes. Other than that, I generally see little difference between Eastern and Western European nationalists. I respect both Eastern and Western European nationalists.

I look up to them. I expect more from the East though, because they have healthier societies to work with. For countries like England and France, Germany and Sweden, Italy and Spain, the path to national renewal will be much more difficult.

RK: Which strategies work best for nationalists?

GJ: In politics and warfare, one must attack the enemy where he is weakest and you are strongest. Right now, our enemies have never been stronger in terms of wealth and sheer brute power. Nationalists, by contrast, have very little wealth and power at our disposal. However, the establishment has never been weaker in terms of its intellectual and moral underpinnings, and the intellectual and moral case for nationalism has never been stronger. Moreover, the people who run our countries are utterly cynical and corrupt, not to mention downright insane and quite easily parodied, whereas nationalism increasingly draws the most intelligent, upstanding, and idealistic people in all European societies.

Therefore, the battle at present has to be metapolitical: we need to destroy the dominance of anti-nationalist ideas, and we need to organize a vital nationalist movement, which must consist not just of political parties, but a whole subculture, with families, schools, businesses, think tanks, cultural events, publishers, artists and craftsmen, etc.

Since nationalism is based on objective facts and moral principles that our enemies flout, they can only grow weaker, and we can only grow stronger, until the point when we can take political power, protect our borders, repatriate outsiders, and reverse our demographic and cultural decline.

RK: How soon would you predict the success of nationalism all over Europe, and where will it begin first?

GJ: It is dangerous to make precise predictions, particularly because the one thing history teaches us to expect is the unexpected, i.e., the unpredictable. We don't want to be like the millenialist sects that kept predicting and postponing the Apocalypse. Failed prophecies can be deeply demoralizing. Instead, the best way to sustain our efforts is not to offer overly precise predictions or rosy forecasts or to foster the illusion that we can completely control events. That we've got a plan that we can just set in motion. Step one, step two, step three, and then victory.

Instead, we have to follow the Aryan ethic of duty that you see in the Bhagavad Gita and Immanuel Kant. We have to do the right thing and detach ourselves from the consequences, which we cannot control. Keep fighting. Never get discouraged. Never soil ourselves with compromise. Always remain morally worthy of victory. We can control that. We can control our own actions, and our own worth, better than we can control external events. And then we have to let the gods sort out the contingencies. It is hubris to think that we can completely predict and control events.

An allied attitude that also detaches itself from this hubris is to regard the struggle not just as a moral duty but as a game, as a source of joy, thus as something that can be sustained as an end in itself, regardless of consequences. Laughter is key. Laughter is glorying in our own superiority. We do not believe we deserve to win if we cannot laugh at our enemies. And they richly deserve mockery. This playful spirit is particularly attractive to young and creative types. It is the source of the endless wealth of memes, parody songs, videos, and podcasts, and troll campaigns that are now reshaping the parameters of political debate. This is cultural struggle — metapolitics — in action.

We can, however, make very broad predictions. I am very optimistic that nationalism will break out somewhere in Europe and spread. Why? Because nationalism is the political philosophy best aligned with our own nature and with the facts of reality, including the most pressing political problems faced by white people everywhere: problems like demographic decline, mass immigration, crime, and ethnic conflict. Multiculturalism brings conflict, chaos, poverty, and misery wherever it is tried. The only solution is the ethnically homogeneous sovereign state.

We have won all the intellectual battles. Our leaders are intellectually and morally bankrupt. But our people don't know it yet. Once we awaken enough of our people, and once the power of the increasingly hollow and brittle establishment to intimidate us into silence and conformity wavers, rapid political change is possible. We saw that with the collapse of Communism, which was just another version of the same lies that rule today.

RK: What would be your advice for a small country like Estonia that lies between the Moscow and Washington/Brussels spheres of influence?

GJ: The main reason why Eastern European countries are receptive to the EU and NATO in particular is their desire to secure themselves against Putin's Russia. This is bad because NATO and the EU are vectors of western decadence. Central and Eastern Europeans may be militarily and economically weaker than the West, but they are racially and culturally much healthier, and the latter factors are more important.

Therefore, I believe that Eastern Europeans need to take control of their own security. Already, Poland, Slovakia, the Czech Republic, and Hungary are part of the Visegrád Group, an economic and defense union encompassing four of Central-Eastern Europe's most dynamic economies and more than 60 million people. I would like to see this independent bloc expand.

The Baltic countries should be the first to join, as they are well-matched in terms of economic and educational factors. Eventually, such a bloc should encompass Ukraine, Romania, Moldova, and Bulgaria, as well as Belarus if it leaves the Russian orbit. Greece and the former Yugoslav republics are also candidates. Austria too. Fully extended, such a bloc would have close to 200 million Europeans, more than a match for Russia's 145 million, many of whom are non-Europeans.

This geopolitical bloc was the idea of Polish inter-war leader Józef Piłsudski, who called it Intermarium. There's an excellent recent article on it at Counter-Currents.[1] For Piłsudski, of course, Intermarium was an imperial dream: the resurrection of the old Polish-Lithuanian Commonwealth. No sovereign state will sign up for the revival of the Polish-Lithuanian Commonwealth or Austro-Hungarian Empire. But a federation of sovereign states

---

[1] Émile Durand, "Toward a Baltic-Black Sea Union: 'Intermarium' as a Viable Model for White Revival," https://www.counter-currents.com/2015/10/intermarium/

spanning from the Baltic to the Black Sea would obviate the need for Central and Eastern European nations to join NATO and the EU.

An Intermarium bloc would allow the racially and culturally healthiest part of Europe to stop following the West into decadence and instead start leading it toward renewal. The East needs to get over its inferiority complex. It needs to rejoice in its health and strength. Matt Parrott once said something very wise to me, which is applicable here: "Sometimes you have to set aside your humility and lead."

RK: Well thank you very much Greg. It has been very inspiring. You have given hope to nationalists in Estonia and the whole of Europe. So as Greg said: be brave, do your duty, and laugh at your enemies. They're just there so you can laugh at them. So have a good night.

GJ: Thank you so much. I really have enjoyed this.

WHAT IS WHITE NATIONALISM?

INTERVIEW WITH
GEORGES FELTIN-TRACOL[*]

GEORGES FELTIN-TRACOL: Isn't White Nationalism a theory specific to a North American context?

GREG JOHNSON: As I define it, White Nationalism is the advocacy of sovereign homelands for all white ethnic groups, which applies just as well to Europe as to North America. North Americans are not simply generic white people. We are Americans, Canadians, and Québécois. Just as Europeans are not generic white people, but members of different ethnic groups as well.

Now, to be precise, I regard ethnic sovereignty as a pragmatic principle for conflict resolution and cultural development, not as a categorical imperative. Some ethnic groups may get along well in a multiethnic system and not aspire to sovereignty, for instance the peoples of the Swiss Federation. Not every tribe of American or Siberian aborigines needs a seat at the United Nations.

But when multiethnic societies lead to conflict or the destruction of identities, and particular peoples aspire to their own homelands, then as a White Nationalist, I say give it to them. Give it to them in an orderly, peaceful, and humane manner like the partition of Czechoslovakia, so they do not have to arrive at the same conclusion by the Yugoslav route of war and bloodshed.

White Nationalism is politically realistic enough to recognize that a completely peaceful world might not be possible. But we think that giving all peoples their own homelands, where they can live in a manner that befits them without outside interference, is the best way to minimize needless strife and lay the

---

* This interview with Georges Feltin-Tracol appeared in French translation in *Réfléchir & Agir*, no. 55 (2017).

foundations for peaceful cultural and economic development.

GFT: Does White Nationalism have a vision of economics?

GJ: White Nationalists differ in their views of economics, and many of us, unfortunately, are still mentally mired in libertarian, "free market" economic thinking, since most of us start our intellectual journeys on the libertarian and conservative Right, and we carry that baggage with us. One of the most important agenda items for Counter-Currents is to promote the exploration of the rich tradition of critiques of capitalism from the Right: social credit, distributism, guild socialism, populism, agrarianism, the economic innovations in Fascist Italy and National Socialist Germany, and so forth. My own economic views are most influenced by the Social Credit school, as can be appreciated in my essay "Money for Nothing."[1]

GFT: What do you think of liberalism?

GJ: Individual self-actualization and freedom are important things. But they are not as important as liberals make them out to be. I believe that the common good is a meaningful idea, and that liberalism is absurd to claim that the common good either does not exist, or does not matter more than individual interests, or cannot be imposed on individuals without tyranny, or comes about spontaneously though individual selfishness, so we do not need wise statesmen imposing limits on individual freedom whenever it conflicts with the common good. In the illiberal society I envision, there will be wide latitude for individual freedom and self-development, but only as long as they are consisted with the common good.

GFT: What do you think of globalization?

GJ: Globalization is a profoundly destructive process. It is destructive of everything that the Right holds dear: traditions, hierarchies, particular identities, national sovereignty, etc. This is one reason that the Left promotes it, at least the Left that focuses on identity politics. But it is also destructive of much of what the

---

[1] In *Truth, Justice, & a Nice White Country.*

Left holds dear as well, at least the older Left that cared about workers.

Globalization destroys the genuine progress that has been made by the labor movement, all of which took place in societies that practiced some measure of economic protectionism. Globalization means removing those barriers to trade. That means that labor costs in the First World and Third World will tend to equalize, which will mean a slight improvement in Third World living standards and a catastrophic drop in First World living standards. This will lead to the liquidation of the white working and middle classes to the benefit of an elite of rootless plutocrats.

Leftists who want to stop globalization need to recognize that the natural stopping point is the nation state. For more on this, see my essay "The End of Globalization."[2]

Globalization is also deeply incompatible with technological progress. One of the main spurs of technological progress has been high labor costs, which encourage capitalists to create new technologies, which make labor more productive. As long as labor has the collective power to appropriate the benefits of these productivity gains, technological progress leads to a rising middle class. Cheap labor removes that spur to innovation and rising living standards. Globalization is thus leading to technological stagnation and a low-tech, low-wage plantation economy.

My goal is to create a utopia where machines put us all out of work, by means of economic nationalism and protectionism, which keep labor costs high and spur technological innovations. But the productivity gains made possible by high tech will be distributed to everyone in the form of a social dividend, which will give everyone the purchasing power to keep the economy running and the leisure to pursue higher aims: family life, creativity, self-cultivation, political activism, science, technology, exploration, and the like.

GFT: You state in your book *New Right vs. Old Right* that "your nation is your race." Isn't it a reductive statement, since many white people stand for immigration, multiculturalism, and interbreeding?

---

[2] In *Truth, Justice, & a Nice White Country*.

GJ: All "my race is my nation" means is that I believe that the survival and flourishing of our race is the highest political good. Of course, there are many white people who disagree with that. But they remain our flesh and blood, members of our greater racial community, just as I regard misguided white Americans as members of my greater national community. They simply have mistaken political opinions.

The goal of White Nationalists should be complete cultural and political hegemony. We must aim at communicating the relevance of our ideas to all white constituencies and securing their loyalty. There is no need to end political pluralism as long as white identity and interests become sacrosanct and throughout the political spectrum, no matter how many other issues might divide us. I am all for the maximum political and cultural pluralism, as long as the degradation and destruction of our race is not one of the possibilities.

I see the task of White Nationalism as rationally persuading an active minority of people of the truth of our views and the necessity of politically realizing them. We can persuade a somewhat larger minority of our people of our views through non-rational factors. Then, if we gain power, we can secure the loyalty of the broad masses by offering them security, prosperity, and peace.

There will always, however, be a minority of our people who will never accept our views. But if our ideas become culturally and politically hegemonic, we will deprive that remnant of all political power and social influence. They will be as alienated, marginalized, and powerless as White Nationalists are today under the current multiculturalist hegemony.

GFT: Do you believe that American White Nationalism can help the cause of Europeans on all continents?

GJ: Yes, because White Nationalism as I define it defends sovereign homelands for all white groups that aspire to sovereignty, no matter where they live. Indeed, ethnonationalist principles apply to non-white peoples as well.

GFT: Some neocons contemplate the "Anglosphere," as the

union between the United Kingdom, USA, Canada, Australia, and New Zealand. What about you?

GJ: Although the Anglosphere does share a common language and a common history up to a point, Englishmen, Canadians, Australians, New Zealanders, and Americans are now different ethnic groups, some of us separated by thousands of miles. Thus, the idea of any sort of politically unified Anglosphere strikes me as absurd and contrary to ethnonationalism. Any necessary cooperation between Anglosphere nations can be secured by trade, diplomacy, customs unions, intergovernmental organizations, and military alliances. There is simply no need for a common sovereign state.

Neocons, of course, are a tiny minority with an immense will to power. Thus, they desire the centralization of power, even if it increases strife between different peoples subject to the same system, since such unification allows a small group to dominate many different peoples. Thus they feel threatened by all forces demanding decentralization and ethnic-national sovereignty.

GFT: What do North-American White Nationalists think of an *Alter Europe* based on identity?

GJ: We are for it, as it follows of necessity from our basic principle of supporting the national aspirations of all white ethnic groups.

THE SHADOW OF TRUMP

INTERVIEW WITH
FRANCESCO BOCO*

FRANCESCO BOCO: On August 28, 2016 Professor Thomas J. Main wrote an article in the *Los Angeles Times* entitled "What's the Alt-Right?"[1] Professor Main said: "The main challenge to our way of life today now comes not from the radical left, but the Alt-Right" and "The Alt-Right represents the first new philosophical competitor to liberalism, broadly defined, since the fall of Communism." It seems that in just a few years the American Alternative Right has succeeded in becoming important and influential. What do you think about that, and what is the true and authentic strength of the Alt Right?

GREG JOHNSON: Professor Main is more correct than he knows, for the Alternative Right offers a more fundamental critique of and challenge to today's multicultural liberal democracy than Communism ever did. The Alternative Right is a broad umbrella term for those who reject the mainstream conservative movement in America. But the ideological core and animating force of the Alt Right is White Nationalism. And from a White Nationalist perspective, both Communism and liberal multiculturalism are based on the same false premise that different races are able to live together harmoniously within the same political system.

The strength of White Nationalism is that it is based on the truth about human nature and society. White Nationalists believe that racial, ethnic, and religious diversity within the same

---

* This interview with Francesco Boco appeared in Italian translation at *Il Primato Nazionale*, http://www.ilprimatonazionale.it/esteri/lombra-trump-intervista-greg-johnson-sullalternative-right-americana-52343/#10tBBObOyv2pApFz.01.
[1] http://www.latimes.com/opinion/op-ed/la-oe-main-alt-right-trump-20160825-snap-story.html

political systems lead inevitably to conflict and the destruction of unique identities. Therefore, to reduce ethnic conflicts and preserve distinct identities, we believe in the creation of racially and ethnically homogeneous homelands for all peoples that aspire to sovereignty over their destinies. This means a return to nationalism and an end to the racially and culturally homogenizing processes of globalization.

The Alternative Right's rise is being driven by the destructive consequences of multiculturalism and globalization. White Nationalists offer the best account of why these forces are destructive, and we offer the only workable alternative. As long as these problems persist, our movement will continue to grow. We will continue to raise and channel awareness of these problems until it becomes politically possible to fix them.

However, as it stands now, I would not characterize the Alt Right as influential. Yes, our memes have altered mainstream political discourse. Conservatives wince at the epithet "cuck." Hillary Clinton took to the stage to denounce us. Our echo brackets (((()))) and cartoon frog have been added to the ADL's index of hate symbols.

It's a great start. But it is a long way from actually shaping political policies. To do that, we will need to be much better organized and funded. In the past few years, the number and quality of people listening and contributing to our message has increased dramatically. But in terms of organization and funding, we are only slightly better off. When we have the ability to capture and productively channel more money, I am convinced that the reach and influence of our ideas will grow dramatically. But that will not happen unless people with money stop wasting it on mainstream conservative organizations.

FB: To most Italian readers the Alt Right is a complete novelty, but you and other authors and activists have been working for many years. Please give us a short account of your political activism and Counter-Currents Publishing. What will be your next steps, and which objectives you want to achieve in the future?

GJ: I have been involved with White Nationalism since the year 2000. From the start, I was guided by the conviction that political change depends on metapolitical preconditions. People have to believe that a political proposal is necessary, moral, and practically feasible, or it will simply be dismissed. Beyond that, for White Nationalism to be politically possible, whites must think of themselves as whites, i.e., as a particular race—a race with a distinct identity and interests, some of which conflict with those of other races, such that separate homelands are the best way to avoid conflict—not just as members of a universal and homogeneous "humanity" that can exist in a borderless world as long as we have sufficient consciousness-raising and progress.

Late in 2000, in discussion with some friends, I began thinking of creating a metapolitical journal that would lay the foundations for White Nationalism in North America. In 2001, *The Occidental Quarterly* was founded, and I regarded it as largely fulfilling that need. In 2007, I became the editor of TOQ. In the Spring of 2010, I founded Counter-Currents Publishing with Michael Polignano. In 2013, I became the sole owner. The purpose of Counter-Currents is to create an intellectual platform for White Nationalist metapolitics, broadly conceived so as to encompass not just political philosophy and the human sciences but also history, art, literature, etc. We believe that we are the legitimate heirs and guardians of the whole of European culture. It is our tradition, and only racially conscious whites will be able to carry it forward. Counter-Currents is really about everything—the whole viewed from a racially-conscious European point of view.

The webzine of Counter-Currents is called *North American New Right*. Initially, I also planned to issue an annual print journal, *North American New Right*, and one volume appeared in 2012. But I came to believe that the last thing that our movement needs is another print journal. I don't publish anything unless I think that it will contribute to saving our race—and, really, saving the world along with it. And if I really believe that, then obviously it should be published online immediately and for free rather than being held up for months and subjected to the artificial scarcity of print publishing just to make a buck. (I will bring out the second and final volume of NANR in 2017.)

As for the future of Counter-Currents: we have been around for more than 6 years, and we have kept up a steady pace of print and online publishing with significant growth in our readership. I expect this trend to continue.

Counter-Currents is also involved in creating real world gatherings. Starting in June of 2010, we began a tradition of Francis Parker Yockey Memorial Dinners in San Francisco. In 2011, we started a tradition of annual weekend retreats. In 2015, we started a tradition of monthly "Toastmasters" style gatherings in New York City. And in 2016, we inaugurated the New York Forum, modelled on the London Forum. Soon we will inaugurate the Northwest Forum. In 2017, we plan six New York Forums (on odd numbered months) and six Northwest Forums (on even numbered months). All of these gatherings have been quite successful in stimulating thought, creativity, networking, and solidarity. We put a special emphasis on bringing together racially conscious people who share the same communities and who can enjoy regular fellowship. We hope that these models will be emulated all over the white world.

FB: The Alt Right seems to build upon the European New Right. Alain De Benoist, Guillaume Faye, Jonathan Bowden, and Francis Parker Yockey are often quoted in your books and articles. What differentiates the Alt Right from the European New Right?

GJ: Again, I will not speak about the Alt Right as a whole, since there are plenty of people today calling themselves Alt Right who have never even heard of the European New Right. But what differentiates White Nationalism from the European New Right is a greater importance of the concept of race, which makes sense in the context of European colonial societies in which peoples from different European ethnic stocks blended together and in which the presence of non-whites led people quite naturally to think in racial terms. In Europe, by contrast, nationalist movements think of themselves in ethnic rather than racial terms.

But this difference is really more a matter of emphasis than a hard and fast distinction. After all, Americans, Canadians, Australians, and other European colonial peoples are not just generic "whites." If all we were is generic whites, then there would really be no difference between Americans and Canadians or Chileans and Argentines. Yet there are differences, and they are not merely racial, attributable to different settlement patterns from different parts of Europe. There are genuine ethnic or cultural differences between Americans and even our closest neighbors and cousins in Canada. Americans, in short, have a distinct *ethnic* identity, an identity which *presupposes* whiteness but cannot be *reduced* to it.

Moreover, European nationalists do not think solely in terms of ethnic identity. There is more to being Italian than simply being a white man, but no non-white can be Italian. Whiteness is a necessary but not a sufficient condition for belonging to any European ethnic group. Non-whites are Americans or Italians or French only because of legal fictions, the untenability of which is increasingly obvious with each passing day. European ethnonationalists also have a sense that our distinct nations have common origins, common enemies, and a common destiny—an awareness that we hope will help us to avoid the petty fratricidal wars of the past and meet the challenges of the burgeoning and increasingly mobile non-white populations.

When I speak of White Nationalism, I mean ethnic nationalism for every particular white ethnic group—Italians, French, Americans, Canadians, etc.—not some sort of European Imperium and melting pot, an idea which is revolting on the face of it, since it replicates all of the problems of globalization merely on a smaller scale, and which could never be realized without the fratricidal European wars it is supposed to prevent. If advocates of a white Imperium want to prove that it is more than a pipe dream, they can demonstrate this by first putting Yugoslavia and Czechoslovakia back together. If they can manage that, I will take them seriously.

FB: From a European perspective Donald Trump seems a histrionic and ambiguous person. A capitalist that talks about stopping immigration and making the USA great again. Is he really the candidate of the Alt Right, or he is, to you, something different? Maybe an opportunity to grow as a movement and gain more influence in American society? Do you see a real change, regarding public opinion, in respect to past elections?

GJ: I see Trump as an immense opportunity. He does not want the kind of society that we want, but we want some of the policies that he wants. Trump is a civic nationalist not a racial nationalist. He believes that the United States should be governed in the interest of all its citizens—a citizenry that embraces different races and is defined in legal rather than racial terms. However, the majority of Americans are white, and by being pro-American, Trump cannot be against the white majority, whereas the Democrats and mainstream Republicans both promoted policies destructive of the white majority.

Beyond that, Trump's proposals to build a wall on the Mexican border, deport millions of illegal aliens, and ban Muslim immigration would slow the demographic displacement of whites, giving us a few extra decades before we become a minority in our homeland. We can use that extra time to rally our people and create a consensus around policies that will halt and then reverse our demographic decline.

Trump is popular because he is giving Americans what we really want: populist nationalism, not degenerate liberalism or "free market" conservatism. Trump does not represent a change in American political preferences. Instead, the change is that he has broken the power of the political establishment, which is based on a gentleman's agreement not to give the people what they want.

FB: How do you envision the future of North America? What should be the guidelines for renewal? Can European roots still find fertile ground in the USA?

GJ: White Nationalists will reclaim North America for our race. We were a tiny minority on this continent when we founded Jamestown more than 400 years ago. Yet we conquered a continent. With far greater numbers and resources at our disposal, we can reconquer it. It is merely a matter of political will. There is no question in my mind *that* this will happen. *How* that happens will be determined on November 8th.

If Donald Trump is elected, he will slow down the demographic displacement of whites which will make it possible for White Nationalists to salvage the United States and turn it into a white homeland. If Hillary Clinton is elected, she will enfranchise millions of illegal aliens and throw open the borders to the Third World, rapidly driving whites into minority status, which will make it impossible for whites to save ourselves within the current political system. That means that we will have to go to Plan B, which is to break up America, carve out homogenously white homelands, and create a new political system to ensure white survival and flourishing. Donald Trump is not the "last chance" for whites in North America, but he is the last chance for the United States of America.

INDEX

This index lists all occurrences of proper names plus definitions and discussions of important concepts. Numbers in bold refer to a whole chapter or section connected to a particular individual or topic.

ABOUT THE CONTRIBUTORS

GREG JOHNSON, Ph.D. is Editor-in-Chief of Counter-Currents Publishing Ltd., as well as Editor of *North American New Right*, its webzine (http://www.counter-currents.com/) and occasional print journal.

He is the author of *Confessions of a Reluctant Hater* (San Francisco: Counter-Currents, 2010; second, expanded ed., 2016), *New Right vs. Old Right* (San Francisco: Counter-Currents, 2013), *Truth, Justice, & a Nice White Country* (San Francisco: Counter-Currents, 2015), *In Defense of Prejudice* (San Francisco: Counter-Currents, 2017), and *The White Nationalist Manifesto* (San Francisco: Counter-Currents, 2017).

His writings have been translated into Czech, Danish, Dutch, Estonian, French, German, Greek, Hungarian, Norwegian, Polish, Portuguese, Russian, Slovak, Spanish, Swedish, and Ukrainian.

FRANCESCO BOCO is an Italian identitarian journalist who writes for *Il primato nazionale.*

MIKE ENOCH is the co-host of *The Daily Shoah* at The Right Stuff Radio, therightstuff.biz.

GEORGES FELTIN-TRACOL is a French identitarian journalist who writes for *Réfléchir & Agir.*

DENNIS FETCHO is the host of *Inside the Eye – Live!* at insidetheeye-live.com.

RUUBEN KAALEP is the leader of the Estonian identitarian youth movement Blue Awakening (Sinine Äratus).

MATT PARROTT is the Director of the Traditionalist Worker Party.

LAURA RAIM is a French socialist journalist who writes for *Monde diplo, Regards, La Revue du crieur, Hors-Série,* and other publications.

ROBERT STARK is the host of *The Stark Truth* at Stark Truth Radio, starktruthradio.com.

TOMISLAV SUNIĆ, Ph.D., is a Croatian scholar of the New Right, whose books include *Against Democracy & Equality: The European New Right, Homo Americanus: Child of the Postmodern Age,* and *Titans Are in Town.*

www.ingramcontent.com/pod-product-compliance
Lightning Source LLC
Chambersburg PA
CBHW031427270326
41930CB00007B/603